# Nature I Loved . . .

### BILL GEAGAN

North Country Press
Unity, Maine

Nature I Loved

ISBN 978-1-943424-75-7

LCCN 2022941681

Illustrations (including cover illustrations) by the author

# Foreword

For his birthday on April 16, 1953, my mother gave my father a recently published book by Bangor writer Bill Geagan titled *Nature I Loved*. The author had inscribed it to my dad, with whom he was acquainted. Eighteen years later, at age twelve, I discovered the book on a shelf in our house and read it. And I reread it, again and again.

That book, along with Jean Craighead George's *My Side of the Mountain*, essentially changed my life. Well, perhaps I shouldn't say they changed my life, but for a young boy with a craving for time in nature and a youthful desire to strike out and test myself in the woods, these two books certainly guided me on a path of adventure.

Bill was in his early twenties when in the 1920s, he struck out to try to find himself, living in a derelict cabin on Hermon Pond in Maine. Supported in the endeavor by his mother and nearly estranged from a father who was losing patience with his son, Bill worked hard, contemplated, pontificated (if only to himself), and survived and thrived on the shores of the lake (Hermon Pond is technically a lake). *Nature I Loved* is a loving testimony to Bill's time in the woods—fishing, hunting, exploring, existential soul-searching, and even falling in love for the first time are chronicled in his story. The book spoke to me.

Easily impressionable, I became driven to live in the woods by myself for an entire summer vacation, using only rudimentary tools and my wits. When I approached my father with the idea, he (knowing I didn't *have* any wits) suspected that I would likely be dead in two or three weeks, and after thinking it over for what seemed like a bit too long, decided against it. Even with eight children at home, it hadn't escaped my father that my nose was in *Nature I Loved* much of the time, and he suggested we consult Bill after church the following Sunday. We did, and when my father told Bill my plan, the author smiled at me and regarded me with a respectful, if not amused, gaze. I remember Bill offering me words of encouragement, and, in retrospect, he did so without making me feel absurd. Which I was. Eventually, it was agreed that it would be better if I acquired some skills first. Bill recommended I attend the Penobscot County Conservation School at Branch Pond in Ellsworth, Maine, a summer camp emphasizing backcountry skills and woodscraft. I wanted to go, but Mom and Dad didn't have the money to send me. After a couple of weeks, Bill called my father over after Sunday service and offered to sponsor me to the summer camp program. I think the arrangement made my mom a little uncomfortable—she had been raised a Baptist and wasn't one to accept charity.

I did go to the summer camp, and although I certainly didn't win the "Camper of the Week" award (I swear to God I thought I'd outgrown the bedwetting), I also wasn't kicked out of the program and sent home early, so I considered the whole endeavor a triumph.

For several generations of Mainers, *Nature I Loved* became a subtler homespun version of Thoreau's *Walden*. But Bill Geagan, at the time more a fly fishing bum than a transcendentalist, worked very hard at his cabin. While Thoreau's mother and sister delivered his meals and firewood so Henry would have the time to think things over, Bill eked out an existence by any means he could find. He eased his existential angst through hard work and by leaning on his faith. He grew crops, ate the fish, deer, and rabbits he killed, and earned what little money he could from guiding, writing, and illustrating. Such an industrious attempt at finding oneself appealed to thousands of Mainers who read his book, as it did to me.

Bill went on to write two other books, but *Nature I Loved* is his greatest legacy. He and his wife Alice never had children of their own, but they had their books to which Alice contributed greatly.

Bill died in November 1974. I was a sophomore in high school, and I had sadly watched his health, battered by cancer, deteriorate. True to his unassuming way, the family's obituary in the Bangor Daily News was only fifty-seven words long. A short time later, his friend Bob Leeman wrote a lovely, heartfelt piece about Bill in the newspaper in his *"Needles from the Pine"* column—the name of which was inspired by Bill years earlier. Every writer who has written about Bill's life tells of how the author of *Nature I Loved* was buried with a sprig of pine needles in his hand because that is too cool not to mention.

I started writing my first outdoor-themed book at fifty, the same age Bill was when he began *Nature*. Years later, decades after Bill and Alice had passed away, I investigated Bill so I could write an affectionate essay about the writer's influence on me. The research became a story in itself. Initially, I thought it would be enjoyable to find the location of Bill's cabin, see if I might draw a little inspiration from the place, and fish some of the spots the author described in his books. In the end, my quest for the cabin's location—the site long reclaimed by the forest and occupied now by modern lakeside camps—became a story about the man beyond his influence. It became about the author's follies, triumphs, and perhaps more importantly, legacies.

I learned many new things about the author while researching him for the essay. Reading through his papers, I learned that he was an incredibly thrifty man, often recycling old, used pages of paper for his first drafts, sometimes even using the backs of envelopes. I discovered that he never learned to drive and that Alice or his fishing and hunting friends had to transport him everywhere. And that he was fond of good whiskey. While not poor, I also learned that he and Alice never had much money and that the $300 he paid for my sponsorship at the Conservation School must've been a hardship for them, and it made me appreciate the gesture even more. As a writer, it took me several books to get to the point where I could make any money from writing, and during the struggle, I would often recall a passage from *Nature I Loved*: "Money, fame, and power aren't everything in this world. Many men of only very moderate success who live in comparative obscurity, but who enjoy what they are doing, are very often the happiest." Those lines buoyed me, just as his summer camp scholarship had done decades earlier.

*Nature I Loved* is a beautiful book that stands the test of time and is still beloved by many people. When Maine native Paul Kelleher decided it was high time that somebody produced an e-book version of it so that new, younger generations of people throughout the country could discover and learn from the book, I was thrilled. Paul had the credentials and the desire to see the project through, and now North Country Press in Unity, Maine, has stepped in to place the physical book back onto bookshelves in Maine, where it belongs. Bill would be proud and grateful, and my being asked to write the foreword for this anniversary issue is one of my greatest honors.

Every couple of summers, I go back to Hermon Pond to fish and explore places Bill described in his books. Time has changed the landscape and changed me (I've grown up...and out), but the same streams, brooks, and meadows are there. I often sit in my canoe or climb up on a rock on the banks of the lake and wonder what it was like there in 1922 when only a few log cabins dotted the shoreline. I think about the long-gone tiny town at the head of the lake that once had a post office, a train station, and a store. I wonder about the lives of the people that lived there and what it was like for them at the time, their heads still swimming from the ravages of World War I. And I imagine Bill, unsure of himself, untrained in any trade, canoeing up and down the lake in a leaky boat, trying to figure out what the heck to do with his life.

Bill Geagan went to Hermon Pond precisely a hundred years ago to find himself. I went there ten years ago to find *him*, but what I found was that he had always been right where I left him...in the pages of *Nature I Loved*, along with his words of encouragement, his reverence for nature, and his kindness.

Dee Dauphinee
April 2022
Bradley, ME
www.ddauphinee.com

# Editor's Introduction

Bill Geagan's *Nature I Loved* has been on my father's bookshelf for as long as I can remember. Although I knew it to be a hallowed book, I never cracked the cover as a kid. I wasn't a reader then, and I preferred to experience the outdoors the old-fashioned way.

Many years later, and two decades removed from my life in Maine, I have come to lean on the written word when pining for a dose of home. I have read and reread E. B. White's dispatches from his salt water farm in North Brooklin, as well as his perfect essay, "Once More to the Lake," about a trip to the Belgrade Lakes region with his son. Then one day it hit me: I should finally read *Nature I Loved*. It has been in the rotation ever since.

Sadly, Geagan's book has been out of print since 1977, and copies are not easy to find. As of this writing, for instance, not one is available for sale on Amazon.com.

It is a bad thing for a good book to be unobtainable. It is worse to be forgotten entirely. *Nature I Loved* teetered on the brink of both. I am therefore delighted that North Country Press is publishing this 70th anniversary edition. I'd like to dedicate this edition to my father, who used to bring my brother and me to fish in some of the waters described in Geagan's book.

***

William "Bill" Geagan was born in Maine on December 1, 1903. After graduating from Bangor High School and feeling unsure about his path in life, Geagan tried his hand at a string of conventional occupations—lumberjack, cobbler, cigar maker, shop clerk—and jibbed at each. Running out of options and chafing at the prospect of a mainstream life, he escaped eleven miles to a two-year stint of self-reliant brooding on the shore of Hermon Pond.

The gambit worked. Having consummated his passion for Nature (his capitalization), Geagan assembled a modest resume as a writer and illustrator of articles for national outdoors magazines. Upon leaving the woods, he spent a year on staff at a Boston newspaper. Returning home, he joined the *Bangor Daily Commercial*, first as a reporter and cartoonist, then as a columnist. In 1936 Geagan was successfully recruited by the *Bangor Daily News*, then Maine's largest newspaper, which gave him the modest charge to "pioneer the field of outdoor writing". His nationally-syndicated Associated Press column, "On The Trail", followed in 1940.

After decades of filing semiweekly copy, Geagan resigned his *News* position as sports editor in 1947 and settled into a long and successful career as a freelance journalist, combining bylines in *Field & Stream*, *Fishing World*, and *Outdoor Life* with continued contributions to several Maine newspapers. Geagan released *Nature I Loved,* his first book, in 1952, and followed it with *The Good Trail* (1954) and *Seed on the Wind* (1957), all published by Coward-McCann.

Throughout his career, Geagan was often credited with establishing and nurturing the field of wildlife conservation in Maine. Commenting on this, he once said: "They call it 'Conservation', but it's really ecology or the relativeness between the various species of wildlife, from the mosquito right on to the moose." As he writes in the last chapter of *Nature I Loved*, Geagan felt a calling "to protect those priceless gifts from all who through ignorance, carelessness, or greed would destroy them, by preaching with the written word the gospel of conservation, and if necessary fighting for them in the same manner."

In 1973 Geagan was elected an honorary member of the New England Outdoor Writers Association. In its citation, the Association confessed to the "admittedly selfish" desire "to consider you one of us. You have nailed down your reputation as a titan in the craft. We respect you. We have envied your talent and studied your technique."

Geagan died a year later in 1974.

\*\*\*

As editor of this new edition of *Nature I Loved*, I must acknowledge that the book contains some discourteous remarks concerning members of a Native American hunting party that Geagan observes from afar in chapter 20. Although I am convinced that Geagan revered Indigenous people and their intimate knowledge of the natural world, even admirers can commit what we now call microaggressions. It is not my place to apologize on Geagan's behalf or to make excuses for what he chose to write in this part of the book. Nor is it appropriate to redact it. Progress is made by confronting the past, and working to do better. Despite its flaws in this and other respects, I sought to make *Nature I Loved* available to a new generation of readers because it is a tender meditation on what the Wabanaki people—Maine's first people—loved and stewarded long before Bill Geagan arrived on the scene.

Upon that background, I wish acknowledge the land described in this book—the land known to Maine's Indigenous peoples as Wabanakeag, the Land of the First Light, the Dawnland. I acknowledge too these peoples—Passamaquoddy, Penobscot, Micmac, Maliseet, and Abenaki. Members of these groups experienced forcible removal from their ancestral lands and were made to endure unthinkable harms for the sake of settler colonialism. Maine remains a land where sacred sites are routinely disturbed, and where Indigenous rights to water, territory, and economic opportunity remain unfulfilled. I encourage those reading this book to learn how they can make meaningful efforts toward restorative justice in their own communities. An excellent resource for those in Maine is firstlightlearningjourney.net.

Paul Kelleher
April 2022
Madison, WI

# About the Text

The text of this book was digitized from the original 1952 edition using the optical character recognition engine Tesseract. In preparing the manuscript for publication, I have made a limited number of editorial adjustments, mostly to fix the occasional misspelling and to rearrange, delete, or add commas. Geagan is a clear writer, but his use of commas was at times idiosyncratic and liable to trip up modern readers.

Readers may access and download a pdf scan of the original 1952 edition of *Nature I Loved* at: paulkelleher.net/geagan/

TO MY WIFE, ALICE

I WANT particularly to thank for their encouragement to write this book and for their advice during its writing Edwin Valentine Mitchell, DeWitt MacKenzie, Ben Ames Williams, Marjorie Mills, Allan Wood, Jr., Mrs. Sylvia Ross, and George J. Stobie.

I strove with none, for none was worth my strife.
Nature I loved and, next to nature, Art.
I warmed both hands before the fire of life,
It sinks, and I am ready to depart.

WALTER SAVAGE LANDOR

# 1

IT SEEMS there is nothing that plagues the human mind so fiercely as being completely lost when time is precious and fast running out. It's like wandering through a madhouse of mirrors while an important engagement awaits outside, or through a tangled forest swamp, with only a little daylight remaining.

I found myself in just such a predicament five years after graduating from high school. I wasn't bewildered by numerous images of myself in glass nor was I wallowing aimlessly in a sprawl of wilderness slop and trees; but I was every bit as badly lost—lost hopelessly, it seemed, along the twisting and cluttered trail of life.

Nearly all of my friends who had left school with me had found their places. They knew what they wanted to do and were doing it. I envied them—not because of the particular types of work or study they were engaged in, but because they had decided on definite goals and were striving to reach them.

Like all who are lost I had tried many ways to get out—to find myself and get started on a solid and definite trail leading to somewhere. Any man who is going to amount to anything should, it seemed, be well on his way at the age of twenty-five. That thought dug deeper and deeper into my mind like a talon as my frustration became greater.

I had tried work of many types, and I had studied art in Boston schools during summer vacations and with my mother, a very good artist in any medium. I thought for a time I wanted to become a cartoonist on one of the great newspapers. I tried too, that is to the extent of shipping bales of my work to big city newspapers and asking for such a job. Rejection slips, and a few kind notes from more human and thoughtful editors, finally convinced me that I wasn't ready.

I don't think I really felt too badly about it after all. Anyhow, I probably wouldn't have worked long at such a job, for in just those few weeks during the summers of studying in Boston I disliked more and more the heat, the clamor, and the seemingly senseless rushing about of the people on the streets, in the restaurants, and in the subways. I made very few friends but not because those people were unfriendly. I think that big city people have been misjudged in that respect. They are really just like those people back in the towns and villages, but they can't be friendly simply because they haven't got the time.

All people living in large cities appear to me like high-geared toys wound up to the bursting point, and controlled by alarm clocks, whistles, and train schedules. Such a hurried and crowded life wasn't for me—a Maine boy who loved the outdoors. That much I was sure of.

I had taken a fling, mostly to please a very patient mother and father, at learning the trades of making cigars and moccasins, and later trying to work up to a job as shipping clerk with a local dry-goods wholesale house. I really tried to make a go of those jobs but the interest just wasn't there.

Making cigars and moccasins are fine trades for those with a natural desire for them, but I had none of that desire, and the thought of a long apprenticeship devouring more valuable years, and finally a lifetime perhaps as a fair operator despising his work haunted me, and again the search for the right trail was resumed.

Odd jobs in lumber mills, unloading coal from steamers that came up the Penobscot River, swinging the pick, clerking in stores, etc., were taken only to earn a few dollars to pay my board at home and put clothes on my back.

One long cold winter as a lumberjack in the great north woods completely extinguished a flickering desire for such a life. I liked the big woods and thrilled at the sight and sound of towering spruces crashing in billows of snow and branches. The food although plain was excellent and was served generously three times a day. I enjoyed too the after supper stories and songs of the old lumberjacks and the little entertainment programs they gave on Sundays after the boiling and washing of our clothes was done. On those Sundays when a thaw sweetened the air I amused myself by following the tracks of the many wild things and reading Nature's storybook written on the snow.

I didn't, however, like the loud and seemingly cruel "roll-out" call before daylight, the hurried wolfing of breakfast, and the long, silent hike in single file through the fierce cold of the starlit morning to the cutting yards, with the rough and ignorant men.

I disliked most of all, though, sleeping on straw in the rough board bunks arranged in tiers along either side of the huge and very squatty log cabin. The damp warm air was polluted with the awful odor of perspiration that oozed from the pelts of the dog-tired men who snored and groaned as they slept. I hated too the lice that came during the night and set up housekeeping inside my union suit. It was impossible to keep clean no matter how hard you tried.

Two and a half months of that life was enough for me, and one cold, sun-flooded morning I shouldered a heavy knapsack, pocketed a bit less than two hundred dollars, and hit the long white trail on the first leg of a sixty-mile journey to the outside and the railroad. The hundred-mile ride home was devoted to thinking, worrying, and brooding.

Finally home there came more days of loafing, of trying this job and that, of hunting and trapping a bit, and of wondering and worrying some more. I think my good folks were a little discouraged with me. I most certainly was with myself. One old neighborhood gossip remarked to others of her kind that "Ann and Henry Geagan would have been much better off if they had raised a pig instead of Bill for they could kill and eat the pig."

Another winter melted away and another spring found me still wrestling with the problem that was now, it seemed, bigger and more difficult than ever. I was low in spirit, and miserable. I couldn't sleep. The loss of appetite and weight followed under the pressure of burning nerves. Something had to be done and soon.

The family doctor told me nobody could help me but myself. Finally in May I decided that I would get into the woods somewhere alone and there think it over and perhaps arrive at a decision as to what sort of work I wanted to do to earn a good and respectable living.

I heard of a man in town who wanted to sell an old log cabin on Hermon Pond, about twenty miles from my home. I called on him and we talked. He gave me the key, told me how to get there, and said that if I liked the place I could have it for a hundred dollars. I discovered after my first inspection of the place that it was quite a bargain.

Maine's many waters have been carelessly classified and named. Hermon Pond is one of them. Stretching three miles in length and more than a mile at its widest points it most certainly is a lake. It is the largest body of water in a sprawl of six, which are connected by small streams and drained by the large Souadabscook Stream, which finally winds down to the Penobscot River at Hampden. The other waters are really ponds. They are Patten, Ben Annis, Tracy, Hammond, and George.

Most of Maine's many waters were named by the Indians. Although the spelling and pronunciation of most of those names have been changed several times by the white man, the following tongue twisters for lakes are still to be found on the map—Mooselookmeguntic, Alamoosook, Megunticook, Nicatous, Sourdnahunk, Cuxabexis, Caucomgomoc, Wesserunsett, and countless others. Streams and mountains too bear Indian names equally strange.

Those lakes, ponds, streams, and mountains were all named for some reason or other. They all mean something according to my Indian friends of the Penobscot, Algonquin, and Passamaquoddy tribes. But even the oldest are not sure of the original pronunciation, how they should be spelled, or exactly what they mean.

One of my closest and oldest Indian friends, Chief Henry Red Eagle of the Algonquin tribe, tells me the waters, mountains, meadows, etc. were named by the early redmen because of conditions or the amount and the species of fishes and game. And he believes that Hermon Pond and the others in that vast area of forests, bogs, and sprawling heaths did at one time have Indian names.

He believes as I do that perhaps because of the length and difficulty of pronouncing those names the white men who settled there finally changed them to those of persons, like the town of Hermon.

The great lazy stream that drains the region still bears the Indian name, Souadabscook, however, which Red Eagle says might mean, "place of many waters." But one very old woman member of the Penobscot tribe once told me she thought it meant a place of much food and fur because of the great abundance of pickerel, migrating sea fishes, and muskrats to be found there at that time.

The white man made many changes and he certainly made a mess of classifying and renaming many waters of the state. For example in Hancock county, twenty miles southeast of Bangor, there are two trout and salmon waters both nine miles long, one of which is called Branch Pond, and the other Green Lake. And so it goes up and down and across the state.

The man who owned the cabin told me of the excellent fishing for pickerel, smallmouthed black bass, and white perch in all of the waters in the area and of an abundance of wild ducks, grouse, snowshoe rabbits, and a few deer. He explained that he built the place with the help of a group of friends years before for a fishing and hunting camp, but because a couple of those friends had died and the others had moved away he had no more interest in the place. It held nothing for him but memories that hurt, he said, and he hadn't been near it for two years. That's why he was willing to sell it at such a "low figure," he explained. And that included besides the cabin, an old eighteen-foot canoe, also dishes, furniture, and bedding.

It seemed like a bargain regardless of the condition of the place and although I had only sixty dollars in the bank I jumped at the chance to get the old place and hurried home with the key and the good news.

My folks agreed it sounded like a bargain if the cabin and other things were in any condition at all, and my father even offered to give me the forty dollars I needed to make the hundred. He said it would probably make a nice summer place for me and the rest of the family. But both he and my mother appeared stunned when I told them of my plans to live there alone. I did of course tell them they would be welcome at any time.

They protested quite vigorously and finally tried to separate me from the idea with ridicule. They said it couldn't be done—that I would have no money and would either starve or freeze to death.

But I was determined and after a rather lengthy debate, which flared quite hot in spots, they agreed that if the place could be made livable and I insisted on trying it during the summer, it would be all right with them. My young sister Helen later told me she overheard my father tell my mother that I would become tired of such a life even if I could get food enough to eat and that when the cold days of fall set in I would be back home in a hurry and ready at last to settle down and go to work.

I planned to visit the place and inspect it the next day and if I liked it to return and try to beat the price down to somewhere between fifty and sixty dollars. When the early morning train hauled out of Bangor I occupied one of the chairs in the smoker along with a knapsack that contained bacon, beans, biscuits, a small tin can for brewing tea, a belt ax, and a roughly penciled map the camp owner had drawn so that I might have no difficulty in finding the place.

I didn't read nor did I smoke during the train ride. I was too busy thinking. Thoughts and plans raced back and forth through my mind in such numbers and at such speed it seemed they would cause a traffic jam. The time rushed by and suddenly the train whistled into the station, squeaked to a stop, rested briefly, and hauled out leaving me and a couple of bags of mail on the pine-plank platform.

It was May and the morning was blue and golden. The outdoors was coming to life after the long winter sleep. The bird choir was at its best. Tiny green leaves trimmed the hardwoods, and the air was sweet with the fragrance of damp earth, fresh water, and growing things. It seemed that Nature had opened a million bottles of perfume.

Behind me in the little station I could hear the monotonous blathering of the telegraph apparatus. An old man under an eye shade was bending over it at a cluttered desk. The window was open. I walked over and looked in. The man lifted his fingers and his eyes from the keys.

"Nice mawnin' son," he drawled. I agreed enthusiastically, and inquired if I could rent a boat somewhere in the vicinity. He said there were no boats available that he knew of, but after I told him what I wanted one for he became more friendly, and said that if I could handle a canoe I would be welcome to use his during the day.

There are many, including fishermen and hunters, who cannot handle canoes and who really are afraid of them. It seems that the slick, streamlined craft invented by the Indian has been given a bad name that sticks stubbornly simply because greenhorns, drunks, and show-offs frequently swamp them or roll them over.

There's no excuse for any such mishaps, for the well-made canoe of cedar and canvas, properly loaded and handled, is perfectly safe. I would much rather take my

8

chances in such a craft on any inland water and under any conditions than in most of the much larger and heavier so called rowboats I have seen.

The station agent's canoe was an eighteen-foot guide's model with a keel. It was turned bottom-up under a spruce on the nearby bank of a wide, lazy stream called Stanley Stream by the natives, Black Stream by a few others, but which is really a part of the great Souadabscook that drains the vast area.

With the bow carefully weighted down with stones placed on a piece of old canvas I was away swiftly with a fast and easy stroke on the light spruce paddle. The stream twisted serpentine for more than a quarter of a mile through wild meadowland, stands of bog maples and alders, and finally spewed me into the head waters of Hermon Pond.

My arrival was greeted by the roar of hurrying wings as three pairs of mating black ducks climbed out of a long tongue of bullrushes.

I studied the map the owner of the cabin had sketched for me, pointed the bow toward the west shore, and sliced swiftly along on a light chop kicked up by a cool northwest wind. That west shore was heavily forested with old spruces, hemlocks, pines, and oaks that crowded down to coarse gravel beaches and great sprawls of sprouting water weeds. A few small summer camps, none of them occupied, crouched here and there back in the woods.

I saw none, however, on the last mile and a half of the three-mile journey. That pleased me for if I were to buy the cabin and live there I would not want to be bothered by the shouting of bathers and the roaring of motorboats. Above all I would not want neighbors or visitors. There would be no time for social activities or playing, for I had a problem to solve—the same problem that all men must solve lest they become mendicants existing miserably on the generosity of more fortunate fellow men until the coming of a merciful death.

It seemed at that time that I would never be able to solve mine. And I wondered how the many men I knew had found themselves, secured jobs they could work at year after year, and how they could raise families, buy automobiles and homes, carry insurance, and meet the many other responsibilities of married life.

The roar of more startled ducks banished that gnawing thought from my mind as the canoe rounded a grassy point. I was suddenly in the quiet water of a yawning cove on the shore of which stood the cabin in which I was soon to live alone with the problem of how to make an ample, respectable, and pleasant living, and gain at least a measure of security.

The cabin was typical of those used by lumberjacks and trappers in the northern wilderness. I became suddenly happy as I walked up the little trail toward it. It was what I had wanted all of my life. It squatted low under towering pines and white birches and the little clearing in which it sat was rimmed with a dense mixed growth that was steadily crawling back to reclaim the land.

The logs were peeled spruce from seven to nine inches in diameter and were notched and laid horizontally. They were grayed and cracked by the weather but testings with my ax and belt knife found them to be as sound as a nut, including those used for sills.

The cabin sat very close to the ground on six large flat-headed rocks and the walls were very low. The roof, covered with a heavy, red sanded roofing material sloped gently well beyond the walls, and it pushed out front on the same spruce ridgepole to cover an eight-foot platform veranda. The cabin itself was eighteen by twenty-five feet.

That's really quite large as woods camps go, and unusually large for one person.

I was further enthused by a fat stone chimney that sat hunched on the middle of the roof, making the cabin appear even lower and cozier.

My enthusiasm faded, however, when I turned the key and shoved open a heavy log door. As I had feared the place was a mess and a rendezvous for spiders, squirrels, bats, and mice. My heart sank like an anvil in a hogshead of molasses.

The smoke-blackened mouth of a huge and very crude fieldstone fireplace yawned hideously at me and one of several crazy bats that roared out of the dark crashed against my shoulder and flopped under an old couch.

The place was cut up into a large living room, a kitchen, and a bedroom. Three quarter partitions of small standing fir logs or poles separated the rooms. It had been a fine place once but it certainly was a dump then.

There were three windows in the spacious living room, one on each side of the door, and a very long one on the north side. They were filled with eight by ten inch panes of glass, some of which had been broken. Two little single beds with cedar log posts and the old couch were shoved against the living room wall, and a large table covered with a faded green tapestry cloth, which in turn was covered with bark and bug dust from overhead beams, stood near the middle of the floor.

Beyond the table in front of the crude and rustic fireplace sprawled the largest braided rug I had ever seen. It had been soaked with rain that came through a leak in the roof, but it was in good condition. I loved it.

Battered chairs, both wooden and stuffed, were scattered about, and the mounted head of an eyeless buck deer hung from a spike on the fireplace chimney. The beams, all ax-scarred spruce logs, were heavily bearded with dust-laden cobwebs.

In the kitchen I found a large range with a hot-water tank on the rear and a warming shelf above. Rain that had dripped through another break in the roofing had rusted it badly. A little black iron sink was also red with rust caused by the dampness and roof leaks. There were three little wooden chairs and a leaf table covered with a ragged oilcloth, and an open-faced cupboard loaded with a weird assortment of dishes and smoke blackened pots and pans.

Several panes of glass had been blown out of the one window by the winds and a curious wild rosebush had climbed up, peeked in, and tumbled onto the floor. It was still alive and sprouting little pink buds. The back door had apparently been forced open some time or other, tearing out the lock and splitting the casing. It had since been strongly spiked.

The stove pipe, which curled up to the fireplace chimney, was broken in the middle and one section of it lay on the floor in a heap of soot.

I turned to the bedroom to find it soaked with rain and snow water that had poured in through several openings in the roofing. There were two windows with several broken panes, an old white iron bed, two cots, and an old bureau. A heap of blankets, quilts, and pillows, some in cases, were thrown over a dusty rafter, and a white pot big enough to accommodate an elephant glared at me in the darkness under the bed.

My rummaging also revealed in the cabin and in a little log shed several kerosene lamps, two lanterns, several cans and pails partly filled with paint and varnish, paint brushes all stiff and hard, a roll of rusted chicken wire, two ice chisels—one of which had a wooden handle that was cracked—window glass, an old ax, chains, rope, roofing tar, rusted tools, nails, spikes, tacks, and a heap of other odds and ends.

A well-worn trail wound into the woods to a two-holer with a leaky roof, and another trail twisted away to a large and very beautiful bubbling spring. Back in the camp my neck was nearly broken when, standing on a rickety chair, I hauled the old eighteen-foot canoe down from its resting place on the bedroom beams for inspection. One of the chair legs caved in and with the bow of the canoe trying to divide my chest I went crashing flat on my back onto the living-room table.

As I had guessed, the old canoe was in pretty bad shape. It had been patched in places and the bottom had been badly clawed and scraped by rocks and underwater stumps and stubs. I found three punctures near the bottom amidships, and the thin strip of brass called a bang plate was broken and protruding at the base of the stern. There were two spruce paddles that, like the ribs and planking of the canoe, were badly in need of varnish.

I stood at the front door gazing in silence at the depressing mess I could call my own for a hundred dollars or perhaps less. I wondered if I could ever clean it up alone and make the place livable. The inspection tour continued in the afternoon after a lunch cooked outdoors, and I crawled from the wreckage convinced that it could be accomplished in time and determined that I'd stick to it until it was.

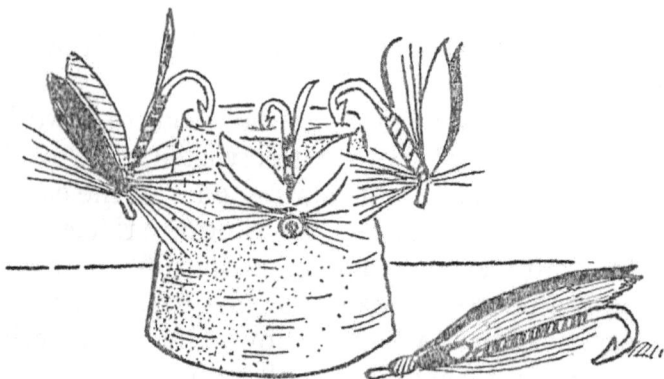

# 2

THE DAY was old and I was very tired when I had finished inspecting the cabin and the grounds. Completely absorbed in the rather fascinating task I had lost all track of time. The train that was to have hauled me back to Bangor had gone and there wouldn't be another until early the next morning. There was nothing to do but make preparations to spend the night there, and with the chilly spring dusk moving in rapidly I had no time to lose.

I wouldn't have slept in the damp, dirty, rodent-ridden cabin on a bet. All good woodsmen such as guides, timber cruisers, and game wardens avoid such places. Back in the big woods of the north country most of the abandoned cabins were once used by old trappers or timber cutters and are usually filthy and crawling with lice and rodents.

I too had learned my lesson and like those veterans of the woods I prepared to camp out. This particular cabin having been used only by sportsmen harbored no lice, but it was in no condition to sleep in.

Dry wood was abundant on a flat spot under the pines down near the big spring and so were fir boughs, which I hacked off to build my bed. Two blankets taken from the cabin were thoroughly shaken and hung up for airing near the little supper fire. There was only a little food left and it was necessary that I eat sparingly so that there might be a bit for breakfast the next morning.

Night crawled through the woods to chase away the shadows, and a bloated moon, like a huge brass gong floated up in the east to bring them back again. A fox barked sharply back in the hills and the haunting hooting of an owl rolled out of a swamp. The little fire burned a ragged orange hole in the night and added fragrant wood smoke to the perfume of the outdoors that sweetened my blankets.

Rolled in one with the other spread loosely over me, I was comfortable and strangely happy as I lay on the soft and fragrant bed of boughs watching the dance of the flames and wondering if perhaps the old fellow at the railroad station was worrying about his canoe.

It was the only real happiness I had known for a long time, and I wondered if perhaps God's great outdoors was the only place I could find it—if it were the place where I belonged.

I recalled what an old woodsman had said to me years before. Every word of it came back to me. I had met him at a little lumbering operation and accepted his invitation to have lunch and rest after a strenuous morning on a trout stream.

Men who live in the woods do not talk much. They become almost as silent as the great trees that make up their world. This is due of course to the fact that there are not many to talk with and not much to talk about. But they do think and from that deep and constant thinking sprouts surprisingly wise and comforting philosophy.

That old fellow was typical of the Maine backwoodsman as were the other members of the very small crew. It was after lunch as we sat in the summer sunshine on the bank of the stream that he spoke those words that returned to me there by the little fire.

I had told him of my love for the woods and of how I was happiest when roaming through them. He looked at me and smiled. Then very slowly as though weighing his words he said, "Son, there's nawthin' better'an the woods. They make a man big and clean just like they are. But if you git into 'em young and stick to 'em long enough, they'll put their mark on you, and you'll come back to 'em eventually no matter where yer go or what yer doin'. Yer jist can't keep away!"

I took that statement with the proverbial grain of salt, regarding it as just another of the many strange little ideas that grow in the minds of such men. But as I lay there happy by the little fire in the quiet woods and recalled those words I wondered if perhaps he might have been right after all.

Like waves washing footprints on the sand, time erases from memory much of our past. Yet, there are incidents that defy its powers and continue to blaze brightly despite the years that soon come and go all too swiftly.

If my earthly span were to be extended to ten times its natural length I would hold always the memory of my self-introduction to the woods. I can recall as clearly as though it were yesterday, how a touseled-haired boy of nine stood saucer eyed in a lush green wonderland of entrancing odors, scampering wild things, and brooks that laughed.

My home was but a scant two miles from a great tract of woods, and being an average American boy it was only natural that sooner or later I would be attracted to them. And, for the same reason, it was only natural that I carried in a back pocket of my faded blue overalls a jackknife. It was an old knife with a broken blade. My father had discarded it. That knife gnawed down my first fishing rod, a crooked alder sapling. And it notched the tip that I might attach a length of soiled wrapping cord, and with a small safety pin and wriggling worm seek the fat speckled trout that fanned lazily in the quiet black pool of a brook that passed under a little log bridge in the old tote road.

It was my first adventure with fishes. I had watched them for a half hour before deciding to try to catch them. And it was during that first adventure that I learned that if you can see a trout the trout can see you, and will not be easily taken.

Sprawling on my belly and back from sight on the little log bridge, I dropped the worm-baited pin over the edge. It landed with a plop in the black water of the pool below. Almost instantly a vicious tug bowed the sapling. My heart pounded furiously, and two small berry-stained hands, paled under pressure, yanked hard.

I heard a splash of water, and a fat, ten-inch trout twisted high in the air. It slipped off the safety-pin hook and bounced in the green ferns on the bank. Quickly retrieved lest it flop back to the water, the fish was stuffed into a pocket and the great adventure continued.

When I told the story to my mother and showed her eight fat trout she scolded me for wandering into the woods alone. Later when she found the crude little rod and line she kissed me and whispered something to my father who was grinning like a Cheshire cat as he dressed the trout for supper. I thought I detected a light of pride in their eyes.

From that moment on I was a fisherman—an enthusiastic disciple of the immortal Izaak Walton, and a lover of the great outdoors. Two days later I was the proud owner of a half dozen little snelled hooks and a roll of green line, which my Dad had purchased for me in town.

Since that day on the little trout brook I have wandered far afield in my quest for piscatorial pleasure and the peace, contentment, and health that goes with it. My cup is filled always to overflowing whether I am taking the tigerish tuna of the broad Atlantic or the lowly yellow perch of a languid lily pond. It will always be so.

My first gun, a little single-shot .22-caliber rifle followed closely my first fishing rod, and a kind and patient father, now gone, God bless him, instructed me in the proper use of both.

Frost-spiced autumn mornings when the hardwoods were ablaze found me pussyfooting along old woods' roads where plump grouse awaited the warming sun. Many a squirrel also bit the dust, and in winter the big white snowshoe rabbit was my quarry.

More and larger guns came later as the years rolled on. With them I sought the swift, whitetail deer, the lumbering yet very elusive black bear, the majestic moose, and the many smaller species of game. The annual autumnal call of Diana always has a strange effect on me. But although I still enjoy shouldering my rifle or shotgun and wandering afield with or without my dogs, I find that now, much in the manner of water oozing from a paper bag, the desire to kill is leaving me.

Although for a time I was at a complete loss to explain this, I now feel that perhaps it is caused by an increasing appreciation of natural beauty and the realization that

American wildlife is becoming scarce as our frontiers recede before the relentless push of civilization.

Fishing too has felt this push in some places where once prolific waters have been ruined by pollution. But there is still much good fishing to be found in nearly all parts of the country, and in some sections State Fish and Game Departments and sportsmen's organizations have launched programs to clean the polluted waters and have them restocked.

Because of these cleanup projects and the extensive stocking programs I believe there will always be fishing for the millions who indulge in it, for it affords matchless sport and the healthful recreation. It will continue long after hunting is but a pleasant memory.

I had gone to the woods early and returned to them many times, and again I was back, this time on the shores of Hermon Pond, and despite the plaguing problem that faced me, I was quite happy.

Finally as I lay there reviewing my life the night sounds faded and I fell into the deepest sleep I had known for many months. I awoke cold and shivering just as the dawn wind came up to blow out the stars. The little fire was reduced to warm white ashes. The train would be leaving in a little more than two hours and I had no time to waste. A scanty breakfast followed a cold washing in the lake and with the old canoe, its leaks patched with adhesive tape, trailing on a short rope, I paddled the one I had borrowed swiftly up the lake nearly three miles to the station.

I hauled up the kind man's canoe and turned it over where I had found it. Mine was placed along side of it. I would use it when I returned to begin my experimental sojourn in the woods.

The old station agent appeared greatly relieved when he saw me swinging up the trail from the stream. He waved me down when I tried to explain and offer my apologies for keeping the canoe over night.

"That's all right, that's all right," he squeaked. "I warn't worried about the canoe. But I was afraid you might have upset or somethin'."

Lest I intensify my parents' disapproval of my plan to live in the woods alone I didn't report an entirely accurate picture of conditions as I had found them at the old cabin. But I went all the way when I reported to the owner the next day. I told him the truth and perhaps a bit more in the hope that he might drop the price to within my reach.

He wasn't surprised, or at least he didn't seem to be, when I told him that the place was in very bad condition and that it would require some money and a great deal of work to make it fit to live in.

He nodded understandingly, smiled, and pulled a faded photograph of the camp and a crowd of fishermen out of a drawer. "That's the cabin and the gang in the good old days," he said, still smiling. "I realize that the past few years must have taken a lot out of the place and maybe it isn't worth a hundred dollars."

I took advantage of a pause to tell him what I wanted the place for and to report my financial condition at the time. "Well," he drawled, "the old place doesn't owe me a dime, so if you want it for fifty dollars cash I guess you can have it."

I was back that night with the money, bought the place, grabbed the deed, thanked him, and hurried homeward through the dark. Most of the night was devoted to examining and packing things I would need, which included fishing and camping equipment, outdoor clothing, towels, dishcloths, washing powder, soap, etc. I also packed ten dollars' worth of food, which included potatoes, bacon, corn meal, salt pork, bread, flour, baking powder, lard, onions, prepared pancake flour, butter, prunes, canned beans, sugar, canned milk, and canned fruit. And for my two fox hounds I stuffed into the load a supply of dog food.

A friend with a small truck hauled the load to the railroad station. My father and I walked down with the dogs. I knew he didn't think I would stay in the woods long—no longer than I had ever stayed anywhere—and that I would soon be back home ready to forget my "nonsense" and go to work on a permanent job. He repeated again what he had said many times before, "Very few working people are doing what they want to do. They are just making the best of it and trying to be happy."

I began to believe that perhaps he was right but knew that I couldn't get along under such conditions. I didn't see any reason why I couldn't be one of the "very few" he mentioned.

I refused the ten-dollar bill he tried to stuff into one of the breast pockets of my black and white checked wool shirt. But to ease his and my mother's mind I promised that if I needed money or food I would get in touch with them. But I promised myself that that was one thing I would not do for by so doing I would again be flying the flag of failure.

That promise was the makings for a little white lie which I hoped would never mature. A few extra dollars I had in my pocket went to pay for railroad transportation of myself, my dogs, and my duffel. I sat in silence on a back seat in the smoker listening to the monotonous clicking of the wheels as they sped over the rails. Each click was taking me farther away from the ones I loved—into an adventure on which it seemed my future, my life depended.

I looked down from the coach window at my canoe lying where I had left it on the bank of the stream. Dogs and duffel were dumped from the baggage car, and there I stood amid most of my worldly possessions and without a penny in my pocket, watching the hurrying train being slowly devoured by the distance.

"What in thunder is happenin'. Is there a circus in town?" It was the station agent. He was coming down the long platform with a bundle of mail in one hand and a can of switch lamp oil in the other.

He tied up the hounds in the little station for me while I made several trips with the supplies to the canoe. It would be necessary to make at least two trips down the lake, and with the hope that a heavy blow wouldn't come up I pitched into the work of carefully packing the first load into the old craft. I decided to take the hounds with that load and tie them up at the old cabin until I returned with the next.

One of the dogs was a large and very handsome black, tan, and white Walker foxhound named Jack. He would run either foxes or the big snowshoe rabbits, and I had known him to run bobcats on a few occasions.

The other was a medium-sized black and tan foxhound named Drive, who would hunt foxes and raccoons. I wondered as I piled the two prancing and whining canines into the canoe if I would be able to feed them for they both had fierce appetites and were used to two meals a day. Most of the owners of sporting dogs I know feed them only once. I never liked that plan. It always seemed cruel to me. I wondered too if I would be able to feed myself.

With all bundles tied as small as possible and with the heaviest on the floor of the canoe I stuffed my pipe, touched it off, and was away on the paddle with a heavy cargo that shoved the old craft deeply into the water. It's really amazing how much can be carried in a canoe when it is properly loaded.

A light northwest wind helped me along down the lake, and I hoped it would not increase before I returned for the second load. The restless hounds, sniffing, drooling, and tumbling over one another gave me a hard time, and before I was halfway to the cabin the old canoe began to leak quite badly.

Finally arriving at the place the canoe was eased up sidewise to the shore and the job of unloading was quickly underway. Fortunately the water that had leaked in hadn't reached the flour or sugar. Everything was in good shape. It was piled under a pine on the shore and the dogs were tied up on long ropes to another tree where they could protect but not reach it.

The canoe was leaking along the keel. I applied more adhesive tape and shoved off after the remainder of the supplies. It was afternoon when again the old craft ground onto the gravel shore in front of the cabin. I had paddled a total of nearly ten miles and was tired and ravenously hungry.

The hounds too were hungry, and they wolfed fiercely the water-soaked mash I had mixed for them, while I devoured with gusto bacon, fried eggs, bread and tea prepared at the little fireplace by the spring.

There after some struggling I pitched my small tent, made an outside table of an old board door by resting its ends on log cleats spiked to a pair of pines. There I would live with the dogs until the tremendous task of cleaning and putting the cabin into condition was completed.

And soon it was time to eat the evening meal. With soap and towel I walked slowly down the trail past the cabin to the shore of the lake. Across the yawning cove, the towering hardwoods, wearing crowns of young green leaves, seemed to be standing on tiptoe to watch the blushing sun go to bed. A cool, plum-blue dusk crowded in to devour the brassy afterglow as I watched in silence. A lonely loon called, and the stars came out.

I liked it there. It was quiet, beautiful, and clean and from it all I would wrest a living—and much more, I hoped. I had come back to the woods to live. Not as Thoreau who went to his Walden Pond to subsist on beans, berries, and a wonderful philosophy, but much in the manner of the bachelor who maintains a village home. At least I would try.

# 3

NEVER in my life have I worked harder than I did during those next five days. Armed with brooms, a mop, washtubs and buckets of hot water, shore sand, soap, scouring powder, and muscle I attacked the old cabin from early morning until well into the night.

The cobwebs, the dust, broken glass, a mountain of mouse and squirrel manure, and loads of worthless junk, including broken chairs, cots, dishes, etc., were cleaned out. Broken windows were replaced and washed along with all of the dishes and pans I wanted to keep.

One of the first things that got the bums' rush was the old white iron bed. I have always hated the sight of the thin, spidery looking things. It was dragged, piece by piece, far back into the woods to a swamp where I established a dumping place for all the rubbish I would be unable to burn.

The huge old pot followed the bed. I wouldn't have been caught dead squatting on that thing even on a night when a blizzard howled. If I should ever become so tender that I couldn't snatch up a lantern and dash to the little outhouse and get it over with man-fashion then there would be no place for me in the woods. I reaped a sort of fiendish enjoyment from standing off and smashing the silly looking thing with rocks.

When the tremendous task of house cleaning and repairing was over I had the two rustic cedar-post beds in the bedroom with a little table between them, a cot on the other side of the room near the dresser, and the old couch out in the living room under the wide window.

The place was full of kerosene lamps. I used a large one with round wick and wide white shade on the living-room table, which I left covered with the heavy and, although a bit faded, rather pretty green tapestry cloth.

A large bracket lamp with a reflector was spiked to a wall log on the other side of the room and another of the same kind was near the sink in the kitchen. The others could be toted about and placed wherever they might be needed. I had plenty of light—soft yellow lamplight. I loved it, and still do.

The sprawling braided rug was spread in front of the fireplace hearth near the center of the floor. I liked the old fireplace. It was very roughly built of jagged field stones and was very large. Adding more to its rustic beauty was a three-inch-thick oakplank shelf on which sat a large and very old clock that was out of whack. It would keep time fairly well but for some reason or other the striking apparatus and the hands never could agree.

After I moved in that old, smoke-stained fireplace shelf plank became the resting place for a weird and tangled assortment of odds and ends which included old bird nests, old hornet nests, fly-tying material, all the Indian relics I could find, bottles of fly oil, pipes, etc. When in desperation I cleaned it off, it would soon be cluttered again. It was just too handy.

The doors and windows were left open during the house-cleaning period that the fresh air and sunshine might sweeten the place. I continued to live in the tent nearby while I banished the bats and mice. The hounds were kept on the long ropes for I had neither the time nor the desire to go racing through the woods to haul them off the trails of foxes, rabbits, or raccoons.

A few little back-breaker traps found in the log shed were steadily reducing the mouse population, but I was anxious to increase the catch and get it over with that I might move in and set up housekeeping. When I found one that had dropped into an old ten-quart pail and was unable to climb out, I decided to use the pail to take them wholesale.

The first step in making the trap was to pour water into the pail to the depth of a few inches. That was enough to drown those that tumbled in. I then stretched tightly, in the manner of a drumhead, across the top, a sheet of brown wrapping paper and fastened it with a few windings of cord around the top of the pail. A little cross was slit in the middle with a sharp hunting knife and bits of bread, butter, and bacon were tossed onto the paper. Pieces of boards were arranged like ramps for the mice to climb on and the contraption was set and ready.

Up they came and down they went through the slits in the paper head to be quickly drowned. The great population was reduced to a scattered few in less than a week, during which time I patched the rips in the roofing, did more scouring, and discovered under the kitchen linoleum a trap door and a one-man cellar. The hole was about six feet square and five feet deep. A little fir log ladder served for steps. The men who built the cabin years before must have dug the hole for a storeroom of some sort or perhaps they had planned to sink a pipe and point down below the level of the pond so that they could pump water into the kitchen.

The little cellar smelled strongly of tar and damp earth. I found in it an old sledge hammer, a rusted shovel, and a large wooden box of oakum, which apparently had been left over after the calking of the logs had been done.

Oakum is tarred hemp fibers used for calking between the planking of ships to keep out the water and between the logs of cabins to keep out the wind and cold. The oakum is shoved between the logs with the fingers and pounded in tight with a wooden wedge and a mallet or hammer. When oakum is not available around woods cabins long-rooted swamp moss is used and makes a very good substitute.

I was glad to find the oakum for there was considerable calking to be done. There were also many other little things that must be done, but with the heavy work out of the way and the cabin ready for occupancy, I could take care of them at my leisure.

Old pieces of sandpaper, buckets of shore sand, and kerosene took much of the rust off the kitchen stove. I planned to give it a coat of stove paint and then some polishing as soon as I could get around to it.

It was late afternoon the day I moved into the place to live. A brisk blaze was kindled in the stove and the first meal was cooked. Little drumsticks of rain were beating on the roof as I washed the dishes and it was cold and windy outside. It seemed like a good night to try the old fireplace.

Sweet smelling cedar kindling soon roared and snapped in the sooty old stone cavern and caught quickly one of the very dry and very few three-foot birch logs I found in the shed. The flames and sparks shot upward through the heavy black smoke but turned quickly to shoot outward and up over the front of the fireplace. Smoke rolled out in great clouds and the room was soon filled with it.

The frightened hounds went yelping and sprawling, with tails between their legs, out the door, and I floundered blindly after them. I snatched up a pail, rushed to the lake, scooped up some water, and dashed breathlessly back to the cabin. Flames from the white-birch log were roaring upward and licking crazily at the plank shelf. Smoke rolled from the lighted door in blinding billows. It looked bad from the outside. I wouldn't have given a dime for the place at the moment.

The one-man bucket brigade continued as fast as I could run, fall, and get going again. My heart was pounding so hard I thought it would kick out my ribs, and my fiercely dry mouth seemed too small to accommodate a good-sized olive.

I think it required seven pails of water to completely extinguish the blaze. Perhaps it could have been accomplished with less but I was frightened and wasn't taking any chances. Most of that water flooded back over the floor and under the huge braided rug, carrying with it ashes and bits of black charred wood.

It took a lot of coaxing to get the dogs to come inside again. With the smoke finally out and the mess mopped up, I discovered with the help of a half-dead flashlight that a huge iron damper as big as a dinner plate was tightly closed.

It squeaked as it turned reluctantly on a rusted shaft. With it finally open I tried the draught by lighting a sheet of newspaper and found that despite the heavy air of the rainy night it drew very well. I later discovered protruding between the stones on one side of the chimney the ringed head of a bolt for adjusting the damper.

It seemed to me it should have been farther up in the chimney but being one of the most unhandy persons in the world I decided to leave well enough alone.

I slept soundly in one of the little cedar-post beds despite the disturbing experience. The next day was spent in making little repairs and changes about the place, and the night found me again in the battered easy chair before the blazing fireplace which was performing much better. The hounds, however, would have nothing to do with it and snoozed out in front of the kitchen stove.

All lamps blazed brightly, the water kettle sang and the fireplace clock ticked merrily. It was very comfortable there. I studied the old cabin as I lounged in the big chair admiring my work of cleaning and repairing, and checking other jobs that must be done. I liked the place and most of all because it was large and roomy. I had always promised myself that if I ever did take to the woods I would not live in cramped and squalid quarters like most hermits.

My cabin was far from being beautiful. But it was at least big and light and clean. I vowed there before the fire that it would be kept clean. And while in the mood I also vowed that I would keep myself clean of both body and mind, guard always against becoming what is commonly known as "woods queer," and remain a bachelor regardless of any success I might attain or wherever the path of life might lead me.

Most men who live alone back in the woods become more or less "woods queer." It's a strange mental condition caused by the lack of association with people, the great silence, and the loneliness. The victims usually become very shy, talk to themselves, and avoid other persons. I have met a number of them. Some kept their places spick and span and were very fussy about such little things as how the stove was polished, the lamp chimneys cleaned, and even how the sticks were piled in the wood box. Others lived in depressing squalor.

I remember one old fellow who fled from his cabin and hid in the woods all one day and night when he learned that a friend and I were going to call on him and try to hire him as our hunting guide. Another of the victims of the strange malady whom I had engaged as a guide used to crawl out of bed and leave the cabin every night about twelve o'clock and be gone for nearly a half hour. Perhaps I was gambling with my life one night when I followed him down a moonlit trail. There standing at the base of a huge pine with arms waving and voice low, he was talking to the tree. I was on my way home the next day.

An old woodsman with whom I was discussing the subject once said, "It ain't so bad if yer talk to yerself, but when yer start answerin' back, yer a gonner!"

I was sure I wouldn't even talk to myself—well at least no more than the normal man might do when he trips over his kid's toys, nicks his face with the razor while shaving, or bangs his thumb with the hammer.

I would be completely normal in this respect, I promised myself, and should I discover the slightest symptoms of becoming "woods queer" I would make occasional calls on my only friend in the region, the station agent, and talk myself, and him, too, into a state of exhaustion.

Marriage of course was not a problem for I had decided against it. I had yet to find a way to support myself not to mention a wife and perhaps a few kids. But, although I had established a fairly comfortable little home of my own, I did have an immediate problem which I discovered much to my amazement when, before retiring that night, I found my supply of food very low.

Absorbed in the work of fixing up the cabin I hadn't paid much attention to the condition of my larder. It was a very serious situation too, for I was dead broke, game was out of season, and although I might catch a few fish, I couldn't live on them alone. And too the dogs must eat and there was nothing puny about their appetites.

The more I thought about it the more I realized what a really tough spot I was in. There was no one I could borrow from, and the owner of the little general store far up at the head of the lake certainly wouldn't trust a stranger for a large order of groceries. Anyhow I wouldn't have the nerve to try, and I just couldn't pack up and go home to admit failure. I couldn't go back anyhow for I didn't have train fare. And there I was hungry, alone, and mixed up worse than ever.

I rationed the remaining food for myself and the dogs so that it would last for a few more days, and tumbled into bed to spend a restless night.

I had seen porcupine droppings on the ground in a stand of huge old hemlocks back in the woods from the camp, and with a little slide-action repeating .22-caliber rifle I eased down the next morning hoping to bag one of the quill pigs for the dogs. There were four of them perched high in the trees and I brought one crashing to the ground with the third shot. They are tough creatures. That one weighed about fifteen pounds.

Porcupines are very durable animals and they are messy things to skin because of the thousands of needlelike quills on their backs and in their tails. I managed, however, after a time, and returned to the cabin with the huge, fat carcass and large liver. The meat and fat boiled and mixed with what mash was left would stretch the limited supply for the dogs and keep their bellies filled for a few days.

I could have killed another for my own use, for although far from delicious the flesh of the porcupine properly cooked is fairly good and, unlike most wild meat, packs considerable nourishment.

Although this slow-moving, stupid-looking animal is despised and killed on sight by most sportsmen and farmers because of the damage he does, I never kill one unless it is absolutely necessary for it is the only food a man lost in the woods without a gun can kill with a club. I shall never forget that my own life was saved three different times by the coarse and fatty flesh of the porcupine.

Contrary to the general belief, the porcupine cannot throw its sharp, barbed quills. But he can release them at the slightest touch, and he also can drive them deeply into the flesh of an enemy by slashing his tail. Many a fine dog has been ruined after making the mistake of attacking one of the quill pigs of the woods.

Those quills, which have about a dozen tiny barbs along the business end, when driven into the flesh of an enemy while the porcupine is alive will crawl through the body unless removed at once. I have found both furred and feathered predators who had won, yet lost in battles with the porcupine barely able to move about. And they included the great horned owl, the red fox, the black bear, and even that skillful killer the fisher or "black cat" which is credited with being the only wild creature that can attack a porcupine and evade the sharp quills. They, too, make a mistake, it seems.

A fondness for salt causes the porcupines to chew up ax handles and canoe paddles which have been held in sweating hands. And they'll chew up a camp in those places where there are any traces of dishwater or fat. I've known them to eat the tires off an automobile parked back in the woods, and even get under the hood and devour the loom on the engine wires. But I still spare them because of the fact that they have saved my life and might again.

With the porcupine killed and the dogs fed, I lined up one of my fly rods—a five-ounce, eight-and-a-half-foot, split-bamboo Montague with plenty of backbone—and with a roll of small streamer flies set out to try to add a fish or two to the almost empty larder.

White perch were protected until the twenty-first of June, when they would be off the spawning beds in the streams and back in the lake and ponds. The small-mouthed black bass, too, were spawning but the Maine regulations permitted the taking of three a day on the fly from the first day of June to the twenty-first, after which the ten-pound daily bag could be taken on all legal lures. It was the second day of June so I could legally seek the belligerent bronze backs.

The pickerel, which were also busy reproducing their kind, are not protected in Maine and at that time there was no bag limit. A limit, which I helped bring about, has since been set at ten fish a day.

A seven-foot, three-pound test gut leader was tied to the tapered "D" line, and a small Supervisor streamer fly was attached to the business end of the leader.

The bass spawn on gravel beaches along the shore shallows and after the eggs are dropped by the female, the male fertilizes them with a thick white fluid called milt, and stands guard during the incubation period. At that time he'll attack savagely anything that comes near the nest. Not being familiar with the lake I spent some time locating a spawning bed, and the very first cast brought a rise. The fish, a two-pounder, struck hard and fought furiously in and out of the water. A three-pounder was the next to nail the fly. He was a terror on the light tackle and waged a thrilling and spectacular battle for nearly ten minutes before he was finally subdued and led to the landing net.

Others were taken and released along the shore line. But two was enough to kill at a time, for unlike meat, fish is best when very fresh. It was quite evident that I was to have very good fishing, at least on that body of water. And in what little prowling I had done in the woods it seemed that game, too, was quite plentiful. The game of course was protected until the fall and although fish is excellent food I would need meat and potatoes and bread and other things, and most of them wouldn't be found in the woods or the waters. They would have to be bought at the store. But where the money was coming from was the problem—a great big problem that would have to be solved very soon.

# 4

LIFE IN THE great outdoors will improve the appetite of even the most finicky person. The desire for food of almost any kind, and plenty of it, is caused by the exercise in the clean, fresh air that is spiced with the fragrance of the forest, the earth, and clean water.

My dogs and I didn't need any appetizer. The scanty fare on which we had been subsisting for days wasn't nearly enough to satisfy our pleading stomachs. I was tired of eating bass and pickerel and bits of corn bread washed down with weak tea. And I guess they were pretty well fed up with greasy porcupine flesh.

The situation had reached a point where I could no longer remain at the cabin unless I did get food or money to buy it. It seemed I would either have to give up the experiment and return home to take any job I could get or wander into the back country seeking work on some of the small, scattered farms. I didn't want to do either but had half-decided on the latter when a human voice broke the stillness.

It was the first I had heard since I said good-by to the station agent more than two weeks before. It was the voice of a man. It sounded strange—a bit frightening. I almost jumped out of my skin.

"Good morning," he said softly. I looked up from my wood chopping on the shore. He was a small, middle-aged man dressed in typical fishermen's clothes that appeared to be brand new.

"Ah, er—ah, good morning!" I sputtered, trying unsuccessfully not to appear startled.

"I don't like to intrude but I thought you might tell me what sort of flies you are using on the bass. You see," he explained, "my wife and I have rented a cabin near the head of the lake for a week of fishing and so far we haven't been doing too good."

He said they had watched me with glasses from the window and saw me take some "good ones." They had been wondering, he said, if perhaps I had some sort of secret feathered killer or something new in technique.

"I decided to hike down the trail today and ask you for some information," he drawled with a wide grin. "Of course," he added hastily, "if it's your own secret, I wouldn't blame you if you would rather not reveal it. But being new to the sport I certainly would appreciate any tips you might give me. I, er, I'd even be glad to pay for such advice," he concluded softly.

But as softly as he spoke I heard him very distinctly, and the word "pay" exploded like a bomb in my ears. There standing on the shore only a few feet away was a man with money and he wanted to give me some of it. For a moment I was afraid to speak lest I awaken myself and be returned to my poverty. It seemed that God had sent him.

Finally gathering my wits but still unable to speak I dropped the ax and reached for my battered hat resting on a huge rock. Several streamer flies bristled in the band. I plucked out a small Parm' Belle and passed it to him.

"That's what I'm having my best fishing with," I said slowly. I watched him closely as he examined it.

"Well, for heaven's sake!" he drawled.

"I've taken some bass on these patterns too," I said pointing to a Gray Ghost, Green Smelt, and a nameless creation of my own. "But," I continued, "at this time of year they should rise for almost any kind of fly if properly presented."

He showed me a book of very large, very gaudy, and very heavily dressed wet flies tied on huge hooks that somebody had unloaded on him. And I learned during our conversation that he was not using a leader but was attaching the flies directly to the thick level line. This was accomplished, he explained, by scraping the enamel off the end of the line, thereby making it small enough to be shoved through the rather large eye of the hook.

I sold him six new streamers from my roll in the cabin, and four seven-foot, three-pound test gut leaders I had tied myself, for five dollars. I told him he could have them all for three dollars, but he insisted and I didn't try to talk him out of it. I threw in the fishing tips, loads of them for nothing.

That five-dollar bill looked as big as a horse blanket. Clutching it tightly deep down in my pants pocket I watched the man walk slowly up the rocky shore. He waved and turned into the woods.

The bill got a fast ride up the lake to the only little store for many miles around. It bought a good supply of groceries, which included potatoes, onions, bacon, bread, canned beans and fruit, stew meat, tea, coffee, canned milk, ketchup, and dairy butter. We often read of the so-called delicious homemade country butter, but I never could go for it. I have found it too strong and usually too salty for my taste. Then too I always wonder where it was made and by what sort of person.

I bought a supply of fine-cut tobacco too. The kind I could smoke in my pipes and also twist into cigarettes. There was a feast for all hands at the old log cabin that night, but the food problem had been only temporarily solved and I wondered as I lounged before the old fireplace if and how I could find a fairly steady source of income. I wouldn't need much money, but a few dollars from time to time would be necessary if I were to continue to live there.

Rain fell heavily during the night and in the morning I faced another batch of trouble. The mosquitoes were hatching. The hatch gets underway every year in early June, and the tiny winged devils rise in clouds from the swamps and other wet places.

The air was full of them, the cabin was full of them, and so was my mouth much of the time. I gave blood transfusions to the pests all morning as I hustled madly about trying to get the windows and doors screened. The black fly hatch which started the week before was heavier, and both species of stingers would be about to make life miserable for man and beast until the hot dry weather of July.

I found screen doors for the front and back but both were in pretty bad shape. The frames were pulling apart and the wire screening was rusted and broken in spots. They required a lot of tinkering and patching before they were ready for service. There were only two window screens, both in bad shape, and enough cloth screening for one more window. The others would have to be kept closed until I could get money enough to buy more of the cloth stuff at the store.

The winged blood suckers were doing a job on me as I worked, and were drilling into the dogs in certain places. I took them off the ropes that they might seek shelter. Both of them headed immediately for the lake and began to wade and lap the cool water.

My face and hands were covered with huge white welts. One behind my left ear bulged like a small potato, and another was shoving down the lid of my right eye. And the attack of the singing blood drillers continued. I wasted no time in splashing into the pond for a bath and swim, and there, sitting up to my neck, I was quite comfortable for the first time all morning until they suddenly found me again and went at my head.

Other insects were hatching and rising along the shore shallows, and small fishes were dimpling the water as they rose and grabbed them. To the fisherman fly time is trout time, but so far as I knew the only trout water in that region were a few small brooks. There were none in the ponds and I didn't know of a good wading stream within fifty miles of the area. It would have been suicide dunking worms in those little woods brooks with the mosquito and black fly hatches at the peak. They would have gnawed me down to my skeleton.

But in addition to the mosquitoes and black flies, the trout bug was also biting. The sight of those fly hatches was too much for me, and I wondered if perhaps with the water of old Souadabscook Stream still holding the spring chill I might find some trout at the mouths of the incoming brooks. I decided to do a bit of exploring the next day.

A threadlike trail that twisted from the cabin clearing for a bit less than a quarter of a mile ended in a sprawling field rimmed by heavy woods. Several men had planted corn there for a canning factory in the town of Hampden, and the crows were flocking in every day to feast on the seed corn and sprouts.

I had brought an old single barrel twenty-gauge shotgun along with me to the cabin and a large number of old shells of various loads that had been piling up in my den at home for a number of years. I bagged two crows with the little gun in the field one morning while doing a bit of exploring and decided to take another fling at the sport that afternoon.

The crow is without doubt one of the wariest, if not the very wariest, of all birds. When a flock comes into a field to feed there are always one or two sentinels on the lookout high in a nearby tree. A sentinel crow can spot a man a mile away and the alarm is quickly sounded.

Crouched down out of sight in a rank growth of leafing alders and young firs where the cornfield met the woods I rubbed on some fly oil and waited for a circling flock to move in. Down they came finally to land quite a bit out of range.

Three of the black raiders finally walked toward my hiding place, pulling corn as they waddled along. As they moved into range I stood up, swung the gun as they rose startled and squawking furiously, and brought one down with a thud. A single "O" buckshot shell, which I held in my hand, was quickly inserted and I "reached" for one of the robbers that trailed the scattered and swiftly retreating flock.

A midget could have flattened me with a pine needle when that bird crumpled and came down. It was one of those lucky shots all wing shooters make occasionally.

Crows are tough too, and that one was no exception. He
limped and flopped with one wing dragging, all over the
cornfield. A load of number-six pellets ended his flopping,
his suffering, and his life of crime.

"Nice work, son, nice work," drawled an old man who
had come up from behind an island of raspberry briers,
chokecherry bushes, and locust trees that sprouted in
bewildering profusion from an old stone cellar that once
shouldered a little farm home.

A younger man and a husky boy joined him. I jacked
out the empty shell and walked toward them. Behind them
in a little grassy road that led from the woods into the field
stood a pair of stout horses hitched to a long, faded-blue
wagon that was plastered with manure.

"You don't mind my shooting these crows here do you?"
I inquired.

"Mind? Hell no!" gulped the old fellow with a grin.
"Keep right at it, son, and maybe we'll get some corn out of
this piece after all."

Upon learning that I was living at the old cabin alone
the old man said that if I planned to remain through the
winter I should plant some vegetables to store away.

When I said I would like to have a vegetable garden but
had neither the land nor the knowledge for raising crops,
he looked at me in silence for a full minute, then he spouted.

"Tell yer what, son, if you'll bang away at these damned
crows once in a while till the corn gits up in good shape,
you kin have a garden over there on that narrer piece of
land near your trail. We ain't gonna plant there. It's been
fertilized and harrowed and is richer than hell. It'll give you
a fine crop of vegetables if you take care of it. And hell," he
continued, "anybudy can raise a few pertaters, and carrots,
and stuff."

He hauled one of several burlap bags of potatoes from the wagon and set it at my feet. He explained that they were for seed and that if cut in pieces so that each piece would have an eye in it, they would produce more than I would need during the winter. He cut a couple while I watched and then watched me as I tried cutting a few.

I shouldered the bag and headed for the cabin to select and cut up the potatoes, which I would plant later according to his instructions. The "piece" of land was about fifty feet long by twenty feet wide. It was brown, slightly damp, and rich looking. I liked the smell of it, too.

I would need seeds for other vegetables, also a cord for lining off the rows and a hoe for keeping down the weeds. I had the cord and an old hoe at the cabin, but I didn't have the seeds or the money to buy them.

The hand to mouth existence was becoming discouraging. That evening I paddled up the lake to call on my friend the station agent and perhaps in desperation borrow enough money from him to buy the seeds there at the little general store. I hated the thought of it and more than once decided to turn back and forget about the garden. But those vegetables would come in very handy during the long cold winter ahead, I reasoned, and I kept on.

In a cove off the mouth of the stream that flowed down from the railroad station and into the head of the lake I saw the man who had bought the flies and the leaders from me. He was standing in a rowboat casting for bass. After watching his sloppy performance I decided that what he needed more than flies and leaders were instructions in casting.

His back casts were falling and he ripped the line and fly out of the water with great force. As a result the forward casts were tumbling in great loops of line which piled up on the water in front of him. If a large bass had suddenly snatched the fly on one of those low back casts he would have plunged into the water with a broken back. Anyhow, it would have been sprained.

On two occasions during the short time I watched him from behind the long point of bullrushes he actually slammed the rod tip against the water in front of him. He was casting furiously with his arm instead of working the rod gracefully with his wrist, and his performance was becoming worse as he became tired. There was little wonder he took no fish.

I moved on quietly up the stream. At the landing near the old spruce I saw the station agent and another man standing on the shore.

"Well, well, my boy!" shouted the station agent, "where in thunder have you been all this time? I haven't laid an eye on you for quite a spell."

"Aren't you working today?" I inquired.

"Workin', sure. But my trick is from seven in the mawnin' till three in the afternoon," he explained.

"This here feller's in a peck of trouble," he said, tossing his head in the direction of the very serious looking man standing at his side.

"Maybe you could give him a lift to his camp, son, if yer ain't goin' nowheres," he continued with that big grin of his that I liked so well.

The man then explained that he had come out from Bangor to open his camp for the summer and that, while trying to take a few bass along the stream, he had broken one of his oars. The two pieces were lying in a heavy and very old flat-bottom boat.

"Why not paddle with the good one?" I suggested.

"Paddle, huh, this old rig is much too heavy for paddling, and the other oar is all patched and about ready to snap. The kids must have raised hell with them last summer," he growled.

"If you are coming back downstream later and would just as soon paddle me back to my camp I'll wait here, and I'll make it right with you," he almost pleaded.

I explained that I wasn't going anywhere in particular and said I would be glad to take him to his place at no charge. I could have hammered myself on the head for letting "no charge" slip out.

Thinking that he might be wondering why there was no bow seat in my canoe, I hastened to explain that I had sawed it out as I had planned to do some guiding during the summer and fall and, like all guides, had substituted a movable back rest of cedar bow and slats so that the passenger might sprawl against while sitting on a cushion on the floor. That was all right with him, and in he piled with a large split-willow creel and a very old and very whippy wet fly rod.

The man's camp was at the head of the lake on the west shore. It was a bit more than a mile from the stream landing. We moved swiftly along in the old canoe into the crimson flush of the sinking sun. He had planned to fly-fish for bass during the next three days with a friend who was coming from Portland on the early morning train. But without oars for his boat he was licked, he said.

"Thanks a lot, son," he said as I set him ashore in front of his place.

I had told him there would be no charge for taking him there. I might have had a couple of sorely needed dollars if I had kept my mouth shut. But that seemed to be that and I backed slowly into the lake as he walked up the path to his camp. It seemed that God had again tried to help me and that this time I had ruined the plan.

Then it came to me like a flash. God was helping again. "Say," I shouted through cupped hands, "I just remembered that I have a pair of oars at my camp that you might have."

There was no reply but he turned quickly and jogged down the path to the water. I moved swiftly in on the paddle. That was it. He was as happy as a kid with a bulging Christmas stocking.

"Great, wonderful!" he almost yelped. "I'll buy them from you gladly!"

In five minutes we were on the way to my cabin and a half hour later we had the oars, a pair and an extra, and were on the way back to the landing on the stream where he had left his boat. After a bit of shaving with my belt knife the oars fitted the locks on his boat perfectly.

He had a ten, and four one dollar bills in his pocket. I got the four ones and a fat cigar, thanked him, and was away on the paddle down stream through the plum-blue dusk.

Not wanting him to know of my financial condition I took a trail farther downstream leading to the store and was soon buying the seeds I wanted. It was late when I arrived back at my cabin with a load of seeds, a little free booklet on gardening, and a few groceries. The hounds, apparently hungry and a bit worried, rushed down to the shore to meet me.

Potatoes, carrots, beets, bush beans—which I could eat green or keep until dry—turnips, winter squash, chard, cucumbers, and onions were carefully planted the next morning. I put in a lot of time and it was afternoon when I had everything the way I wanted it. The little garden didn't look bad at all and I was quite proud of it. Like just about everybody, I love green corn, but I didn't plant any because the old fellow who had planted the big field told me to take what I wanted to eat any time.

The pawing around in the earth whetted my appetite and I ate ravenously, then wandered back to the cornfield to hunt crows and woodchucks unsuccessfully until late afternoon.

I prayed hard to God that night for His help in bridging the gaps, and fell asleep to dream of lush vegetable gardens.

# 5

THE RISING SUN was pushing a blood-orange flood through the windows when I awoke the next morning. Handsome red-winged blackbirds were singing to the new day, and the feet of scampering squirrels drummed on the roof. Growing things added to the fragrance of the dew-drenched morning, and the placid pond borrowed blue from the sky.

A soaping and plunge into the cold water of the pond was invigorating, and a brisk rub with a rough towel brought a warm, tingling glow. A new black fly hatch was underway and they competed with the mosquitoes for my flesh and blood. The trout bug also was stinging again, and I decided it would be a good day for the trout-seeking trip which had been postponed because of the garden planting.

Wet and dry flies and small streamers in my favorite patterns were stuck in the band of the old hat, and tapered gut leaders, fly oil, and line dressing were tossed into a battered split-willow creel. My choice of rod was a smart and very spunky little four-ounce Thomas, one of the two I owned at the time.

A small, rust-colored knapsack bulged with tea pail, a few slices of bread, a small block of bacon, a brace of hard-boiled eggs, and just in case I took a few trout, a handful of corn meal and a small frying pan. There's nothing more delicious than a good feed of freshly caught brook trout fried over an open fire on the bank of the stream. I didn't plan on such a feast, but I had hopes.

I didn't even take time to wash the breakfast dishes. The hounds, filled with food, were snoozing in the sun on the sandy shore. I should have been underway in the dawn I thought. But still with no definite destination it would make no difference. After all I was only hunting for fishing water.

And I might not find any trout water at all save those little woodland brooks. I certainly didn't want to fish them at that time with the mosquito and black-fly hatches underway. I would seek the speckled-finned treasures of their deep black pools when summer's searing breath had dried out the woods and the survivors of the hatches had retreated to the places of damp shadows.

The adhesive tape patches dabbed with green paint, and the swelling of the cedar planking, had tightened the old canoe pretty well, and it leaked but very little. A bit more work and it would be in pretty good shape. Weighted with stones in the bow the old craft knifed swiftly along through the slick water of the lower part of the lake and into the yawning mouth of a mile-long thoroughfare which is really a part of Souadabscook Stream that curls deep, slow, and black through forested bog and high land to Hammond Pond.

Wisps of night mist crawled away over the water like frightened ghosts, before a rising wind. It carried the sweet breath of damp woods and fresh water. Gawky blue herons and meadow hens waded on pipe-stem legs in the shore shallows, and noisy kingfishers plunged crazily for minnows. Black ducks and the very handsome wood ducks, too, were breakfasting in the weed patches. They flushed in pairs on the lazy bends.

Here and there a swimming muskrat split the stream's mirror with a silver wake, and fat frogs made noises like stoppers being pulled from jugs. Small birds of many species poured liquid notes from lush green trees, and crows called back in the pines.

An osprey, his big white head gleaming in the sunshine, split the morning wide open in a power plunge from the blue to smash the flat face of Hammond Pond and seize a small pickerel.

The osprey, or fish hawk as it is commonly called, is an excellent fisherman. He spots his prey with gimlet eyes far above the water, then with great speed bullets downward and grabs it in sharp and powerful talons. To lessen wind resistance on the flight to the nest in some towering pine stub, this smart bird streamlines the victim by arranging the position of his stout legs so that the fish's head will be pointing forward.

The much larger eagle who also is very fond of fish but who is unable to catch them himself sometimes attacks the osprey as he flies away with a fish, causes him to drop it, then swoops swiftly downward to grab the finned dinner in mid-air. I have watched such hijacking performances many times.

Wildlife was everywhere—flying, swimming, and scampering through a scented and greening wonderland, bathed in the warm gold of the spring sun. It was strangely unreal, seeming at times like a place I had read about in a child's book or had seen in the stupor that precedes sleep. Mighty old Souadabscook really got underway there at Hammond Pond. I found it hauling out deep and black on the eastern shore. From there it twisted serpentine in ever changing moods for nearly six miles down to the great Penobscot River.

On and on it flowed through sprawling cranberry bogs, alder-cluttered heaths, and great stands of hardwood, spruce, fir, and white pine. On a wide, lazy bend where the little alder-choked stream struggled in from George Pond I went ashore to inspect a beaver house and wander for a time through a bewildering sprawl of felled poplars and their pointed stumps. The industrious little engineers of the woods didn't need the trees and limbs to build a dam there for the water was quiet and very deep.

They were felling those trees that they might have the tender bark and twigs to eat, and because according to Nature's strange arrangement, they must use the big incisor teeth every day to prevent the chisel-like and fast-growing things from excessive growth and, consequently, excessive overlapping.

I have in my years of prying into the family affairs of the wild things learned that if, because of illness or injury, gnawing animals such as the beaver, woodchuck, and porcupine are unable to use those big teeth for a period of time, they overlap to such an extent that the animal is unable to open its mouth and dies slowly of starvation. If because of a tooth injury they fail to meet properly the upper incisors that curve inward sometimes curl into the mouth cavity and occasionally pierce the roof of the mouth and go up through the skull.

The teeth of gnawing animals grow much in the manner of the human fingernail, and the hoofs of such animals as deer and moose. Man trims his nails, and the deer and the moose prevent excessive hoof growth by traveling and pawing. If forced to remain off their feet for a long time those hoofs will grow rapidly, finally curling up at the ends like children's double runner skates.

I have found a few dead and dying deer in overbrowsed winter yards with such hoofs. And I once found a sick old doe, with such skatelike hoofs, who had been chased onto the slick ice of a lake by a hungry bobcat.

During a discussion of this subject with a noted sportsman-physician while on a fishing trip in the Canadian wilderness some years ago, he said something that I have never forgotten. He explained that if man would break away from his soft and easy living and give all of his internal organs, teeth, and muscles the sort of a daily workout they are supposed to have, he would seldom if ever be ill. I have found that to be true.

After a few miles of enjoyable paddling through an unspoiled, almost untouched wilderness I felt a strong pull of water. The stream was moving quite fast and ahead I heard the roar and babble of rapids. Around the next bend a long sprawl of boulders of various shapes and sizes loomed above crazy white water like so many headstones in a snow-blanketed cemetery. The stream was more beautiful there than at any other point on its course from the pond. It became a wild and lovely living thing.

I experienced a strong desire to run that fast water, but being unfamiliar with the channels I couldn't afford to try it with my old and only canoe. And anyhow canoes with keels were not built for running fast water. They are fine on the lakes, ponds, and quiet streams, but the smooth-bottom river canoe is the only model that can be used successfully in running white water.

The canoe was hauled ashore and turned over. Shouldering the small knapsack and the creel I struck off with fly rod in hand along the brushy bank. Seemingly weary from its rushing, the stream finally yawned and relaxed in a great black pool trimmed with hissing froth patterns and bursting bubbles. It looked trouty, and my hopes were high, but I had my fingers crossed.

A brook hurrying in from the west belched its ice-cold contribution into the stream at that point. That was exactly the sort of place I had in mind. Having neither hip boots nor waders I put belt knife, pipe, tobacco, and matches into the little knapsack, and wearing only moccasins, old khaki pants, and checked wool shirt, I plunged in to wade.

Before me sprawled a stretch of water that all trout fishermen dream about. Never before nor since have I seen more promising looking trout water. My hopes were high. They slumped, however, like a tallow candle in the breath of a blast furnace after more than an hour of fruitless casting with my favorite wet flies in singles and casts of three. The wet fly is supposed to look like a drowned insect and I fished them that way, very carefully, across and up to drift down naturally with the current, and straight across to be retrieved in little jerks. But there was nothing doing.

I continued to wade, slipping and floundering as I went and wishing that I had worn my old rubber sneakers instead of the slippery moccasins. Finally it was high noon—a hot, bright, sun-plastered noon. On a bulge of high land where the breeze sifted through open hardwoods near the mouth of another, but much smaller, brook that curled in from the east, I built my lunch fire. The mosquitoes and black flies were not so numerous there and the smoke banished those that did come to feast on my perspiring pelt.

Appetites are fiercely sharp in the woods and that lunch of cold boiled eggs, with a few strips of fried bacon, bread soaked in the grease, and stout tea brewed in the smoky little pail was downed with gusto.

I wandered a bit in the woods after lunch, watching the little wild things, and in a small brushy clearing in which the tumbled remains of a trapper's cabin stood I found delicious wild strawberries blushing down deep in the grass.

Fierce black clouds that sent large, cold raindrops ripping through the leaves like buckshot sent me scurrying back to the canoe. I crawled under it and for more than an hour I kept dry and fought off the mosquitoes and black flies with bug oil, pipe smoke, and busy hands. And I wondered if the heavy shower would wash out the seeds in my little garden.

A new hatch of both mosquitoes and black flies was underway after the rain. I resumed my wading downstream sometimes to my knees and sometimes to my armpits, rolling out my favorite wet flies. The bugs were killing me despite the frequent applications of oil and continual puffing on the pipe until my tongue was raw and swollen. I used every trick in the anglers' book and some of my own but raised only three chubs and two male white perch that squirted milt all over the pool as they fought. They were carefully released, even the worthless chubs, and I moved on.

With hope of taking trout all gone I turned and fished halfheartedly upstream. The day was old and the sinking sun was shoving shadows across the water. The cool, sweet breath of the woods was refreshing. Ahead on the wide pool where the second brook came in, a fly hatch was underway. They were May flies, and off the mouth of the brook fish were rising for them.

It doesn't take much to raise the hopes of the ardent angler, and I was no exception. The line, soaked after hours of fishing sunken flies, was a bit heavy for dry-fly fishing, but I had no other.

With the dusk moving in there was no time to lose if I were to try for what might possibly be feeding trout. Dry-fly fishing is short line fishing and, in my book, always upstream behind the fish. So, wallowing to shore I dried out as best I could by briskly rubbing with a large red bandanna handkerchief about thirty feet of the tapered line. A coating of line dressing was applied with the pad in the little box and with an artificial May fly attached to the business end of an eight-foot tapered leader I returned to the stream and moved slowly toward the squirming tail of the pool.

The fly was dipped in the little bottle of oil, dried with a few false casts, and sent sailing over the slick water and down into the thick of the hatch off the mouth of the brook.

It bristled cockily on its stiff hackle and floated slowly toward me. I collected the slack with my left hand that I might have a straight line and immediate contact between rod tip and fly should a fish rise. Rising fishes were still dimpling the water across the yawning pool, which was then streaked with wavering brass and salmon-pink wisps of the afterglow.

I worked the little floater close to the mouth of the brook. It rode slowly back then suddenly it was gone in a soft bulge of water. I felt a sharp tug on the line. The hook was instantly set with a light lift of the rod tip and I was into a fish. It sliced across the black pool, sounded, then bulleted upstream toward the incoming fast water. It acted like a trout, but I was still doubtful. Having no net I worked the fish downstream to a bit of sand beach, hustled it ashore and snatched with a shaking hand a handsome ten-inch brook trout. I was very happy, I had guessed right. My hunch was paying off.

I admired the beautiful finned thing, slipped it onto the creel, and with enthusiasm high went back into action. Closely studying the pool I called my shot on the next cast, placing the fly on a spot just below the brook mouth and close to shore where I had seen what appeared to be a large fish roll and take a natural. The water boiled and again I connected but my fish, if it was the same fish I had been watching, wasn't nearly as large as I had expected. It was, however, a bulging bellied twelve-incher with brilliantly marked body.

I continued casting into the fading flood of the after-glow and when the lamp of day was sputtering out I had seven beauties from nine to thirteen inches on the damp ferns that lined the creel. Fish were still rising and rolling but by that time it was almost impossible to follow the tiny fly as it floated back on the slow current.

By crouching down in the moving water I could watch it fairly well in spots, and casting short I continued to roll it out to those faintly lighted places. The hatch was about over and there were few rises on the water. But the hard-bitten angler finds it difficult to give up. I watched with straining eyes then suddenly, as the black smother of the velvet night settled, a fish boiled under the fly. It struck hard and there in the dark I had a time for myself.

That fish had a lot of tricks and he used all of them. The fine little rod was equal to the task, but in the dark, I wasn't. I could feel him surge and sound. And I could hear him splash in the shallow stretches but I couldn't see him. The rod was bowed and trembling, and I could see faint flashes of the ferrules.

I tried to hurry him and finally worked him down to the little sand beach but running him ashore wasn't so easy. He had other plans, it seems, and he slashed furiously. I would have given a lot for a landing net. I had him about halfway out of the water on the sand and in desperation I clutched at him with my left hand. I'll admit it was terrible technique, entirely unworthy of such a finned aristocrat, and I would have been embarrassed had any but the eyes of the wild things seen me.

It was a trout and a beauty. I guessed the weight at more than two pounds. He was plump and hard, and fiercely cold. He was slippery too, and a mighty flop freed him from my grasp and the hook, too. He sloshed away through the shallows and was gone.

There I sprawled on the bank, soaked and muddy in a bed of fragrant crushed mint, and lacy little ferns, catching my breath and listening to the pounding of my heart, which sounded like a sledge hammer banging against an empty hogshead.

The roar of the rapids upstream led me to the canoe on the shore and I pushed off under the stars on the return journey to the cabin. I was delighted with my discovery of good trout water, and became increasingly glad that the finned monarch of the pool had escaped and was still back there with all of his cunning and great power with which he might again sometime meet the challenge of my little rod and feathered lure.

# 6

THERE IS something strangely fascinating about an open fire. The ballet of the flames in red and blue and orange jackets, the continual blinking of red-eyed embers, and the pinpoint sparks that billow from little explosions cause the eyes to stare restfully, and the mind to labor, but, usually, in a velvet harness.

Chilled by my wading in the cold water of the stream, I relaxed in dry clothes before the sooty old fireplace that night. But as I watched, the happiness and enthusiasm I had enjoyed only a few hours before were slowly devoured by a creeping realization of the very little progress I was making in my search for a place in the world of men.

I thought of home and my parents, of my young sister in high school, and of those friends who with each passing day were moving steadily onward toward definite goals. I was getting nowhere fast, and time, cruel and relentless, was not waiting. Those thoughts plagued me fiercely and I squirmed in a hell of frustration and fear.

I hated everything including myself, and particularly those damned little flames that were dancing on my logs and making me miserable. I would have dashed water onto them had the night been warm and my body not chilled. I could in that way stop their tormenting. That would be one thing I could accomplish.

They were left alone to their dancing, and a long walk with the hounds through the night along the lake shore brought some relief. But I could not brush from my mind the gnawing thought that I was wasting time—that I was loafing, and fishing, and enjoying myself like one of means, while others toiled. I was doing no more than I had always done.

Sleep evaded me like a will-o'-the-wisp. I piled out of the blankets, brewed refreshing tea, and finished the trout. Again I went outside—this time with a lantern and bucket down to the spring for fresh water. A loon laughed crazily out on the lake—perhaps at me, I thought, like people back home probably would do as time went on.

Such nights are the longest of our lives. Most of us have experienced them at sometime or other. I vowed in anger that I would experience no more like it, and with the coming of a blazing dawn I rolled up the proverbial sleeves determined that I would cease all playing and smash relentlessly at my problem until I had beaten it to dust at my feet or had gone down under its great pressure. At least it would be a fight—a real fight, and to a finish.

There was still quite a bit of work to be done on the old cabin, and although a bit groggy from lack of sleep I pitched into it mostly on my nerves, thinking and planning as I toiled. A check up on the garden found some of the beans washed out by the rain that fell heavily the day before. They were carefully pressed back into warm, damp soil, and I returned to the cabin to try to create some sort of substitute for an icebox to protect such perishable foods as butter, canned milk, eggs, pork, and the like.

Although always one of the most unhandy persons in the world, I finally managed to build a very simple sort of food chest, which I carried to the big spring in the cool, dark woods and sank about halfway down in a hole dug close to the outlet stream. The box from which I fashioned my crude refrigerator was one from a cracker bakery that operated in Bangor years before. It was about two and a half feet long, eighteen inches wide, and fifteen inches deep. It had a tight fitting cover that had been torn off and I couldn't find the hinges. I found the old box in the shed. It was full of old books and magazines. Hinges, three of them, were made of pieces of thick leather cut from an old moccasin I found, and I covered the bottom with bright tin cans cut open and flattened out. Others were tacked along the sides about halfway up. They would keep the food clean and would hold the chill from the cold running spring water and the damp earth. A stone of about five pounds was placed on the cover just in case an inquisitive and hungry animal came along.

As I returned to the camp clearing I saw the two dogs sleeping in the cool, green grass and, lo and behold, less than twenty feet away sat a large brown snowshoe rabbit watching them. Then all of a sudden things began to happen. Hearing me, big Jack the Walker looked up. As he did so he saw the rabbit. Like a flash he was onto his feet and after the intruder at high speed and yelping furiously. The other hound joined in the chase and away they went yodeling and baying behind one of the fastest rabbits I have ever seen.

The hounds were running by sight but finally the high-geared rabbit began to stretch the distance between his bobbing, powder-puff tail and the dogs. When they could no longer see him, old Jack who ran both rabbits and foxes slowed down and began to follow the scent trail left by the bunny's big feet on the damp floor of the woods. I listened to his deep, bell tone baying that recalled many happy days with him when the ermine of winter robed the land and the trail was warm.

Drive, the black and tan who would run only foxes, and occasionally a raccoon if the trail was hot, soon lost interest and returned to the camp. Jack ran that rabbit most of the day. It was apparently an old buck who knew all the tricks and who seemed to enjoy the chase. He came into the camp yard many times during that summer where he would sit until Jack saw him. Then away they would go bounding through the woods to resume their little game.

What convinced me more than anything else that the rabbit enjoyed having the dog chase him happened one afternoon when Jack gave up the chase because of poor trailing conditions, and the rabbit returned to the camp yard a few minutes behind him. The poor dog went crazy mad when he saw the rabbit that time and away they went for another session. I never laughed any harder in my life. That strange little game was one of the very few sources of laughter I found during that rather bewildering first year in the woods.

I continued my tinkering about the place each day. I ripped from the log walls of the cabin such corny decorations as pictures of bathing beauties, college pennants, comic postcards, etc. There were a number of old calendars with large reproductions of oil and water-color paintings of hunters, fishermen, and log drivers in action. Others were of wildlife in natural haunts. These pictures I cut out and carefully arranged with tacks on the walls, and then, just as carefully, framed them with pretty white-birch saplings. I sawed the saplings in sections and split them down the middle. Four halves tacked around a picture made the frame. They were very attractive and added much to the appearance of the camp. I had never seen anything like them before.

I did another cleanup job in the old log shed, and plastered with a mixture of blue clay, rooty swamp moss, and wood ashes those places between the ragged rocks of the old fireplace, where the cement had fallen out. The mixture hardened in the heat of the fires, and held very well.

I had noticed several times what appeared to be a long, narrow platform, called a boat slip or dock, caught in some alders on the shore at the foot of the lake just a short distance below the cabin. I decided to look it over and, if it was worth repairing, tow it back to my place and use it.

It was a good one that apparently had been left to freeze in by a careless camp owner, and had been carried away far down the lake when the ice broke up in the spring. It consisted of three peeled cedars about fifteen feet long, across which four-foot boards were nailed.

I waited for a day when the wind was strong from the south that I might be assisted in my towing with the canoe, and dragged it slowly up to my landing. I repaired it and decided to use it. If the owner ever did come and ask for it, I would give it to him, I told myself. But he never did.

The end at the butt of the logs was set onto flat stones on the lip of the beach and the other end was swung out straight into the lake. The logs rested in the water and the whole thing was held firmly in place by four stout cedar stakes, two on each side, driven into the bottom mud and spiked to the side logs.

It was a very handy addition to the place. I could walk to the end of it to dress fish, wash potatoes, or dive into the deeper water for a swim. It made a good place to work on the old canoe, and the dogs loved to sprawl there and sleep in the sun. Some days I would lie face down on the end of the long platform and for hours at a time study the actions of the sunnies, yellow perch, small bass, and other fish that fanned under it in the shade. It was an interesting show and I learned a lot.

I fished only for food, killing what I wanted of white perch, trout, bass, and pickerel and hurried back to my work around the place. At night the eels and horned pouts would move in to feed on the heads and entrails of fish thrown into the water where I had dressed them on the end of the slip. I remember very clearly while taking a cool bath there in the lake one dark night something eased up and grabbed savagely at the wiggling big toe of my right foot. It took a jump out of me and I let out a wild yelp. As I did so I kicked hard bringing my foot out of the water. A large eel let go of the toe and splashed back into the pond. The toe was badly torn by the sharp teeth and, although carefully dressed each day, it caused me considerable discomfort for some time. From then on I wore an old pair of ankle high sneakers when taking my after dark baths.

The work I was doing around the place wasn't very important to be sure, but it kept my mind occupied, leaving little time for worrying and above all for pitying myself and becoming discouraged. And, too, each little job completed was an accomplishment. At least I wasn't loafing. I was doing things. That thought helped a little.

Wildlife has always interested me. I wanted to know how all species of those creatures in feathers, fur, and fins lived. I wanted to know what they ate, when they ate, why and how they fought, and about their mating and breeding, etc. I had spent considerable time in prying into the affairs of all the creatures in the strange and mysterious outdoors world; even the bugs, the snakes, and the turtles. But I had learned very little, it seemed.

Living there in the woods alone, with time heavy on my hands, gave me an excellent opportunity to continue that study. One morning, while watching some noisy crows that appeared to be teaching their young to fly, I found one of the youngsters sprawled helpless in the deep grass near the shore of the lake. The other crows, old and young, flopped back into some nearby pines when they saw me. I had never known crows to desert one of their kind before. They usually fight savagely like wolves in a pack to protect each other and particularly their young against man or natural predator. Perhaps they didn't know that one had fallen. Or perhaps the mother thought he was a weakling and didn't care what happened to him.

Anyhow he was left behind. I pitied the poor little fellow. He was of good size, and in his bluish-black feathers rather handsome. He squawked and pecked at me with his huge beak when I picked him up. When I found neither wing nor leg broken I guessed that he must have knocked himself silly by crashing into an old oak stump that bulged in front of him in the grass.

I placed him between my feet in the canoe and took him to the cabin. I fixed up a box for him in the shed and fed him canned milk, bits of cooked fish, small pieces of bacon, bread, and a little raw egg.

He began to eat and drink the second day. But he was still very unfriendly. Whatever his ailment might have been he appeared to be completely recovered in a week. And when two weeks had passed he was flying all over the camp yard. I hoped he would fly away, but he would go no farther than the big pines and white birches on the rim of the clearing. I couldn't drive him away.

The dogs gave him several maulings when he pecked at the rivets in their collars while they were sleeping, and waded into their food dishes while they ate. But nothing bothered him. He was a saucy thing, and like all crows, a born thief. He would waddle into the cabin, fly onto the table and carry off food. And he would also snatch and carry away any bright object he could lift. Such things seemed to fascinate him. He would steal fishing flies that had a silver tinsel body, reel screws, bright nuts and bolts, and even nails. He would take them into the trees, set them down on a large limb and stare at them with head cocked to one side. When I shouted at him and pounded on the tree trunk he would pick up the object and fly to some other tree back in the woods. I don't know whether he stored them all in a hiding place or finally lost interest in them and dropped them onto the cluttered floor of the forest. But whatever he did I never saw them again.

The day he grabbed my sun glasses off a table on the veranda of the cabin came very near being his last. I was really sore. I needed those glasses to protect my eyes against the glare of the sun on the water, and I would need them even more to prevent snow blindness with the coming of the winter. I had the shotgun loaded and was about ready to touch it off when he accidentally dropped them from his perch in the tree. Fortunately they landed on a patch of soft green moss and were not broken.

If I took the canoe to go fishing he would flutter down and perch on the bow, and after watching me cast awhile would return to camp probably to bother the dogs. When I went to the garden he would follow me and torment me while I worked by yanking up the small plants. He would perch on my head or shoulder when I went to the spring for water, and he was always down on the boat slip to meet me when I came in with the canoe.

I began to like the foolish thing, and I called him Sammy. He ate table scraps and also foraged for himself along the shore and back in the woods. He ate small frogs, mussels, and mice and he was a nut on grasshoppers.

I took on another load of trouble shortly after adopting Sammy, when I found a baby skunk with its little head stuck fast in a bean can on the backwoods dump. Apparently the old mother skunk had taken her youngsters to the dump in the night to search for food and had abandoned that one when she found him half canned. Skunks are frequently caught this way in cans and jars when they push their heads too far in after a bit of food.

The poor little stinker was in a bad way. I had to cut open the can with my belt knife. If his musk sac had been developed he surely would have sprayed me for I did handle him pretty roughly. He was what trappers call a "short stripe," having a small white spot on his head and a little white V running down the back of his neck to his shoulders. Such pelts are worth more than those with stripes all the way down the back and along the tail. The only other white on his handsome little black pelt was the tip of his bushy tail.

He was only a little fellow but he had reached the stage where he could eat anything, and believe me he did. I fed him table scraps, canned milk, cooked fish, oatmeal, and an occasional raw egg. As he grew older he eased the drain on the scanty camp larder by catching mice, toads, frogs, little snakes, crickets, and grasshoppers.

He was a handsome and very friendly little fellow, and after a time the dogs seemed to love him as much as I did. He never did get along with foolish Sammy the crow who was forever stealing his food and pecking him on the head as he slept curled up in the sun. I called the little fellow Waldo.

He was a better pet and was cleaner around the place than any cat or puppy I ever had. He slept most of the day and prowled most of the night. During the time he was awake in the day he would follow me around like a little dog, and always close to my heels. He threw his foul smelling musk only twice that I know of while I had him. The first explosion took place one evening down on the shore in dense brush, at either an owl or a mink that must have frightened him. The second time was one day in the fall when Sammy landed on top of him and began to steal the food from his plate. Sammy half flopped and half ran, blind and squawking through the woods and didn't show up at the camp again for two days.

Waldo used to get terribly mad at me when on those mornings he was around the place I would grab him and make him take a bath with me in the lake. He hated it. But his protest amounted only to fast pacing and the furious stamping of his hind feet on the dock. He would then run as fast as he could back to the camp yard to hide.

After a time he knew what was going to happen when he saw me coming toward him in the early morning, and he tried to run away but he was always captured, and down we would go on the run for a plunge head first together into the water. Waldo would swim swiftly back to shore soaked and skinny looking and I would pile out after him, lather him with soap and toss him back in again. Then lathering myself I would dive in behind him. He would be raging mad.

After those baths and a brisk drying with an old towel his coal-black fur shined brightly and he smelled like a little gentleman. But although he didn't enjoy the baths he seemed very friendly and frisky after them.

*Nature I Loved*

Those were good days—days which, as I dream back, were really the happiest of my life despite the fact the future looked black.

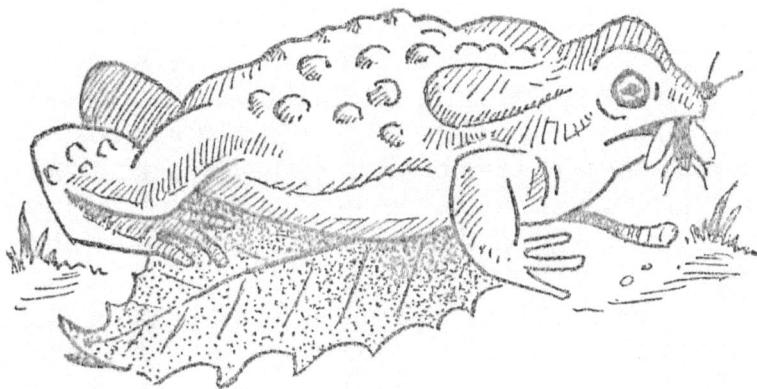

# 7

SPRING MELTED slowly toward summer and the study of wildlife really got under my skin. I found it extremely interesting and was at it day and night regardless of weather.

In the daytime I would watch the mud and snapping turtles dig holes in the sandy shores of lake and stream, back up to them, and fill them with eggs that reminded me strongly of tiny potatoes.

It seemed that the raccoons, too, knew that the turtles were laying eggs for with the coming of night they would come out of the woods, sniff about until they located a nest, dig up the eggs, and devour them.

I discovered, in my prying into their affairs, that all creatures have enemies that prey on them and their young. They live by the oldest of all laws—survival of the fittest.

Nature in her wisdom arranged things that way for proper balance of all wild things and their food supply. It is, in a sense, a cruel law yet sounder than many made by man.

I also discovered that the cute and harmless little red squirrels that scampered into my cabin unafraid looking for crumbs, were robbers of birds' nests. I watched them many times as they scurried through the trees seeking the nests to eat the eggs and if they had hatched, to eat the young.

The squirrel, too, has his troubles for both young and old are hunted and killed by owls, hawks, crows, and weasels. The populations of nearly all species of wildlife rise and fall on a seven to twelve year cycle.

That is another part of Nature's wonderful arrangement. That year the red-fox cycle was near the peak and the varying hare or snowshoe rabbit, one of reynard's chief sources of food which had been very numerous in the woods for several years, was becoming scarcer. The rabbit was, it seemed, on the down trend of the cycle. The ruffed grouse population also seemed to be on the down swing. The foxes were everywhere. I saw them every day.

By lying on the edge of the woods I was able to watch the females catching mice in the little fields and clearings for their young back in secluded dens. I had seen female foxes many times scooting back to their dens with mouths fringed with dangling mice and I wondered how they could carry so many at one time. Then one day that summer, with the aid of a pair of old field glasses, I watched the crafty animals catch the mice and very carefully lay them on the ground in two bunches with all the tails crossed. By grabbing all the tails in her mouth the fox would have a bunch of mice on either side and away she would go through the woods.

I also saw foxes carry young grouse and farm chickens by the same plan of crossing the little necks as they did the tails of the mice. I spent many hours watching the clever red rascals catch ducks, both wild and domestic. It was indeed an interesting show. Spotting a flock of ducks swimming close to the shore of a pond, the fox would come out of the woods and, paying no attention to the birds, would begin to play on the shore. He would leap about, chase his tail, roll over, and dash up and down near the water in short sprints. The birds would become increasingly curious and swimming in little circles would move closer to the shore.

The wise old fox, watching them out of the corner of his eye but still pretending not to notice them, would move farther back from the shore to continue his antics. Finally the foolish birds completely overcome with curiosity would waddle out of the water to get ringside seats to the show. Then with the speed of lightning the fox would be upon them to grab the nearest bird and throw her over his back with a broken neck. The other ducks would flounder and flop back to the water in great confusion. Their quacking and squawking would be deafening. Like a flash the red rascal would strike at a second bird. But, although I have seen a fox catch up to three domestic ducks in this way, I never saw one that was able to kill more than one wild duck at a time.

Getting back to the turtles and the raccoons, I recall one late afternoon when I witnessed one of the strangest battles I have ever seen in the realm of wildlife.

I was sitting on the edge of the woods that rimmed the shore of Souadabscook Stream examining a few Indian relics I had dug up during the day. Suddenly a medium sized raccoon came out of the shadows a few yards below me and began sniffing about the sand. Finally he located what I guessed was a turtle's nest and began to dig. I sat there barely breathing lest he see me and run away. It was a nest and there were eggs in it—a lot of eggs and very large ones. The raccoon ate one and had started on a second when much to my surprise I noticed crawling out of the brush behind him the largest snapping turtle I had ever seen. She was almost as big as a barrelhead. On and on she waddled at a surprising rate of speed. Her wrinkled neck was extended, her ugly head was raised and her mouth was wide open.

The raccoon neither saw nor heard her until the old turtle was at his side. The startled animal turned quickly. Like a flash the turtle struck. She seized the raccoon by the side of the head in a vicelike grip. A furious struggle followed but the powerful old turtle meant business and held on. She turned around and began backing slowly toward the stream dragging the floundering animal with her. Down the shore they went, inch by inch and finally into the water.

The raccoon leaped and yanked furiously in a vain attempt to shake off the turtle. He was growling and squealing as he made the last stand for his life. I was wide-eyed. I wouldn't have believed it if I hadn't seen it. They rolled and splashed about in the water and finally disappeared beneath the surface. A cloud of roil and a few bubbles marked the spot.

Finally a few yards down the stream the drenched gray back of the poor egg thief rose to the surface. He turned partly over and I saw his handlike forefeet. The powerful old turtle was winning, and it seemed the strange battle of the wilderness was about over.

Suddenly I began to pity the poor raccoon, and having no love for snapping turtles I snatched the paddle from the beached canoe and rushed down the shore to try to save the ringtail. But before I arrived at the spot the struggling pair reached the shallows of a sand bar and now with more solid footing the raccoon gave a mighty leap, twisting as he did so and broke away, leaving the turtle holding only flesh and hair in her mouth. I was glad for the poor thing. I watched him crawl away into the woods more dead than alive.

Another strange battle I will always remember was between a female mink and a large eel. I watched it from a ringside seat in my canoe in the very early morning. The mink walked out on a ledge that jutted from the shore of the lake. I saw her look down into the water, watch something a moment, then plunge in. Almost instantly she appeared on the surface with the squirming eel held by the head and the battle was underway.

They rolled and splashed, went down and bobbed up again. The eel finally coiled his strong and slimy body about the mink and they rolled farther out into the lake. They went down again. The snakelike thing was trying to drown the little mink. And he appeared to be doing a pretty good job of it. In fact I held little hope for her for she seemed to be growing steadily weaker.

I guessed that she had young back in a shore den and was trying to get food for them. She fought savagely against great odds. It was another battle by that same old and cruel law—survival of the fittest. I thought suddenly as I watched the last stages of the struggle that that mink and perhaps some of her youngsters would put needed dollars into my pocket when I strung my traps in the fall. So again I decided to interfere in a brawl of the great outdoors.

As I moved toward the struggling pair the eel went suddenly limp. The mink had apparently driven her sharp teeth through the brain. She swam slowly to shore apparently too far gone to be afraid of me sitting in the canoe only a paddle length away. The eel, its head still held fast in the mink's mouth, trailed behind. The poor little mink was completely exhausted when she finally reached the ledge and hauled herself and the eel out of the water. She relaxed her death grip on the eel's pointed head, rested a bit, then seizing it again dragged her limp victim through the dry-ki and over the rocks to her den.

I witnessed many other battles of the wild things, including those between crows, hawks, and mother ducks trying to protect their young, wars between armies of black and red ants, fish on the spawning beds, and others.

I studied fishes and their foods until I feared I would sprout fins. Experiments in catching them on a wide variety of baits and lures under all sorts of conditions following these studies usually paid off with excellent catches.

There were also long sessions of studying the weather and its effect on the birds, animals, and fish, from which I learned a great deal. I had found a strange and fascinating new world—a world of secrets and mysteries known only to God and Nature and the few who like myself cared to probe into them. Although very interesting, this probing is a slow process and the knowledge gained in a long lifetime would be comparatively scanty.

During that first summer I actually made friends with one of the wildest of all birds—an osprey or fish hawk. This huge bird with white head and neck resembles the bald eagle but it is not so large. The osprey possesses amazing fish-catching ability. Soaring high over the water until its sharp eyes locate a fish swimming just under the surface, it will flutter in one spot, take deadly aim, and then much in the manner of a dive bomber, and with seemingly almost as much speed, it will plunge downward. The bird smashes into the water with a great splash, seizes the unwary fish in its sharp talons and rises with it high into the air.

I discovered with the help of the glasses that this particular bird had a stiff leg. It hung down from its body like
a stick and was of little use to him in catching fishes. I
watched the bird plunge and miss the quarry many times.
He scored occasionally with the other foot but the pickings
were rather slim for the poor creature.

I figured the leg had been injured in a fall from the nest
when the bird was young or in twisting out of some pelt
hunter's mink or muskrat trap. But whatever the cause
might have been the poor thing was badly handicapped in
the continual struggle to get a living. He reminded me of
the many persons in our so-called civilization who are
bravely carrying on despite similar physical handicaps.
That bird and that comparison made my own quest for a
living seem much easier, and less important.

Filled with pity for the unfortunate thing I decided to
help it. Every morning when I went out on the lake to catch
a bass, pickerel, or a few perch for the camp larder I would
catch and kill a few chubs, sunfish, or yellow perch and
scatter them on the water. After I had passed, down would
come the hawk to seize them.

After a time that bird actually looked for me every
morning and many times in the late afternoon. When he
didn't spot me on the pond he would circle high over the
cabin. The fish I tossed onto the water were grabbed only a
few feet from the canoe. He trusted me for he knew I was
helping him. It made me feel warm and good inside, not
only because I was helping the poor thing, but because I
had made friends with one of the very wildest of all birds.

Like most people I had always thought that the high-
pitched singing coming from the bogs and meadows in the
nights of early spring was the vocal efforts of thousands of
newly born frogs. But long and careful study that got

underway that year and continued the next revealed that it was the love song of the spring peeper.

The peeper is a member of the tree-frog family, which is seldom found in trees. This rather mysterious amphibian, who is only about an inch long, comes out of hibernation in the mud with the coming of spring and prepares for the annual symphony and the mating season.

For a week or so they tune up with low guttural croakings and then get underway full blast. My curiosity caused me to haul on borrowed waders and plenty of warm clothes and squat on soggy hummocks for hours at a time to listen and try to see by the pale light of the stars and the moon, and occasional flashes of a light, just what was going on.

In such places where the little creatures were numerous the singing was deafening. I discovered finally that during the concerts they have a bubblelike globe of skin bulging at their throats.

Only the males sing and they really do whoop it up from dusk until well into the dawn. When about to pour forth this weird yet cheery song the little frog first closes his nostrils. The skin of the throat then swells as air is forced out of the lungs into spaces connected with the mouth cavity, until it forms the large globular bubble.

The air in the mouth cavity is then forced back into the lungs, the bubble remaining inflated, and the stream of air passing back and forth through the little vocal cords causes them to vibrate, which produces the tone. But how that sound can be so loud is a puzzler.

This little frog has a dark X-shaped cross on its back which, I later learned, suggested its scientific name, Hyla crucifer, or "crucifer the cross-bearer."

The study of wildlife continued night and day, in the woods, in the meadows, in the sky, on the water, and even under it. It fascinated me strangely. I couldn't get away from it. I made notes of all my findings and also many pencil sketches, some of them on white birch bark, of everything from dew drops to deer. All were carefully filed away at the cabin. I didn't know at the time why I was keeping them. I just continued to stuff them away, more and more as the days and nights rolled on.

# 8

I HAD READ how the early Indians fertilized their gardens by burying fishes in the rows, and I followed their example. Such worthless species as chubs, eels, and sunfish caught off the boat slip and carefully placed in the earth near the plants caused them to grow rapidly. I had a fine garden and was quite proud of it. I had some trouble with bugs but solved that problem with an insecticide bought at the little store. The dogs kept the rabbits out of it, and the little twenty-gauge shotgun took care of the woodchucks and porcupines. The crows didn't bother it after the plants had developed.

The hand to mouth existence finally ended, at least for a time, when I accepted a job to guide a wealthy old bachelor from Massachusetts at three dollars a day. My friend the station agent who had known him for a long time brought him over in his canoe to talk with me. He said he had once been a fine actor. The man explained that he had been renting a cabin on the other side of the lake every summer for the past four years. He was a small man of about seventy with a heavy thatch of white hair and a funny little paunch that bulged like a pumpkin in a potato sack.

He told me he had fallen in love with the region when he first saw it and planned to someday build a log lodge there on the lake. He said he liked to fly-fish for bass, cook outdoors, and just cruise about and that he would want me as his guide at least three days each week. Sorely in need of the money I was at his boat slip with my canoe the next morning at four o'clock.

I sat in the stern smoking my pipe and watching the outdoors come to life. Finally the lamp in the cabin went out and down over the steps he came with enough equipment to sink the canoe. He had three rods—two for wet flies and one for dry flies—small streamers all lined up, a loaded tackle box, a split-willow creel large enough to accommodate the carcass of a small shark, a camera, a long-handled landing net, a full-length raincoat, and a big knapsack bulging with food and cooking tins.

I explained as tactfully as possible that I had a net, cooking tins, a guide box for the fish, and plenty of leaders and flies, and that there was no need for him to "bother" taking such a load.

After looking at the canoe he understood and took only the dry-fly rod, a roll of streamers and dry flies, the food, camera, and raincoat. We were pretty well loaded even then.

He was a pleasant man but very quiet. He seemed always to be preoccupied. But he certainly did enjoy the outdoors and all that it offered. He was wild about fishing. He was a very good fly-fisherman, and I enjoyed watching him roll out beautiful casts with streamers, tiny drys, and fat bivisibles.

I paddled up the lake about two miles and nosed the canoe into a narrow flat-faced bog stream that curled lazily out of Ben Annis Pond. It was a small pond almost round with boggy shores and of course, no camps. We saw a lot of wildlife including huge blue herons, meadow hens, wild ducks, muskrats, turtles, mink, hawks, squirrels, and a sleek doe deer.

Buds of the white and the yellow water lilies poked their heads above great patches of pads and the skeletons of tumbled trees cluttered the shore shallows. A dense stand of spruce, bog maples, poplars, tamarack, and an occasional white pine rimmed the pond. It was beautifully wild.

The old fellow failed to raise a bass but, on streamers cast up to the rim of the shore weeds, he took some husky and very belligerent pickerel. An old whopper whose weight we guessed at all of five pounds fought furiously in and out of the water and finally severed the leader with his sharp teeth.

He took several others almost as large along with a number of smaller ones but ordered me to carefully release all but one unusually fine specimen that weighed three pounds. I wrapped it in a wet sugar bag and placed it on ferns in the little fish box.

He snapped pictures of the place and the fish and we headed back for the lake. A bloated, crimson-faced sun climbing out of a clutter of horizon clouds in the east cast a blood-orange flood over woods and water. It was beautiful. The old fellow mentioned it several times.

He enjoyed good sport with the bass and large white perch during the remainder of the morning and at noon on a breeze-fanned point of boulders and birches we feasted on broiled bass wrapped with bacon strips, potatoes baked in the coals, warmed-over biscuits, and tea stout enough to float a double-bitted ax.

He slept soundly on a bed of fir boughs part of the afternoon while I washed pots and pans, and later wandered back in the woods for more wildlife study.

There was a hatch of flies on the lake in the late afternoon and with dry flies and later bivisibles he tangled with a few more bass and perch. He took back to his camp only the large pickerel, to be cut in steaks for frying, and two perch for a chowder.

He insisted on paying me at the end of each day. I liked that arrangement, and dead tired but happy with the three dollars in my pocket I paddled slowly across to my cabin and my pals—the dogs, the skunk, and the crow.

I guided him on fishing and exploring jaunts around the lake and the ponds at least three days a week until late September. In order that I would know what days he wanted me he would tie a white towel to a tree on the shore. It was easy spotting it with the glasses and over I would go.

The day he broke camp and I paddled him and his dunnage to the station he made me promise I would guide him the next summer, and before boarding the train he stuffed a ten dollar bill into my hand. He had already given me a duck hunter's coat lined with sheepskin, a hunting knife, two new pipes, and a pair of moccasins.

On those days when the towel didn't hang from the tree I continued my probing in the realm of wildlife, fished a little, worked in my garden, and built a rustic bookcase out of small cedar logs for the scanty assortment of books I had found in the cabin and a few the old actor had given me.

I made the old shed over for a chicken house, wired in a small yard in front of it and, with some of the money earned guiding, bought from a farmer at the head of the pond a dozen barred Plymouth Rock layers. He told me that if I kept them free of lice during the warm weather and dry and warm when fall came they would produce all the eggs I would need and "right through the winter." Table scraps and a little grain would be all the food they would need, he said.

Food and fuel are the important things when a man is spending the winter in the woods. I had been around enough to know this. And what could be better than fresh eggs for breakfast, and maybe an occasional dinner of fried or roast chicken as the winter waned. Such fare would be a welcome relief from pickerel, rabbit, and deer meat, if indeed I were lucky enough to shoot one of the latter. The fuel problem, however, still loomed before me unsolved.

The plan worked like a charm, too, after I finally got the poor birds down to the camp. But I had one hell of a time doing it, and came very near losing all of them en route and my own life too.

A light south wind that had been blowing in mist since noon was still puffing away in the late afternoon when the farmer helped me down to the canoe with two burlap bags full of chickens and a half bushel of cracked corn.

Each bag held six of the birds for which I had paid seventy-five cents apiece. I placed the bulging bags of squawking poultry on the floor of the canoe with the sack of grain and dug in for the haul of nearly three miles against the chop and the mist. But, when well out on the lake, what had been only a light blow and mist suddenly turned into a gale and a two-fisted rainstorm. The waves were high and trimmed with froth and the cold drops slashing down by the millions beat savagely against my flushed face. It was really tough going, but I was getting along pretty well until the struggling of the hens opened the top of the bag farthest from me and out they came to perch on the gunwales and the bobbing bow. The wind and the pitching canoe caused them to flop furiously to hold their balance and some of them tumbled back into the canoe. I was having all I could do to keep the frail craft quartered into the blow and couldn't leave the paddle for a split second. When the squawking things again mounted the gunwales I did try to brush them back with the paddle but only made matters worse. There is nothing on God's green earth as stupid and excitable as a hen, and those crazy things were no exception.

Just as I waved the paddle blade at them a huge hissing roller with a white cap smashed into the bow and hoisted it into the air. That was the spark that set off the explosion, and hens went squawking and flopping all over the lake. All six of them were on the water at once.

I never saw the rain fall any harder nor the wind blow more furiously. I was in a tough spot. I dug in until I thought the paddle would snap but made little progress. I was drenched with rain and sweat. My mouth felt dry and small and my heart banged like a hammer in my chest. I suppose the sensible thing to have done would be to have forgotten the floundering poultry and concentrated on holding my struggling canoe in the gale. But I didn't. I wanted those birds and I quickly decided to take a chance. My experience in handling a canoe helped a lot, but it was really the kindness of God that pulled me through.

There in the middle of the lake with the wind screaming in my ears and the snarling waves tossing the canoe about like a peanut shell, I worked furiously with the paddle and a long-handled landing net.

The canoe was soon in the trough of the huge waves some of which were piling in over the gunwales. The hens in the other bag were drenched and squawking. Hens can't swim so there was no time to lose. I managed with the net to scoop up four of them. The other two were swept far out of reach and were drowned. Drenched and completely exhausted I worked the canoe and its miserable cargo to the shore at the head of the lake only a short distance from where I had started.

I dumped the water out of the canoe, built a fire with dry cedar behind a huge boulder that bulged in a thick stand of spruces and placed the two bags of hens close enough to feel the heat. I then slumped down on a soggy seat to wish for dry tobacco and wait for the storm to subside.

The wind continued to howl like a crazy witch through the trees and the waves roared in to spend their might along the shore. The plum-blue dusk came early it seemed, to put the dirty little day to bed with its toys of wind and rain, and I resumed my journey on a light chop through the misty black night.

The drenched hens were taken from the bags and placed in the snug home I had prepared for them. They were soon singing and scratching vigorously by the light of a lantern for corn tossed into the straw. I slopped into the cabin to get into some dry clothes and prepare a hot supper for myself and the dogs and scrape up something for Sammy and Waldo.

Friends have often asked me if I ever became lonesome, and how I "ever managed" to keep myself and the old cabin clean. The women in particular just couldn't understand how I ever managed to take hot baths especially in the winter, and to wash, dry and iron things.

I am always quick to tell them that I had my lonesome moments, but that keeping myself and my few possessions clean was never much of a problem.

I took a good soaping and plunge every morning and evening in the lake during the summer and right through the autumn. And once in a while piled into a large galvanized washtub for a hot one. In the winter the baths were taken steaming hot in the same old tub in front of the blazing fireplace every Saturday night. And I came out every bit as clean as I would have from a fancy tub in a scented city apartment.

My teeth were brushed with a good powder at least twice every day and my washings, which never were big, were done regularly and well. I had only the blankets and pillow cases on the one bed I used, along with a few towels, dishcloths, handkerchiefs, and the clothes I wore. And in the summer those clothes amounted to just a pair of either khaki or gray wool trousers, a pair of low moccasins, a battered hat, and now and then a sweat shirt or short rain jacket.

In the winter full-length silk and wool union suits, sweat shirts, heavy socks, and checked wool shirts covered my carcass. All went into the same old tub. There were clotheslines outside between the trees in summer, and in the kitchen and living room in winter. I'll admit I dreaded washdays in winter because of the drying problem, but I finally got used to it. An old flatiron I found in the cabin was used very little.

A good broom, a mop and a bucket of hot water kept the floors bright and clean. And the same broom with a cloth wrapped around the business end took care of any cobwebs that formed on the beams and rafters.

I had my moments of loneliness now and then but managed to banish them along with my spasms of worrying about my future by piling head over heels into work that had to be done around the place.

I got a few newspapers and magazines, and a letter from home once a week. All letters were promptly answered and all carried only good news so that my good and patient folks would not worry about their "black sheep" son.

An almost fierce appetite caused by the life in the outdoors was satisfied with plain but hearty food. I ate very little sweets. The exercise and that food, along with plenty of restful sleep, packed pounds onto my frame. The scales at the store pointed to 160 by midsummer. It was the most I had ever weighed. I beamed only a bit better than 140 when I left the city worried, discouraged, and half sick to set up my bachelor quarters in the woods.

My neck, arms, hands, and chest were thicker, and muscles bulged across my back and shoulders. Almost constant exposure to the sun and wind had tanned the upper part of my body to a deep, golden brown. The occasional sunbaths in my birthday suit had done a pretty good job of staining the rest of me.

I was as hard as the oaks that towered majestically behind the cabin, and never felt better physically in my life. At least I had what many so-called successful men didn't have—robust health. And, too, I had a sort of home of my own. Those thoughts brought me considerable comfort and inspired me.

I shaved when I felt like it, which wasn't very often. My hair, however, was something of a problem. It was dark and sort of wavy and thick as swamp grass. It hung down below my jaws. But I managed to make it look fairly neat, until that day when I could find someone who could cut it properly, by keeping it soaked down with water, parted sharply in the middle and combed back behind my ears in a great soggy pad on the back of my neck. A bit of Vaseline helped a lot.

But like the others, it was a small problem compared to the one I had brought there to struggle with, and which up to then had me on my back.

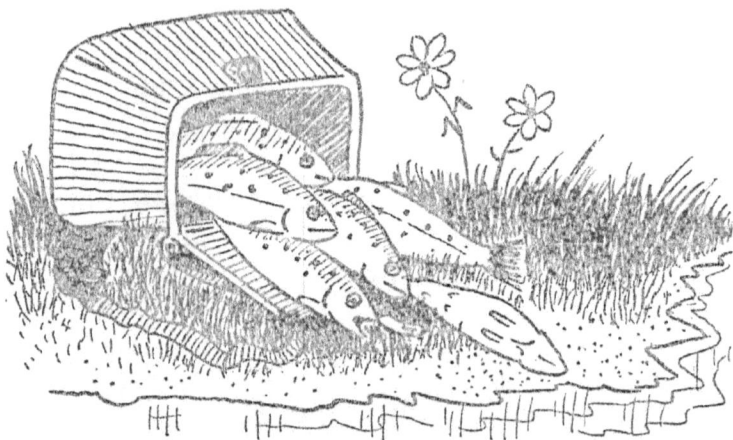

# 9

PERHAPS IT'S because they are constantly before us that we give them only passing notice and fail to realize that it's those many little things along the way that make up all things including our lives. Even such tremendous things as the towering mountain, the restless sea, the desert, the forest, and the prairie land are but a lot of little things put together—little things like drops of water, grains of sand, trees, smells, and blades of grass. And so it is with life, the biggest thing we know, and, if we will but pause to notice and appreciate its little things, it can be made far sweeter and more interesting.

The life in the woods caused me to realize this more and more with each passing day. Those little yet very important things were all about me. I studied them as I found them. To mention all of them would fill a great volume. But I will endeavor to set down here a few of those that impressed me most in the hope that others in reading this book will remember and perhaps enjoy them.

There was the little star imprisoned in a rain pool . . . Old rail fences staggering across lonely fields . . . The dawn wind coming to blow out the stars . . . Tam-o'-shantered acorns under the oaks . . . The ballet of the raindrops across the pond . . . Country cemeteries like little white villages of the dead . . . October's pretty little afternoons . . . Ragged alders crowding down the bank to watch the brook go by . . . The symphony of the crickets . . . The brown corduroy of ploughed fields . . . Proud forests robed in ermine after the storm . . . The setting sun bleeding on the snow . . . Fall winds undressing the trees . . . Fireflies burning little yellow holes in the night . . . Crumbling stone walls . . . The thunder of flushed grouse . . . Gun-metal streams curling through the dusk . . . The frozen pond opening one blue eye to peep out at spring . . . The rain's little drumsticks beating on the camp roof . . . Lakes borrowing beauty from the sky . . . Swooping swallows cluttering the summer evening . . . Purple dusk leading the old day down the stairs of time . . . Blazing autumns . . . Bounding deer flashing white flags . . . The perpetual twilight of the woods . . . Winging ducks driving a black wedge through the afterglow . . . The stream changing its mind to make an eddy . . . The laughter of brooks . . . Rising trout dimpling the pool . . . The cold, green fingers of the northern lights clawing at the stars . . . Distance dressing the mountains in purple robes . . . The moon's golden carpet across the water . . . Aluminum rain dawns . . . Wind songs.

I had always been fond of the outdoors but was actually falling in love with it by late summer. It was big and clean and beautiful, and would give me a living if I would be satisfied with that sort of life. That realization banished much of the fear that had been gnawing at me.

As the summer waned I made friends with a rustic old hermit who lived in a tired old cabin across the pond. He gave his age at sixty-eight, but I guessed it at seventy-five at least. Like most old fellows living alone in the woods, time on its restless wings had rushed past him destroying as it went all but the brightest treasures in his chest of memories.

He never mentioned his past. I don't know where he came from or if he had any relatives. He talked very little about himself. He had a little garden and a few chickens. He trapped and hunted a little, sold a few ax handles, and got a Spanish-American War pension every month from the Government. It wasn't much, he told me, but it helped. He had what clothes he needed, plenty of food, and although his small cabin was cluttered and a bit dirty in spots he appeared to be quite comfortable.

He was a kind old fellow with a keen sense of humor and an almost fierce love for pickerel fishing. He owned an old flat bottom boat that had seen better days, and his fishing gear consisted of a bamboo pole about twenty feet long, a piece of heavy green line of the same length, and a big black hook. I first met him coming out of the stream that curls into the head of the lake. He had a load of pickerel. Some of them were whoppers. There was no bag limit on pickerel in Maine at that time and it was legal to sell them. He told me he was going to keep a few to eat and sell the others to a man who was coming out from Bangor the next day. The sight of all those fine pickerel lying dead and slimy on the bottom of that old boat sickened me.

I later learned that his method was as crude as his equipment. His bait was a strip about three inches long and a half inch wide cut from the belly of a pickerel or perch. One end was fastened to the big hook and he heaved it out over the weed beds. By springing the limber tip of the long pole up and down the bait would skip along the surface. Aroused by the motion and the splashing of the chunk of bait the pickerel would streak out after it and attack it in great swirls. He'd lower the tip of the big pole to give the pickerel a few seconds to swallow the bait and hook and then with a mighty lift he'd hoist the squirming fish through the air and into the boat. He'd let the fish slam against his flat chest which usually caused it to drop off the hook onto the floor of the boat. After a day of fishing his shirt and his bare pelt, too, would be plastered with slime and blood that attracted buzzing flies in swarms. Those fish that were too heavy to lift out on the pole were hauled in hand over hand. He called this method of fishing, "skittering."

When I met him that day at the stream mouth I had never seen him in action. But I did many times after that and really enjoyed each performance except when he took what I thought was too many pickerel.

He was resting on the oars while smoking a powerful old pipe. He was the first to speak.

"Howdy, son, how they bitin'?" he said in a high pitched voice.

"I'm not fishing. I'm just going to the station for my mail," I explained.

"Kin yer stand a few pickerel fer yer supper? If yer kin here they be, all yer wants of them," he said pointing down to the floor of the boat.

I told him I didn't need any fish but that I would like to see his catch, and eased the canoe alongside his battered boat.

"Thuty-three of 'em and most of 'em are beauties!" he drawled proudly. "I kin git a mess of 'em any day up this here stream."

Curious and wide-eyed I asked him how he caught them. "Why thar's nawthin' to it, son—nawthin' to it at all. Alls I do is whale the hell out of 'em all the way up then turn around and whale the hell out of 'em all the way back. Nawthin' to it," he yelped with a small cackling laugh.

The man I was guiding at that time didn't care for the old fellow whom, by the way, was known as just Pop. He said he was a "fish hog." When I was paddling him I was instructed to avoid the old guy. But I liked old Pop just the same and he liked me. At least he seemed to and did many little favors for me.

If it hadn't been for Pop I wouldn't have been able to be away from camp for two- and three-day cruises in the woods. I took them whenever I could make arrangements with the man I was guiding. I traveled by canoe and on foot while old Pop looked after things including the garden, and the feeding of the hounds. And when I took on the flock of hens he cared for them, too. Waldo the skunk and Sammy the crow were then pretty well grown up and were foraging for themselves most of the time.

On those little jaunts I explored a great part of that vast region of woods, bogs, hills, and waters. They provided an excellent opportunity for more wildlife study and I learned many amazing things about the furred, feathered, and finned things. I found little trout brooks fished only by mink and otter and enjoyed wonderful fishing. Using both flies and worms I took handsome wild trout from six to twelve inches. I did a lot of experimenting with flies and baits under all sorts of conditions from which I learned a great deal about this speckled aristocrat of the piscatorial realm. I killed only what I needed for the pan and sometimes a few to take back to the cabin.

I paddled and poled the canoe for many miles and walked many more. I carried a canvas knapsack that contained a small frying pan, tea pail, a fork, salt and pepper, and a supply of canned beans, bacon, bread, a little belt ax, and a notebook. A wool blanket, telescope fishing rod, compass, hunting knife, and a .38 revolver completed the equipment. I regretted many times that I didn't own a good camera.

The woods provided an abundance of delicious raspberries, and water from little springs that was so cold it made my teeth and jaws ache. The cool pools of the brooks were my bathtubs along the way. If it rained at night and I had the canoe at the spot I would turn it on its side and sleep under it. When without it I would make little shelters of saplings and spruce or fir boughs and cover the roof with slabs of bark pulled from the trunks of large old birches and hemlocks that time had felled. The bark kept out the rain and I enjoyed the restful drumming of the drops.

After supper on fair nights I would sprawl on a bed of fragrant boughs and watch the twinkling stars up through the great trees while listening to the sweet wild music of the night birds, the wind, and the hurrying brook. It was wonderful. Now and then the strange symphony would be broken by the soft hooting of a barred owl, the mournful wailing of a tiny screech owl, or the sharp barking of a fox. Woods mice, porcupines, rabbits, and deer attracted by the little fire were frequent visitors. I could hear them poking about in the leaves and brush but they never came beyond the rim of the fire's light.

Only once that I knew of did any of the wild creatures invade the camp site. Tracks in the shore mud of the brook told me it was a large raccoon who had come while I slept and sneaked off with my breakfast trout.

The mornings back there in the woods were beautiful beyond description. Trout strike fiercely when the summer dawn is breaking. I could snag all I wanted in a few minutes. It was simply a matter of keeping out of sight and floating a dry fly onto the pool or dunking a wriggling worm into it.

While the plump little beauties fried slowly to a crispy brown over the small fire I relaxed to watch the new days unpack. Dawn breezes gossiped in the leaves and ushered the wispy night mist out of the shadows. The sun came then to pour blood-orange ribbons down through the pines to mop up the dew. It was then that Nature sprayed her sweetest perfumes, and the bird choir was at its best.

On one of these little trips I visited a country cemetery and the grave of an old family friend at the request of my father. A letter in reply to one in which I had foolishly told him about my wild canoe ride through the storm with the chickens warned me against taking such chances, and reminded me of what had happened to Big Jim. He asked me to visit Jim's grave and to report to him regarding its condition.

The last of Jim's relatives had died in Bangor a year before and my father who loved the big fellow wanted to take over the responsibility of keeping the grave looking well.

A little map sketched in pencil showed the location of the cemetery. It was north of the town of Hermon on the top of a hill. The grave, marked by a circle, was at the far end under a huge white pine.

Jim was a giant of a man, and a truly great woodsman. A kind of crazy courage blazed in his huge chest, and he didn't know the meaning of the word *fear*. He could split a man wide open with his massive fists and sink an ax to the eye in a hardwood log. Yet the same handsome brute would play for hours with a baby, and give his last dollar to a bum. Big Jim was absolute proof that courage and strength are the parents of kindness.

The stars, the sun, and the streams were his only compass when traveling through the deepest woods, and they served him well. He never was lost. He was also a great hunter, and could make the coldest blooded bull moose in the Maine woods fall head over heels in love with his imitation of a mate-seeking cow through a birch-bark horn.

An old timer once said of Jim, "He's one of the greatest woodsmen of all time. Why, the guy can carry a canoe on his big back till hell cracks and keep right on going through the opening!"

No man could handle a canoe better, whether on a wind-lashed lake or the roaring rapids of a wilderness river. He was tops with both paddle and pole. He took my father and me on many trips on water and in the deep woods, and he taught me many things. He was patient and kind and good. I loved him fully as much as my father did. It seems that for some reason or other God doesn't make many men like Big Jim.

The big fellow used to boast that there wasn't enough water in the whole state of Maine to drown him. That tremendous confidence in his own great strength and ability caused him to take crazy chances.

But one black fall night Jim took one too many of those crazy chances. He tried to fight the whole outdoors at its worst. Slashing rain rode the shoulders of a screaming gale out of the southeast. Black, froth-trimmed waves smashed down upon him. Big Jim's heavily loaded canoe, the duffel still lashed firmly in place, was found overturned in the shore shallows of a wilderness lake in the northern part of the state. His hat, and pipe with the stem bitten off, and a broken paddle, floated nearby. The things he had so long defied and beaten had ganged up on him and finally beaten him. Big Jim had laughed in the gray face of death for the last time.

I found the cemetery finally. A rainy dusk was settling when I shoved open the creaking iron gate. It was a large cemetery and the dates on some of the stones told that it was very old.

I could hear the whispering of the rain in the leaves of the elms and maples, and the clear chirping of unseen tree frogs. I don't like cemeteries. I don't think anybody does especially when night is near. The wind up there on the hill whined softly out of the southeast—the very same wind yet in a calmer mood than the one that caused Big Jim to be resting there. I suddenly hated it—and the rain, and the lonely old cemetery. I would have fled from it had my good father not asked me to visit Jim's grave.

My moccasined feet moved reluctantly and I walked slowly down the graveled path—down through the corridors of the dead. I found Jim's grave under the pine. Raindrops ran jerkily down the face of the small weather-grayed stone, and weeds wrestled in great tangles across the mound.

Poor old Jim, I thought. I muttered a prayer for the repose of his soul and hurried back to the gate. The rain was coming down harder as I swung down the road. Two miles of it stretched between me and the little woods trail that led to the stream where my canoe was beached.

The rain hadn't reached the bark and wood I had placed under it, and behind a ledge in heavy growth I kindled a fairly brisk blaze. A scanty supper of beans, bread, and tea was wolfed down. Then drenched and tired I rolled up in the blanket under the canoe to spend a miserable night of shivering and thinking, and in cat naps dreaming about Big Jim, the rain, and cemeteries.

I reached camp late the next afternoon with a fly-bitten pelt, a splitting headache, and a few wizened trout. I had been gone three days. Old Pop waddled down to the shore to meet me.

"Glad to see yer, son. Let's you and me take our fishin' stuff and go some place!" he roared enthusiastically.

"I am going some place, Pop—to bed!" I drawled through hot and cracked lips. Dog tired and half sick, I tumbled into bed with my fever to sleep soundly until noon the next day, when after a cold plunge and a good feed of bacon and eggs I felt much better. It seems a man recovers rapidly when he's living close to Nature.

# 10

I WAS EATING out of my garden by late summer. Fresh young carrots, green beans, cucumbers, little beets, and chard, along with sweet corn from the great field of my farmer friend were welcome additions to the camp menu. The potatoes, squash, and turnips were coming along fine. They would be harvested later to be stored for winter with the large carrots, beets, and dry beans.

It seemed as I made a check of the garden that I had planted too much and would have a large surplus. But anyhow I would have enough and that was important, for the Maine winters are long and severe, and there was no way of knowing what luck I would have in the pursuit of fish and wild meat.

The spacious old cabin was gradually taking on the appearance of a rustic lodge with its huge stone fireplace, bookcase, pictures in birch-sapling frames, and other decorations. Even an old buck's head over the fireplace looked better since I carved out and painted pieces of pine to fill the eyeless sockets. The handmade eyes gave him a surprised expression but that was better than the foolish, blank look he had before.

I used to enjoy lighting all the lamps and kindling a brisk blaze in the fireplace and then lounging back in one of the badly worn but extremely comfortable old chairs and admiring the place. I had always hoped that some day I would live as a wealthy bachelor in one of those English-type lodges with bear rugs, steins, huge fireplace, sporting dogs, etc., I had so often read about and seen in the movies.

I had neither the wealth nor the expensive decorations but I did have the dogs, two of the best in fact, and what faintly resembled the lodge.

I never was in the least mechanically inclined, but by constant tinkering I did manage to make the big clock's hands and the striking apparatus come to a permanent agreement. And I did a pretty fair job of administering first aid to an old box victrola whose turntable wobbled and spun much too fast. But despite this success I was sure that my niche in the world would not be that of a mechanic.

Dancing was one of the many things that never interested me. Perhaps that's the reason I dislike the high-geared, slam-bang type of music. I have always been fond of old ballads and opera. There were many such records in the old cabin. Some were badly worn, others were cracked but most of them were in fairly good condition.

There before the dancing flames in the fireplace and with the lights turned low I listened night after night to the beautiful voices of those great tenors of that era, John McCormack, Henry Burr, Enrico Caruso, and others. McCormack and Burr with their lighter and sweeter voices were my favorites as they rendered such grand old ballads as "I Hear You Calling Me," "Somewhere a Voice Is Calling," "When the Corn Is Waving, Annie Dear," "My Wild Irish Rose," and many others. They were old then, but like most old things they were beautiful. I loved them.

Soft, sweeping waltz music also was on my hit parade. It rested me and caused me to live with sweet memories and to have beautiful thoughts. There was a tear now and then. I let them fall unashamed. I didn't care. There was no one looking but the dogs.

I also am fond of flowers, and tried to keep fresh bouquets of some kind on the tables in the living room and on the veranda. The meadows, little woods clearings, and fields provided blue flags, daisies, black-eyed Susans, buttercups, and others, and beautiful little wild roses crawled all over the cabin.

In the cove that yawned nearby white lilies grew in such profusion that the water appeared to be blanketed with snow. Their fragrance during the day was swept into the cabin. They, too, were among the blooms that decorated and brightened my home in the woods.

The hens were getting along very well and supplying the table with plenty of large fresh eggs. A raccoon that broke into the food chest down by the spring gave them some trouble for several nights, but the hounds finally nabbed him in the yard, despite the fact they were tied up on long ropes. They gave him a good mauling before he hauled himself loose and dashed away into the woods.

The hens didn't like Waldo at first either, but he paid no attention to them and their squawkings and they soon became accustomed to seeing him waddling around the place.

The shorter days with their chilly dawns and dusks, and the drowsy midday songs of the crickets and locusts, brought the realization that summer was passing and that the autumn would soon be moving in to herald the coming of winter. I dreaded that thought, but I had to face it for if I were to remain there I would have to make plans. There would be wood to get, a lot of it, and a heater of some kind, for the cookstove in the kitchen, and the old fireplace in the living room, couldn't keep the old place warm during real cold weather.

There would be many other things that would have to be done, including getting a large supply of food to hold out, particularly during that period when the ice on the lake would prevent the use of the canoe yet wouldn't be strong enough to walk on. The camp larder would have to be well stocked at all other times too, for it would be a long, hard hike over the frozen lake to the little store and back. Then there would be heavy storms and perhaps times when because of injury or illness I would be unable to get out. Fortunately I didn't have any such unpleasant experiences during the entire winter, although on two occasions there was no great pain nor suffering I came very nearly losing my life. There were times when blizzards would rage for days, and when the mercury in my veranda thermometer was down from ten to forty below zero. The ample supply of food looked good to me then.

I took my final fling at fishing in September. I traveled by canoe and on foot to a tiny pond I had heard about to seek trout with the fly. Fall fly-fishing, so called, never appealed to me; in Maine at least, it's the most uncertain of all fishing. I have on rare occasions dumped the piscatorial jackpot but on most of those late-season jaunts got nothing but the exercise and fresh air.

There are no fly hatches then and the trout are preparing for the annual migration into the spawning streams. I used wets, drys, fat bivisibles, and streamers, and one day I managed to raise only five fish in as many hours. They rose for a one-inch Parm' Belle streamer. Only two were keepers. They were identical twins, beaming one pound apiece.

The bass, perch, and pickerel fishing held up very well and casting streamers in a wide variety of patterns I enjoyed fairly good sport on the lake and the ponds and some very good fish dinners on the shores and at the cabin.

Then suddenly that fishing was gone when the annual autumn "turnover" of those waters took place. All lakes and ponds turn over in the autumn. The cold and heavier water on the surface goes to the bottom and the warmer bottom water rises to the top. The change isn't noticeable on most of the sand and gravel lakes, but the waters with muddy bottoms become the color of weak coffee. You can't see a sunken fly as far as you can spit from the canoe. I've tried huge bright spinners, oversize streamers, and just about everything in the way of baits but never got either strike or nibble. I've had a hunch for a long time that perhaps way down deep the water is clear and that the fishes are down there below the roil. But that's only a hunch. Perhaps those lakes and ponds are roiled all the way down. Anyhow I didn't try to learn by very deep trolling or dunking baited barbs from an anchored boat. I just gave up reluctantly and put the rods away.

Those waters clear up again later in the fall but the fishing season in Maine is over then. It gets underway again for pickerel as soon as the lakes and ponds freeze over, and for salmon and trout, the first day of February.

I had enjoyed very good fishing throughout the summer on the brooks, the lake, and the surrounding ponds. I also enjoyed those fine fish dinners. I missed them until the pickerel became legal quarry with the coming of the ice.

Harvesting my crops was a pleasant yet, in a way, rather sad task. The sight of the plump, fresh vegetables heaped on the brown earth brought a sort of warm tingling feeling known only to those who have toiled hard and long and in the end accomplished something really worth while.

The bugs and the weeds had been defeated and I was reaping the fruits of my labors. But the realization that summer was gone seemed to bring a certain sadness that dulled my happiness.

Most of the vegetables were carefully stored in the hole under the cabin that served for a cellar. I left some of the larger carrots and turnips in the ground to be pulled later for the frost wouldn't hurt them, and the turnips would be sweetened by it.

The first frost, a very light one, sent me scampering to a nearby cranberry bog to harvest a supply of the sour little berries to be stored for the winter with the vegetables. I am very fond of stewed cranberries served with plenty of the winelike juice. If I were to have any there was no time to lose for a severe frost would kill every last one of them. The little ground-hugging bushes were loaded with them in the various stages of ripening. Some were a deep red, others were all green, and many of them were half and half. All would soon become ripe when stored.

I had no rake for gathering the berries but managed to claw up a bushel with my hands. I clawed up plenty of leaves, twigs, and bog grass, too, but it was easy to get rid of that simply by holding the basket high and dumping the berries very slowly onto a blanket spread on the ground. Only the berries reached the blanket. The wind took care of the litter.

Frost mantled each blazing morning from then on. The lily pads were rotting in the coves and the sugar maples flamed like giant torches here and there on the ridges. The morning plunges in the lake were hard to take then and the bathing was soon confined to the cabin.

I added a bushel of wild apples to my store and found a lot of beech and hazel nuts that I would gather later if the squirrels, who were also harvesting, didn't get all of them.

During my summer wanderings I had found two bee trees. One was an old pine whose top had been knocked off by lightning. The other was a giant beech that had died a natural death. Both were partly hollow and were occupied by large swarms of the little honey makers.

I knew nothing about taking honey away from mad bees with sharp stingers so I sought the assistance of old Pop who said he knew "a little sumpin' about it."

We took the old pine first and my job was to climb up to the small entrance hole and plug it with rags. We then cut open the bottom and gave them a dose of smoke. Then we felled the tree with Pop's crosscut saw. We repeated the process on the beech and took nearly sixty pounds of wild honey. We worked with gloves on our hands and black cloth screening wrapped around our heads but even then we both got stung several times.

The places where the stingers had drilled into my perspiring pelt burned and pained for a time. But the thought of winter breakfasts of wild honey on flapjacks, along with fresh eggs and bacon, and stout coffee, poulticed out much of the pain.

I found quite a stack of mail on my next trip to the station. Most of the letters were from buyers of raw furs in the large cities to whom I had written regarding the prices they would be paying for pelts during the fall and winter.

One was from home. It carried the usual worry words of my mother and a few lines from my father inquiring about the wild duck situation and a request that if the birds were numerous I invite him to do a bit of shooting with me.

I read the letter down on the bank of the stream near my beached canoe. The blue and golden October day was growing old and as I lifted my eyes momentarily from the neatly penned lines I saw a great wedge of black ducks splitting the pink and brassy flush of the afterglow. The season on waterfowl had been open nearly two weeks, but I had been much too busy to do any hunting. I never did care much for duck hunting anyhow nor for the rather strong and greasy flesh of the birds.

I had noticed the ducks flocking into the ponds from the back woods brooks and marshes where they had nested during the spring. They were quite numerous and included black ducks, blue-wing teal, golden eyes, and a few wood ducks. My father and I could enjoy good shooting it seemed and it would be nice to be with him again.

His letter was answered there at the station and put on-to the night train. I told him of my enthusiasm over the fact that he was coming out to shoot with me and that the birds were quite plentiful. I asked him to bring my 20-gauge double gun and plenty of shells along with some of my hunting clothes. I would be waiting for his reply telling me when and on what train he would arrive.

The old cabin was the proverbial beehive of activity that night and most of the next morning as I scrubbed floors, blacked and polished the stove and sink, shined up the lamps, cleaned the fireplace, straightened pictures, and took care of a lot of other things that would improve the appearance of my home in the woods. I wanted to impress my father who would carry the good news to a worried mother.

I sawed and split wood most of the afternoon to replenish my supply which I had allowed to get rather low, and scrubbed the dried mud and the chalky spatterings of careless birds off the old canoe. The outdoor cooking outfit was scoured and placed in the knapsack and I was ready.

Sunset found me down in the garden with the old single barrel shotgun blazing away at a bean can that swung on the end of a rope from a tree limb. I hadn't had the gun in my hands since the war on the crows and the other creatures that invaded the cornfield and my struggling garden months before. I found myself badly in need of practice for one must shoot fast and well if he is to bag the very wary and fast black duck, and I knew that was the species my father preferred to hunt.

The frost had no effect on my chard which was still flourishing and lush green. I gathered some for supper and gave a generous serving to the hens.

The black and tan slipped his collar while I was washing the dishes and trailed a raccoon all night. It was indeed a merry chase. I was too tired to go floundering after him through the black woods, and lay there listening to his mournful yodeling as he pursued the wise old ringtail through the big spruce swamp and along the ridge to the south. It kept me awake most of the night and at dawn I struck off through the woods to a large old oak where the dog had the coon treed. I spotted him crouched in a high crotch. He was a big fellow and I brought him tumbling down with the third shot from the .38 revolver.

I didn't want the animal at the time but shot him for two reasons. The first was so that I wouldn't break the heart of a fine hound and the second was that Pop my old friend across the lake had asked me to get him some raccoon meat the first chance I had. The excited dog tore into the very dead animal, gave him the usual shaking and was satisfied. I delivered the carcass in the skin to Pop later that morning.

As I walked through a strip of woods after leaving Pop's cabin I flushed a pair of plump ruffed grouse sunning themselves at the edge of the trail. They went up one after the other with a thunderous roar of wings that startled me. It was then that it dawned on me that the grouse season, too, was open. It seemed time was passing me on swift and silent wings. I had lost all track of it.

The summer had slipped away and autumn had arrived with its hunting time and its warning of winter and I had yet to find a trail I could follow back into the world of men. This realization again caused the demons of despair to dance in my brain and to probe with hot forks.

It seemed that the experiment had failed. That I was no farther ahead than if I had remained in the city, and that my father was coming not really for the hunting of wild ducks, but on an errand of mercy—to take a poor, shiftless son back to the protection of his home before a fierce Maine winter murdered him. I broke down and cried hard that night. I finally fell asleep praying.

# 11

SAMMY THE CROW who had caused me considerable trouble gave me another serving of it the next morning and I decided then and there to shoot him and be rid of him for all time.

Having no clothes pins I had made a supply from the small limbs of hardwood trees. I simply cut off a five-inch piece, split it halfway down, smoothed off the ends, and pinched the pin over the line.

Sammy seemed to enjoy walking the clothesline and pulling off the pins with his huge beak. At first I thought it was funny and that I had a very remarkable crow. But on those occasions when I was away from camp and returned to find pieces of my washing scattered all over the ground I became enraged. I really blew my top when he did it again that morning. I came from the spring with two buckets of water to find the pillow cases and sheets for my father's bed and a few other pieces heaped in the dirt and being pawed by the wind. I wanted my father to have the best during his stay and planned to give him my bed all dressed up, while I curled up on the couch in the living room. There I could watch the fireplace and keep it going all night.

The soiled washing went back into the tub for another going over and simple Sammy went winging away into the pines with a charge of number six shot whistling all around him.

I cooled off while paddling to the station for the letter I expected from home. I was glad then I hadn't hit Sammy for I wanted my father to see him.

The morning train that hauled in as I was beaching the canoe carried the letter. It was brief. Only a few lines. He would arrive that night on the eight o'clock train.

Back at the cabin I did more cleaning and arranging and made up the bed with fresh sheets and pillow cases. A limb of red and golden maple leaves was arranged over the fireplace and big bouquets of blood-red bog berries and sprigs of fresh green pine were placed on the tables in the living room and on the veranda. Poor Sammy showed up in the late afternoon and although a bit wary at first I soon patched things up with a little food and some soft words.

I fed the dogs and the hens, took a hot bath in the old washtub and scraped off a two-weeks crop of beard. For the first time in many weeks I was concerned about my personal appearance. I wanted to look my best when I met my father.

With scissors and a small hand mirror I backed up to the large mirror in the living room and managed to trim off some of the great crop of hair that covered the back of my neck. It wasn't a bad job at all. A generous gob of Vaseline and plenty of water followed by a careful combing held it down in pretty good shape and I looked fairly respectable.

I hauled on a clean black and white checked wool shirt, clean khaki pants, white wool ankle socks, and the low moccasins my sportsman friend had given me before he left. I felt wonderful.

The days were much shorter then and I paddled through a chilly dusk to the station. On the way up the lake I wondered how I should greet my father when he stepped off the train. I tried aloud, "Well, well hello, Pa! How are you?"

I tried several other greetings filled with fire and enthusiasm but all seemed just as corny and by the time the canoe pushed into the stream I had decided that perhaps a "Hi" and a handshake would do. Frankly I was afraid to meet my own father. Like all others who live as I was, I was actually becoming woods queer. I hadn't noticed it before.

A flock of black ducks flushed from their resting place in the rushes that towered over me and my canoe. I hoped they would be there the next morning when we would be armed and looking for them and their kind.

I arrived well ahead of train time according to the station clock and returned to the canoe to smoke my pipe and practice talking to my father. I listened to muskrats swimming on the stream in the darkness and becoming chilly started up the trail to the station where a fire of soft coal was burning in a large potbellied stove. As I reached the platform the train whistled far down the track. It was coming and bringing my father—the father whom I had disappointed and who would probably ask me to return with him to the security of his home. A cold sweat broke out all over me. A failure, a problem son was about to meet his father. Those awful thoughts rushed through my mind like wind through a hollow log.

The lighted windows were a golden chain on the black velvet of the autumn night as the train rounded the bend. Then suddenly it squeaked to a stop—the hot and greasy locomotive hissing and panting like a tired monster.

The night station agent spoke to me as he rushed past. I barely heard him and made no reply. The heavy pounding of my heart sounded like a hammer in a hogshead, and my mouth became fiercely dry. There was a sensation of puckering and then of no mouth at all. Only thin dry lips remained it seemed. I thought of dashing away into the night. Away from the terrible feeling. Away from my father. Away from it all.

Then I saw him. He stepped off the smoker behind two other men and talked with the conductor. My father said something and they both laughed heartily. Perhaps he had told the man of me, and that he was coming out to take me home, and they were making light of me, I thought.

The trainmen waved chubby little lanterns. The huge locomotive whistled sharply and, shaking the coaches as if to arouse them from their dozing, dragged them away into the night.

Only my father and I remained on the platform. He was standing beside a pile of duffel and staring into the darkness down the little board walk. Something seemed to shove me toward him. I raced into the soft yellow light that fell from the station windows and shouted with a voice that trembled and broke, "Hello, Pa!"

"Well, well, well, hello, Bill!" he roared back.

A long and crushing handshake followed and my father threw his arm around me and pulled me toward him. Tears were close to our smiles, and as we walked past the last lighted window of the little station I saw a wet streak made by one that had gotten away from him and hurried down his ruddy cheek. Perhaps it would have been better if we had not fought our emotions and had wept in our joy. But men are like that.

My dad was a rugged and fine looking man who dressed well for all occasions. He looked smart that night in his hunting outfit, which consisted of medium high, soled moccasins, khaki breeches, and hunting coat and cap of the same material. He was a veteran sportsman and knew that when hunting the wary black duck one cannot wear bright-colored clothes if he hopes to return with anything in the game pockets of his coat.

We chattered like a pair of squirrels as we shouldered the duffel down the trail to the canoe. We were soon on our way down the stream through the black smother of the night. I was still a bit uncomfortable even though it was dark and I could not see him slumped comfortably in the bow behind the load. He fired a steady stream of questions at me and I answered them as best I could.

As we glided from the mouth of the lazy stream a great copper moon that looked as big as the back of a barn climbed slowly above the blackened spruces that crowded down the eastern shore of the lake. It rolled a shimmering carpet of bronze over the water.

Muskrats split the slick water ahead of us as they traveled back and forth in the weedy coves, and a barred owl hooted softly back in a swamp. The cool, damp air was sweetened by the breath of the woods and bogs over which the frost was spreading. My father sucked in great draughts of it and admired the moon-bathed night.

"Boy, oh boy, Bill, this is the life—this certainly is the life!" he said repeatedly until I became tired of it. I hoped he would be equally enthusiastic about my cabin. During the last half mile I made apologies for it adding that it was rough but very comfortable.

The hounds barked the usual welcome as the canoe was eased onto the beach. I excused myself hastily and raced up the trail to light every lamp in the cabin, unleash the dogs, and toss a match into the cedar kindling and birch logs I had previously arranged in the fireplace. With lighted lantern in hand I dashed back to the shore.

After hearing their names called and doing a lot of hurried sniffing, the barking and growling of the dogs changed quickly to furious yelps of joy. They leaped all over him, nearly knocking him into the water as he waddled from the canoe with his arms full. They knew him, and showed their love for him with a wild and woolly demonstration. Dogs are like that. The kindness and sincerity of a dog could be copied to great advantage by man. The world would be better for it.

I shouldered most of the load because I was the host, the guide, and also because I wanted to show how strong I was. As I had hoped, my father was impressed with my little place in the woods. He also mentioned again and again how well he thought I looked. I was pleased, for his enthusiasm meant that I had at least made some progress.

We talked of many things far into the night. It was after midnight when we sat down to a snack of sardines, crackers, and tea. We should have been in bed hours before, for we had a long and strenuous day ahead of us in the pursuit of the ducks. But it was a rare occasion and we were making the most of it. We could make up the lost sleep the following night.

My father planned to stay with me for several days, one of which would be devoted to visiting the grave of Big Jim. We would go by train, he said. It wasn't far that way. My father continued to talk after we had piled into our beds. I dropped off to sleep listening to him.

He was even more impressed with the place the next morning. We wolfed a big breakfast of bacon and eggs, fried potatoes, toast, doughnuts, and coffee. Darkness still mantled the frosty outdoors as we ate by lamplight.

My father got his first look at fat little Waldo the skunk as we fed the dogs and the hens. He had been on the prowl all night and was returning with a belly full of mice to snooze under the cabin. My father laughed and expressed amazement when Waldo walked toward me and I picked him up. But it was impossible to talk him into handling the little fellow or even coming within ten feet of him. He did take to Sammy the crow, however, who put in an appearance just before we left. And Sammy, apparently taking a liking to my father, perched on his knee until we were nearly halfway up the lake. Then away he went, flying low back to the camp.

It was too early in the season to use the decoys my father had brought along, for although the mornings and evenings were cold and spiced with frost, the days were quite warm. The birds I had seen were still in small family flocks feeding in the shore weeds on the quiet streams and pond coves. They wouldn't join other flocks until the coming of cold, rough weather when they would be preparing for the annual southward migration. That would be the time to use the cedar imitations anchored out in front of the grass and brush hide-outs.

The early season method of hunting the wary blacks on the inland waters is called "jump hunting." The hunter paddles quietly along in a canoe and "jumps" the feeding birds then puts the lead to them as fast as he can shoot. It's good sport and calls for good canoe handling and equally good gun handling.

When two hunters team up, the man with the gun sits in a small, low canoe chair in the bow, back to his companion who is handling the paddle in the stern. They go ashore from time to time to change places. As my father's stay would be short I planned to let him do most of the shooting.

When a hunter is alone the bow of the canoe is weighted down with rocks and he sits in the stern with the paddle and a loaded shotgun carefully placed against the nearest crossbar, which is called a thwart, where he can grab it and swing into action in a split second when the ducks are flushed. I always take two paddles instead of one, and lay the spare on the floor of the canoe.

The black duck is one of the wariest of all birds. Its hearing and its sight are amazingly keen and it flushes quickly and is instantly away on swift wings. The lone hunter certainly has his hands full when stalking them with a canoe. He has two strikes on him before he starts.

The splash of a paddle blade, be it ever so faint, or the bumping or rattling of it against the canoe, will send a flock into the air well out of range of the gun.

That's why I take two paddles. When I hear feeding ducks around a bend I take several powerful but quiet strokes then, instead of trying to put the paddle in the canoe, it is dropped quietly onto the water. The gun is carefully picked up and the canoe glides quietly around the bend. The ducks, surprised at their feasting, rise in confusion usually within easy shooting range. After the bombardment is over I take the spare paddle, pick up any ducks that might have fallen, and drop back to retrieve the other paddle. Then away again to seek other birds and repeat the procedure.

My father, who had hunted ducks since he was a youngster, knew, and nodded in agreement when, as we headed up the lake, I told him of my plans to "jump" the birds on the stream.

We were dressed quite heavily for the frosty morning was sharp, and penetrating fog rose from the slick water that was warmer than the air. Wandering gusts that goose-fleshed it in spots caused shivering birches to gold-leaf the shore. As we entered the stream mouth between towering walls of rushes and swamp grass that reminded me of sword blades, my father loaded his double-barrel 12-gauge shotgun and got into shooting position. I worked the paddle blade quietly, and the canoe sliced silently through the dark, steaming water.

Skinny little grass pickerel swirled ahead of the canoe and scooted bulletlike through the dense weed growth along the shores. Meadow hens, which seemed unusually late in heading southward, and muskrats, too, were startled as they breakfasted. We passed the station landing and pushed on through deathly silent forests, bogs, and lush meadows. There would be ducks along that stretch of the stream. I was sure of that for I had seen the mothers with their youngsters during the late summer.

Neither of us spoke. I was accustomed to the silence after nearly six months of living alone so close to Nature. I liked it, for it had repaired badly shattered nerves that had caused me great discomfort.

Suddenly my father raised his right hand. I stopped paddling and listened. I heard the low quacking of ducks some distance ahead. The canoe was eased close to shore and paddled slowly and ever so quietly.

The quacking became sharper and louder as we moved along through the mist. And finally they were just around a little bend. My father signaled that he was ready. I drove hard on the paddle and the canoe glided swiftly and silently around the bend close to a towering wall of alders, swamp grass, and cat-o'-nine-tails.

There they sat, a mother black and her seven husky youngsters. They were almost as large as she was. The wary old mother had heard something that apparently didn't sound just right and she was looking toward us. The bow of the slowly moving canoe was then less than thirty feet from the little flock. She spotted us through the swirling mist, sounded the alarm, and in a great explosion of hurrying wings and splashing water they rose in wild confusion.

My father swung quickly. His gun roared, smashing the quiet morning wide open. One young bird crumpled in a flurry of feathers and tumbled loosely to the water. Again the gun belched fire and shot but brought down only a few feathers and colored leaves from a small bog maple that slanted over the little cove. They floated down slowly and came to rest on the placid water, then all was quiet. It was a ringing sort of silence that hurt the ears.

My father cussed his "poor shooting." I laughed, picked up the dead duck, and we pushed on, up the crooked stream. We found the birds fairly numerous and although my father showed the need of practice, a sun-bathed noon found us with five fat blacks. The legal bag at that time was ten ducks a day, but he was satisfied and we went ashore near a little spring to brew tea and have lunch. We found the tracks of raccoons, mink, muskrats, and a few deer in the shore mud. I would be after them with the coming of November and cold weather. We both had a few shots at ducks that afternoon but failed to connect and we returned as the sun was nearing the end of its short autumn journey.

My father bagged a plump grouse on a little trail near the camp just before sunset and I knocked one over down by the spring. We fried both of them in butter for supper the next night. They were delicious. No kind of meat, wild or domestic, has the same entrancing and indescribable flavor as the thick white breast of this great game bird.

We had the grouse breasts and the little legs with baked sweet potatoes, cranberry sauce, plenty of gravy, hot johnnycake, hot buttered beets from the garden, and fragrant red tea. It was a feast for the Gods, as were the other game suppers we had together.

It was the first time I really enjoyed eating wild duck. I got rid of the strong odor and grease by skinning the birds feathers and all, and removing the oiler on the rear end. The flesh was quite dry and although far below that of the grouse for quality it was surprisingly good. We stuffed the ducks with a mixture of bread crumbs, sage, onion, and slices of apple. Generous slabs of bacon were pinned to the breasts with long birch slivers and the birds were placed in a very hot oven to roast slowly. When done the stuffing was removed and thrown away leaving only the meat which we sliced off in thick brown slabs.

The black duck, which while on the fresh water is a vegetarian, and the wood duck, which is strictly a fresh-water bird and a strict vegetarian, are the only species of waterfowl I can eat. I like fish very well but I don't want my fish with feathers on them. I do, however, know many people who are very fond of the fish-eating ducks.

We had very good shooting during my father's stay at camp, and we both enjoyed being together again. To one who had lived alone under those conditions for that length of time they were indeed golden days. I made the most of every hour, every minute.

Only one thing marred our highly enjoyable time together. It was a revival of that old argument about me and my future. My father started it the last day of his stay as we paddled back to camp from the station after the visit to Big Jim's grave. He made me feel that I was simply having a hell of a good time playing around in the woods but now that winter was approaching I should pack up and return home to become serious and get some kind of a job with a future. He smiled as he spoke, but his words, which were soft, were skillfully handled and equipped with stinging barbs.

"You simply can't go on like this, Bill!" he drawled with a brow furrowed like a ploughed field, and arms waving loosely in a perfect portrayal of disgust.

"The best you can hope for here is a hand to mouth existence as a greasy, woods-queer trapper and part-time guide!" he exclaimed. "Surely you don't want that, or do you?" he questioned.

I tried, as I had before leaving home, to impress upon him that I was going to live in the woods with the hope that I could pull myself together—to find myself and in time figure out just what I wanted to do in life.

"I'm not lazy!" I told him. A ringing silence followed. My puzzled father just glared at me and smiled weakly. I knew he didn't agree. He also didn't agree, and said so in sizzling words, that there was any hope of a young man deciding what kind of a city job he wanted while "lying around in the woods."

"You've had plenty of time, all summer, to decide on some sort of worth-while occupation. It seems to me that if you haven't done so by this time you never will out here!" he blurted forcefully. "And anyhow," he continued, "you couldn't possibly live in that old cabin in the winter. You'll need a lot of food for yourself, the dogs, and those hens, and you'll also need another stove and a great amount of wood, and the money to buy it. You just couldn't make it, and you'll either starve or freeze to death!"

By this time we were back at the station with his duffel, also a few grouse he had shot, some wild honey I had given him, and the evening train for Bangor was whistling a mile up the track. He put his strong, heavy arm around my slumped shoulders, and with a smile said, "I'm sorry we had the little chew, Bill, but you know how it is. You stay for the hunting season and catch what furs you can and then come on home and settle down. How about it?"

He promised to ship my traps and some cold-weather clothing to me. Completely bewildered at the moment I half promised to return home as he had requested.

Although that night was lighted by a full moon it was the blackest I had ever known.

# 12

THERE WAS a strange emptiness around the old camp for several days after my father left. I found his big pocket knife on the kitchen table where he had left it in the rush to get packed and up to the station. I opened it and found that its stout blades were very sharp. But they were no sharper than the words he also had left behind. They were like burrs in my brain every time I recalled them.

I was terribly discouraged for a time, but as I had many times in the past, I sought and found relief in prayer and hard work. The hard work this time was harvesting wood for the winter. And swinging a three-and-a-half-pound ax all day is hard work in great big letters. I had discovered long before that earnest prayer and hard work are to a man's mind and soul what fragrant soap and warm water are to soiled and weary hands.

There was a dense stand of second-growth white and yellow birch, maple, and beech on a ridge a short distance south of the camp. The owner was the same kind farmer who planted the field of corn and who made it possible for me to plant a garden. His farm was more than two miles away. I walked to his place and asked him how much he would charge me to cut some stove wood.

He smiled and brushed my question away to make room for a couple of his own.

"Well, well, son, how yer gettin' along down there? And how did yer make out with the little garden?" he inquired with his head cocked at an inquisitive angle.

We finally got back to my question about the wood.

"Yer mean thet small stuff down on the ridge the other side of the bog, don't yer?" he inquired.

I told him that was the place, that I wouldn't take much of it and that I would not clean out any one spot but would pick out trees here and there. I also told him that I didn't have much money at the time but could pay him something then and the rest later.

"Listen to me, son," he drawled in a low, sort of confidential tone, "if yer plan to stay in thet cabin all winter yer gonna need a heck of a lot of wood. Thet stuff down there's no good to me so just hustle right into it and cut all yer want fer nawthin'. But," he continued, "yer gonna need some big stuff fer thet fireplace of yours too. When yer git around to it let me know and I'll haul down a good big load. You know, three-foot stuff and plenty big. It won't cost too much and yer can pay me when yer feel yer able."

That old man, God bless him, never knew how happy he made me that day. He was typical of the honest, God-loving men who live close to the land. I thought then and have thought many times since what a wonderful world this would be if all men were like him and his kind. We sampled his sweet apple cider together, shook hands, and I hurried back down the dusty little road and through the woods to the cabin.

At first I decided to clear out a little trail through the woods from the camp to the ridge over which I could drag the small trees after I had felled and limbed them. But on second thought I decided that it would be much easier to do the sawing where I was cutting and transport the wood to the cabin with the canoe.

Felling and limbing trees is rather fascinating, and on frosty mornings it's really enjoyable. I enjoy splitting the big pieces, too. But there is no form of labor I detest more than pushing and pulling on a bucksaw. But it had to be done and the harvesting of that very important fuel got underway. The young hardwoods ranged in size from three to six inches through the butt and of course tapered to smaller diameters as they went upward.

I took the hounds off the long ropes that had prevented them from running off into the woods during the spring and summer when the rabbits, foxes, and raccoons were with their young and protected by the game laws. They were crazy in their freedom—like little mountain brooks when the hands of spring break the bonds of winter.

I could hear them trailing back in the woods, killing nothing but enjoying the chase, and getting into condition for the hard days of serious hunting for meat and fur that were soon to come. The woods resounded with their voices and the ringing of the ax as it bit deeply into clean, hard wood.

I hacked away for several hours every day and at the end of the first week I had a surprisingly large pile of the long, limbed trunks. Another week of steady chopping would give me all the wood I would need to feed the old kitchen range through the winter. And it would take another week or a bit more to saw it up into stove length, split some large chunks, and carry it all in the canoe to the cabin.

That could all be done in any kind of weather and I wanted to enjoy the grouse hunting during those blue-and-golden days, so I halted the fuel harvest and hunted at least a part of every day.

The ruffed grouse is the most mysterious of all birds. Like nearly all wild creatures the population of the grouse is controlled by a cycle arranged by Nature in her great wisdom, but even today, after years of exhaustive research by the most learned biologists, it is little understood.

The rise and fall of wildlife populations is Nature's way of maintaining a balance of her creatures and their food supply. Although the number of years in the rise and fall of the cycles governing the populations of most creatures are pretty well known, no one has been able to learn the number of years in the grouse cycle. For instance the cycle of the snowshoe rabbit is at the population peak every seven to ten years. But the old thunder wing of the beech ridges still has the leading authorities scratching puzzled heads.

But whether it's ten, fourteen, or twenty-four years, the birds were quite numerous that fall. And there were very few hunters in the country I roamed over.

I hunted them mostly in the early morning and late afternoon, working a bit at my woodpile during the middle of some of the days. The hardwoods were then blazing with color and on some of my jaunts I used to wander to the top of a towering ridge at the head of the lake, and there in wide-eyed amazement silently admire Nature's grand masterpiece. It was a great panorama of red, gold, bronze, and brown, broken here and there by towering stands of spruce and pine, and dotted with the fiercely blue ponds and streams that dozed unrippled under the sun's golden cloak.

Far to the east, the south, and the west, mountains that borrowed beauty from the distance sat majestically on the edge of that gorgeous and massive crazy quilt of the outdoors. The nearest and the highest of those monuments of forests and stone was Dixmont Mountain. I had walked to it several times on my summer jaunts through the woods. With its pointed head and rich purple mantle it was a thing of rare beauty as it towered with hunched shoulders above the painted trees that crowded at its feet.

I had seen it many times and I had climbed over its massive back. I had seen it drab and brooding in the rain, resplendent in the sun. Yet I never tired of looking at it. It fascinated me strangely. And there in the golden autumn it loomed again, old a thousand years ago yet more beautiful than ever.

Those old roads with sandy flanks and grass-ridged bellies also hold a strange fascination for those of us who, when the uplands are aflame in the autumn, prowl with fowling pieces in pursuit of wild poultry.

Perhaps it's only a weedy remnant of the lush lumbering days, a rutted trail winding back to an abandoned farm; or it might be the passage to a gravel pit. But whatever its purpose in the past or present, there's something about it that attracts the grouse hunter with the same strong pull experienced by a fox when he scents a hiding hare. They are quiet, mysterious ribbons that curl along between walls of woods, and here and there are dappled with the gold of the sun. It's on these roads that the grouse, fluffed and contented, bask in the sun's warming flood when frost mantles the morning, and wander again for a snack and pebbles when the day is old and the west is inflamed.

And though his time for hunting may be short, or the dusk moving in, the man with the gun cannot, for the life of him, hold himself back from that next bend. He wants to know what it looks like around there and, of course, there might be a bird or two waddling about. And so he eases along, squints expectantly around that bend, and finds it no different than all the others that wind behind him. But, there's another up ahead and, maybe—and so it goes until the autumn dusk hauls a purple robe over the woods.

I toddled along just such a road late one afternoon. It twisted back through the woods to an abandoned lumber camp. It was flanked by towering stands of old and young hardwoods. It was sandy and hard most of the way on either side of the grassy middle, but in places there were greasy mud blots and little pools of old rain.

Around the first bend it became a sun-flooded lane that bored straight away through a leafy tunnel of blazing red maples. The pools, like pieces of broken mirrors reflecting the fierce blush, loomed like basins of blood. And now and then, a leaf surrendering to autumn the harvester, relaxed its grip and came tumbling down.

I stood in silence in my environment of fantastic beauty. All thought of grouse drained from my mind like dewdrops from a wind-turned leaf. I pushed on through the maze of bewildering beauty. There were no birds on the road and I turned back for the walk to camp, turning again and again, to admire that corridor of color that wound through that greatest of all art galleries, the great outdoors.

The dusk dropped its purple curtain. I unloaded my gun and knelt to drink at a little spring. The evening star burned a tiny hole in the sky's deep-blue blanket, and a one-eyed moon unrolled a brassy carpet ahead of me. I had seen a bit of Heaven. There would be other days to hunt grouse.

And there were other days, many of them, when on that same beautiful little road I bagged many a plump bird. There were other days when I sought that great bird in the dense covers—days filled with the thunder of hurrying wings, the smashing report of a gun fired fast, and of thrilling sport. Although quite numerous in the woods that year I had to hunt hard for them at times. I killed only what I needed for the camp larder.

Several days were devoted to "jump hunting" black ducks with the canoe on the lazy streams. I missed many more than I brought down but didn't care much because I never was fond of the meat. I am, however, fond of the handsome and scarce wood duck, which is a strict vegetarian whose diet includes nuts, acorns, and seeds. They are not nearly as wary as the black and some of the other species and are quite easily stalked.

The lack of wariness is perhaps the reason for the scarcity. Because they are few in number, regulations governing the hunting of ducks in Maine permit the Nimrod to kill only one of either sex a day. I killed three in as many days, two gaudy males and one female. Neither greasy nor strong the flesh was delicious. The skins of the males were carefully removed, salted, and put away until the coming of the long winter nights when the beautiful feathers would be used in the tying of fishing flies.

It was slow, hard work sawing the great pile of trees into stove wood and transporting it load after load up the cove to the camp. The wood was heaped by the side of the cabin to dry a bit in the sun. Later it would be sheltered by a roof of boughs raised on poles. As much as possible would be neatly piled on the spacious veranda.

My father was quite prompt in shipping out my traps, warm clothes, wool socks, and heavy boots. I was surprised to find them on a trip to the station. They were all packed in a large wooden box. I rolled it over and over down the little trail to the canoe and then wrestled with the problem of getting it down the lake to the camp. It was much too large and heavy to take in the canoe so there was nothing left to do but rip it open and pack its contents on the floor of the long narrow craft.

The old eighteen footer was loaded almost to the gunwales with a pair of heavy red and black plaid hunting breeches, a red and black checked shirt, two sweat shirts, socks, wool mittens with leather casings to pull over them, two silk and wool union suits, knitted stocking cap, red and black plaid hunting coat, knee-length parka, a leather vest lined with sheepskin, big leather belt, cartridge belt, high moccasins, a pair of twelve-inch hunting boots with soft leather tops and red rubber bottoms, my old .30-30 carbine lever-action rifle, a box and a half of cartridges, a stout belt ax, a large compass, and forty of my steel traps of various sizes.

One thing that I had hoped would be in the box was a note from my father. Everything was thoroughly searched but the note wasn't there. Apparently my patient and puzzled parents had talked it over, become disgusted and given up all hope of ever getting me to return to the city and go to work. They were unhappy and so was I.

The box which was taken apart was later made into a house for one of the dogs. I put a pitched roof on it and covered sides and all with large slabs of birch bark. A house was made for the other dog out of old boards. That too was covered with bark. With dry leaves on the floors they were snug and comfortable. The dogs seemed to enjoy them.

While working on the little houses I recalled what a French-Canadian trapper once said to me. I was hunting with him in New Brunswick. One day when he didn't show up at the camp until noon, I asked him where he had been.

"I was home," he said. Then went on to explain excitedly, "I had to go to de store to buy an empty barrel of flour to make a hencoop for my dog."

I laughed until my sides ached that day. And I laughed almost as hard as I recalled what he said. I guess the dogs thought I had suddenly gone nuts.

A man thinks of many things when he is working alone. I thought mostly of home and my parents who had shipped my things to me but who had failed to write.

Like all men worthy of their salt I would gladly have done everything possible to bring comfort and happiness to my parents. But this thing they asked of me wasn't possible. It seemed I had no control over this strange desire to live alone. It was bigger than I was. I couldn't explain it, yet somehow I knew that out there in the woods—out there near God where it was good and big and clean—I would find my way out of the hellish black maze in which I wandered, and finally emerge into the sunlight that warms those who toil at tasks to their liking.

# 13

THE RAIN AND WIND like harvesters came with November to gather the leaves from the trees and pile them deep across the land. The woods, so beautiful during most of October, brooded in their nakedness, and the birds, heeding the warning of approaching winter, had spread their wings and headed southward. The crows and the ducks were the only migrants that remained.

The swallows were the first to leave. They departed when the fly hatches were over in late August. All of them were gone by September. The little feathered songsters followed along with the herons, meadow hens, and finally those tiny, but excellent game birds, the woodcock, were gone. The robins seemed reluctant to leave and were about in flocks until well into November when suddenly they too soared away.

The shell ice, which was forming over the shore shallows in which the ducks sought weed seeds, mussels, and minnows, caused the last of the flight birds from Canada to start for the open waters of the coast. I watched them leave every day. The crows in great flocks, too, were winging down to the sea. And Sammy, apparently tiring of life with a young hermit and his hens and hounds and a skunk, went with them. I was surprised but not saddened for I knew he would have been an unbearable nuisance during the winter when he would have to be in the cabin much of the time.

The departure of all the feathered things caused a feeling of loneliness. As I watched them soaring away through the sky I felt like crying after them to come back—back to keep me company and live with me forever. And I wished strongly that I were one of them and could ride at will on the wild winds, free of the problems of man's hurrying world.

Pop helped me pile and cover the stove wood I had cut and sawed. The big stuff for the old fireplace would be hauled down by my good farmer friend when snow mantled the ground and the ice on the lake was stout enough to bear the weight of the loaded sled and his horses.

In return I helped Pop pick out a trapline and set a couple dozen muskrat traps and then set the forty of my own. We were far from being experts in the art of setting steel traps and outwitting fur-bearing animals, but the muskrat is not very wary and is quite easily taken. I had trapped them successfully since I was a small boy. We set our traps on opposite sides of the lake and some of mine were strung along the boggy shores of Ben Annis Pond. Apples and carrots were used for bait, and as the animals were numerous we were quite successful.

We worked our lines alone and seldom saw each other. The pelts were bringing about two dollars apiece then and it seemed, as I made the rounds every morning, that I was picking money as I would flowers or berries. Although my hands and wrists were red and badly chapped from constant soaking in the cold water, I enjoyed that harvesting of furs. Catching the rats wasn't the only work involved. They had to be carefully skinned, and the pelts stretched, scraped, and dried before they would be ready for shipment to the buyer.

Most of the skinning was done at night before the leaping flames that filled the throat of the fireplace. The skin is first cut down the inside of each hind leg then peeled off whole in the manner of removing a shirt or sweater over your head. The long hairless tail and the feet are worthless and are left on the carcass.

The Indians and many white trappers I know eat the meat of the muskrat. They claim it is delicious. Perhaps I too would have eaten it and enjoyed it but the name "rat" was too much for me. Then, too, by the time I had skinned a dozen or more rats the sweet and heavy odor from the musk glands had sickened me of them and dulled my appetite for any kind of food. The meat, which is a dark red and very tender, was not wasted, however. All of the carcasses were spiked to trees near the cabin to freeze and to be cut up and cooked for the dogs. I fed them bits of it raw, too, and left pieces near Waldo's den under the camp that he might enjoy a snack of fresh meat, which I know he was finding scarce on his nightly prowls.

Thin box boards whittled to a gradual point at the top were used to stretch the skins. They were pulled over the boards, inside out, tacked along the bottom edge, scraped clean of fat, and hung up to dry away from heat and any mice that might be prowling about.

The fox and the mink, which were much more valuable, were also much harder to trap. I did manage to outwit and capture a few of the latter, but the crafty old brushtails fooled me completely. The few that I did bag were shot ahead of the hounds.

Pop put out a few traps for skunks and on the rare occasions that our trails crossed his success in pursuit of the smelly creatures was strongly evident. In addition to the black and white pelts Pop also took the thick white fat from the carcasses from which he melted oil to use in his constant battle against rheumatism.

When the shell ice along the shores became hard to crash through with the canoe and made trapping difficult, I hauled in my traps and quit.

We both shipped our furs to a house in St. Louis. The company provided us with large tags, and the furs laid flat were first wrapped in heavy wrapping paper, which was in turn wrapped in burlap and tightly bound with stout cord. I managed to break through the shell ice that coated much of the lake and all of the stream with the old canoe and shipped the two bundles of furs at the station.

My catch of muskrat, mink, and fox pelts brought me a check for three hundred-fifty dollars, while Pop's much smaller catch of muskrat, and skunk pelts paid him a bit less than two hundred dollars. I don't remember the exact number of pelts we shipped but I do remember that we had quite a load of them. Some of the rat pelts, we were informed by letters from the company, weren't top quality and of course didn't bring the top price of two dollars. We got a fair deal and were very well satisfied. It wasn't a lot of money, but not bad for a couple of amateur trappers in only three weeks.

My farmer friend took the endorsed checks to his bank in Bangor on one of his trips and returned with our money in small bills, which Pop said looked like a couple bales of lettuce.

The frigid fingers of winter were rapidly sealing the lake, and I wasn't sure when on Thanksgiving night I crashed and paddled through the great expanse of windowpane ice for a little celebration at Pop's camp whether I would be able to get back in the dark. It seemed certain that if I did manage to get back it would be the last ride in the old canoe until spring.

The yellow lamplight from Pop's windows stabbed into the night, and from his squatty chimney a plume of lazy white smoke curled straight up, into a sky powdered with stars. I could hear the old fellow rattling dishes and singing at the top of his raspy voice.

"Well, well, bless yer young heart, yer made it ice and all, didn't yer," he yelped enthusiastically as I stepped into the warm kitchen. The pleasant odors of wood smoke and cooking food rushed into my nostrils.

A bit played out after the battle with the ice, I answered Pop's greeting with a smile and a wave, and slumped into an old rocking chair. Instantly the smoky little room rang with the screaming of a cat. It was Pop's. I had come down on him with all of my weight as he slept. I bounded out of the chair with the mad and frightened feline still yelping and firmly anchored to the seat of my pants with his claws. The poor thing shook himself loose and dashed crazily into a shadowed corner. A crazy kind of cackling laughter poured from Pop's toothless mouth and little tears squirted from his weak red eyes. Finally weakened by this outburst of mirth he sat down to catch his breath.

"That wuz Peter, son," he gasped. "Don't know if you ever saw him afore or not."

"Yes, I know, Pop, and I'm sorry I sat down on the poor thing," I apologized with a silly grin.

"Aw ter hell with him, he's half baked. Allus gittin' underfoot and half squashed ter death then ahollerin' like a panther. I've sot down on him a thousand times and he's got the rump half clawed offen me. If it want thet he's a good mouser I would have heaved him out long ago. I'm gonna have me a good cat someday," he chuckled.

I had never seen Pop looking so clean. He had scraped off a two weeks' growth of gray whiskers, suffered through a bath, and put on a change of clean clothes. I had freshened up a bit, too. It felt good after weeks of skinning wild animals and scraping their greasy pelts.

The dinner consisted of three fried grouse that Pop had saved for the occasion, baked potatoes, mashed turnip, stewed cranberries, fried onions, hot biscuits, doughnuts, canned peaches, and stout tea. It was a bountiful and excellent meal and we enjoyed preparing it as much as we did eating it.

There was one other item on the menu but only Pop enjoyed it. And how he enjoyed it! It was wine he had made from elderberries the year before. It was in a dusty, cobwebbed gallon jug that he dug out of his little cellar hole under the kitchen floor. He seemed very disappointed when he learned that I never drank anything stronger than tea.

"Well now thet's too bad, son," he said slowly. "But," he added hastily, "you don't mind any if I have a swig or two afore we eat, do you? I might have three or four, if it's all right with you," he chuckled with a jack-o'-lantern grin on his weather-whipped face.

I assured him that I had no objections, and lounged back to watch my fine old friend fill and drain a water glass. His Adam's apple bulged like a beet in a stocking, and for a time it looked as though his eyes were going to pop out on the floor. Quickly recovering from the jolt he expressed his apparent complete satisfaction by a lot of loud lip smacking and breath blowing.

Pop was in high spirits when we finally sat down to our holiday feast. We were both hungry and sailed into the food with gusto. Pop, who used the knife instead of the fork, reminded me of a sword swallower I had seen in a carnival side show, and there were times when I feared he would slice his withered throat.

It was a fine meal and we had barely finished when the old fellow was at the wine again.

"Let the dishes go ter hell or somewhere else till we sit awhile and smoke," he squeaked as he filled a glass to the brim with the blue liquid. He was talking louder and faster as the minutes flew by and finally he broke out in song. It was awful.

Pop had cooked most of the dinner and I decided that under the circumstances I should take over the job of washing the dishes and cleaning up the place.

I was surprised that the old fellow knew when he had enough, or perhaps I should say a bit more than enough. I watched him in silence as he waddled over to the trap door, the seat of his pants sagging like the rear end of an elephant, and placed the jug and what remained of the wine into the little cellar.

He returned to the couch on which he had been sprawled and began to talk. He said something about deer hunting but his words soon faded away into meaningless nothings and he was soon sound asleep and snoring like a bear.

It was near midnight by the time I had cleaned up the place, banked the fire in the old ram-down stove, and made Pop comfortable for the night.

The ram-down, so called, is a narrow and long boxlike stove made especially for heating. They come in several sizes, taking sticks from two to nearly four feet long, and they are popular with all who live in northern woods camps. They are sometimes referred to as "schoolhouse stoves" because of their wide use in little country schools.

I wished, as I worked on the fire, that I had one for I knew that the little cooking range and the old fireplace wouldn't keep my large cabin warm during the months of fierce cold that were closing in.

November had been a cold, hateful month, and many of her dirty little days had spit snow in our faces. All signs pointed to an early and severe winter. While running our little traplines Pop and I had carried our rifles and prowled over some promising looking country in hopes of bagging the deer we would need so badly, but neither of us saw anything more than tracks and frosted droppings.

Deer were not numerous in that region then. It is a well-known fact that the white-tail deer follows the ax, and the greater part of the Maine herd at that time was farther north where the many lumbering companies were harvesting the giant pines that made many wealthy and that gave the state its name.

Deer concentrated in those sections where they could feast on the tender twigs and buds of the felled hardwoods, the green lace of the cedars, and the tender green plants and shoots that spring up in profusion in the old cuttings.

There were a few in our neck of the woods, as Pop expressed it, and some of the tracks we had seen along the muddy stream shores and back in the bogs were made by big bucks. But we couldn't find any of them, not even a doe or a fawn.

Perhaps because of our trapping we hadn't hunted hard enough or at the right time of day. We needed badly the money the furs would bring and we also needed the meat of the deer. But it seems we couldn't have both. We couldn't unless our luck changed during the next four days for that was all that remained of November and the legal hunting season on deer.

The laws governing the taking of game and fur-bearing animals were much more generous then and I planned to continue trapping on a small scale throughout the winter. I knew that it would be much more difficult and less productive when the lakes, ponds, and streams were locked in ice and the woods blanketed with deep snow. But it would be interesting and I was sure to catch a few animals which would mean additional dollars. And, too, it would give me an excellent opportunity to continue my study of wildlife and the outdoors, which had never ceased since early spring.

During the spring and summer when paddling alone in my canoe I always carried about sixty pounds of rocks in the bow to hold the craft down on an even keel. On the return trip from Pop's camp that cold Thanksgiving night I found the ice had thickened to such an extent that it was next to impossible to plough the weighted bow through it. And I was following as closely as I could what was left of the jagged path I had made on the way over. I managed to backwater to the shore where I landed and shifted the rocks back far enough so that about half of the canoe would ride up onto the ice and the weight of the rocks would break it. Several times on the way across the lake the ice failed to give under the weight of the canoe and it rolled over on its side. I had a couple of very close calls.

The narrow and very ragged path I had made through the ice on the way over had sealed over, and unable to find it except in spots I headed the canoe straight for the lighted lantern I had left on the shore in front of the cabin. And while hot and dry lips mumbled an occasional prayer, I worked hard but very carefully through the thickening ice field lest the canvas be ripped open or the frail craft rolled over.

I wondered at times, when the canoe riding high on the ice rolled and took in water, if perhaps, as my father had warned, I was that very night to go the way of our great friend Big Jim. I made it finally, and standing puffing on the shore looked through the night across the lake at the ragged path the canoe had made. It curled away serpentine and was suddenly lost in the black smother.

A hasty inspection of the faithful old eighteen-footer in the dim, yellow light of the lantern revealed a badly scraped bottom and two long slits in the canvas near the bow. I turned it over, dumping out three inches of water and walked slowly toward the cabin.

A clammy sort of cold greeted me when I pushed open the door, and again I realized that I would need a good heater if I were to live in the old place during the winter. Other things, too, would be needed including tighter calking between the logs and a deep banking of boughs around the base of the old place. And just to be on the safe side I planned to cut more wood. But all that would have to wait for I had but a short time, four more little November days, in which to try to hunt down and kill the deer that would provide me with meat for the long white months ahead.

I had learned long before that fresh air heats much quicker than stale air and I threw open both the front and back doors of the cabin before lighting new fires. I looked in on the dogs and the hens, then returned to touch off birch bark curls and cedar kindling in both the kitchen cookstove and the fireplace. The place was quite warm and cheerful as I oiled and polished my rifle in preparation for an all-out hunt for a deer that, although having little time to sleep, would begin before the coming of the sun.

# 14

HUNTING WILD GAME is a fascinating and thrilling sport, but when the fatal shot is fired the fun is all over. This is particularly true of deer hunting for from the moment the deer is felled it's all hard work. I feel sure that all who have hunted the animals alone will agree there is no harder work than dragging the heavy and limp carcass through brushy woods. It's a tough job even for two stout men in excellent physical condition. This carrying of a large deer across the shoulders is done only on magazine covers.

Although I have hunted and bagged many kinds of game large and small, in this country and Canada for many years, I still feel a bit sorry for a poor dead thing lying broken and bloody at my feet.

In fishing I can seek, catch, and enjoy the thrill of battle, and even take the victim in my hands and admire it, and after I've had my fun, release it, none the worse for the experience. But in hunting the bird or animal can't be released to live on and perhaps provide more sport another day, for the instant the spiraling lead slug or pattern of pellets smash into the warm flesh that particular creature's life is at an end.

My hunt for that sorely needed deer would be one time that there would be no sorrow after the kill, if indeed there was a kill. The sight of a fine fat buck or even a doe sprawled before me would bring only unbounded joy for I would be hunting to eat —hunting to live, like any other predator of the forest.

I had learned long before that deer are where you find them, and that the hunter never can tell just where he will find them. As Pop used to say, "All yer gotta do ter git a deer is ter be at a certain place the same time the deer is."

Lady Luck plays a part in the hunting of all species of game, but she plays a leading role in the pursuit of the unpredictable deer. She certainly had evaded Pop and me.

I was a bit groggy from lack of sleep when in the frosty dawn of that first of four precious days I loaded the .30-30 and swung down the trail. My lunch that sagged in the game pocket of the red and black plaid hunting shirt consisted of six raw carrots. Hungry animals hunt better, and I would need all of the pep and prowess I possessed. I had always been fond of raw carrots and frequently took a few on one-day jaunts to munch on while I hunted. You can eat them while walking and they don't cause that lazy and contented feeling that follows a full meal or a stack of sandwiches and hot tea. Carrots are nourishing and although not as satisfying as a regular lunch they do a pretty fair job of dulling the pangs of hunger.

I missed the old canoe, for with it I could have traveled faster, reached better hunting country, and if I bagged a deer I could get it back to camp with much less effort. But that first coating of shell ice still held and was rapidly getting thicker.

The frozen and frost-powdered woods was alive with chattering red squirrels. They were busy with the last of the nut harvest. As I watched them dashing to their dens with cheeks bulging I felt that I was indeed fortunate to have the few quarts of beechnuts gathered while running the trap line.

The red squirrel is a nervous little creature. Moving in short, jerky sprints with bushy tail forever pumping, and yapping and yammering as he goes, he reminds me of a small fur bag in which a hundred tiny and tightly coiled springs are letting go all at once. He is little Mr. Twitchy Pants of the woods who burns up enough energy in a day to last a mud turtle a lifetime.

The blue jays, too, were squawking all over the woods. These handsome birds always whoop it up before a spell of soft weather. As usual their prediction was true. The wind swung around into the southwest before noon and the temperature climbed rapidly. By the middle of the afternoon a light rain was falling and by the time I reached the cabin it was belching down in great quantities.

It drummed heavily on the roof all night and it was still drumming when I awoke early the next morning. It was a cold and miserable dawn, and I wondered, as I lay curled in the blankets watching the faint light struggling through, if perhaps Nature had taken sides with my parents in the effort to bring me home.

The warmth of the freshly kindled fires cheered me a bit and a hot breakfast of flapjacks and wild honey, bacon, and stout coffee helped considerably in bolstering my sagging spirits. While feeding the dogs and the hens and gathering the few eggs, I discovered that Waldo had dug a den under the cabin and was living in it. He had set up bachelor quarters for the winter. The light-brown earth was heaped up outside the entrance and when I saw him late that dripping afternoon his front paws and little pointed face were covered with it.

He always seemed glad to see me, but he seemed more friendly than ever that day. It made me feel good inside when he, a little wild creature, hurried toward me, climbed into my outstretched arms, and snuggled his dirty little nose against my neck. I cracked a raw egg for him and gave him what was left of a can of salmon and went to work on the old canoe. It was pretty badly scraped and torn by the ice but with strips of thin canvas cut from the seat of an old chair, adhesive tape, green paint, and a bit of varnish I managed to do a pretty fair job of patching.

When spring came it would need a complete overhauling. I don't know why I bothered with it then. I guess it was because I had nothing more important to do in the rain. I hoped that when spring did come I would be able to buy a little sixteen-foot craft without a keel that I could slide through the small streams, run through fast water, and carry with ease on my back past rapids too nasty to ride through.

Just before the warm and steaming dusk settled, the shell ice, which had sliced open the belly of my canoe and taken a swipe at my life, broke up and in ragged melting chunks was herded cattlelike by the southwest wind toward the head of the lake. The ice in the stream that flowed out below the camp also opened. It seemed good to see water again.

Two of the last four precious days of the deer season were gone. It takes only a split second to bag a deer once you line your sights on the animal, but finding one was my problem. And it was very much of a problem in that vast country where deer were few, and God willing and weather permitting, only two little November days in which to hunt.

The lake was nearly wide open the next morning. It lay placid and blue while the rising sun rouged its face. It had rained well into the night and the forest dripped and steamed as the sun climbed. Such sudden changes in the weather aren't at all unusual in Maine where Nature seems unable to decide what she wants to serve. At that particular time of year she might serve a bit of June for breakfast and dish out a blizzard for dinner. But come what may later, the day and the open water looked good to me and I took advantage of it. I was glad then that I patched the canoe the day before for with it I could travel to what I knew was better deer country than that I had been hunting in.

The paint and the varnish over the patches had dried pretty well, and with rocks in the bow to balance my weight I was quickly away around and between broken fields of thin but tough ice that moved about at the bidding of a weak wind that had sprung up suddenly.

I headed down the stream toward Hammond Pond where I found the way blocked at the mouth by ice that had been shoved in by the wind. Smashing through it with the old craft seemed impossible and I dared not attempt it. A bad rip in the canvas then would have robbed me of most of another hunting day and if the canoe became wedged in the middle of the mess I would have been in a very serious predicament.

There was another problem that had to be solved. A man who lives alone in the woods is confronted by a great many of them—some that come suddenly with a frightening challenge. But he must meet and defeat them without help. That sort of life was at least teaching me self-reliance and giving me confidence in myself, which previously had barely existed.

Alders that crowded down to the shore to watch the stream go by stood in tangled profusion. They sprawled back for quite a distance to a soggy meadow. I would have to hack a path through them with only my belt knife, then shoulder the canoe and carry it around the ice field to the open water in the pond, a distance of more than a hundred yards. The rough and narrow opening was finally made through the barrier of alders and I tested the boggy earth of the meadow for holes and soft spots. The rifle and paddles were lashed to the canoe thwarts and the balance rocks were taken out of the bow. The old canoe wasn't built for river work and portaging in the first place, and with its keel patches, and two or three coats of paint it was heavier than ever—much too heavy to be swung onto the shoulders and carried very far.

By turning it upside down and shoving the stern up to arm's length I was able to get under it and with the paddles resting on my shoulders, and the floor of the heavy old craft on my head, I was finally able to balance it and go staggering and floundering through the alders and across the meadow to the shore of the pond below the ice field.

It was quite a struggle and after dumping it with a splash in the water I slumped down in the coarse yellow swale hay to rub the pain from my shoulders and regain my wind. Unable to find more balance rocks there I had to return to the stream to get those I had left behind. There were seven in all, and were quite heavy and awkward to carry. I had to make three trips to get them all.

I was away on a fast paddle down the pond and finally into the yawning mouth of the deep and quiet outlet stream. On the first bend I flushed a pair of golden-eye ducks, commonly called whistlers in Maine. Unlike the other species of ducks the goldeneyes frequently remain inland after winter has set in just as long as they can find a stretch of open water on which they can swim and find food. I have known these birds to stay all winter on a long stretch of open water below rapids in a big stream.

Muskrats returning home late after a night of wandering and feasting knifed through the slick black water like little tugboats. I saw quite a number of them and decided that if the mild weather continued I would again string the traps for them.

Seemingly endless bogs of cranberry bushes, pucker brush, and islands of nondescript alders and stunted white maples sprawled away on both sides of the stream to meet faraway forests of pine, spruce, and towering hardwoods. Here and there in the tall yellow swale hay of those bogs I could see the trails of deer, and on little tongues of mud stuck out into the water, their few tracks looked like little hearts that had been split in halves.

It was a good day to hunt deer and I promised myself I would go all out in an effort to bag one of the scarce and elusive creatures. Aided by the light current I was soon at the rips below which, at the mouths of the brooks, I had enjoyed good sport with the trout in the spring and early summer. The canoe was quickly hauled up and turned over, and I was away slowly and quietly into the southwest wind.

The white-tail deer has very poor eyes but his nose and ears are extremely keen, and he is ever alert. Because of this it is very difficult to stalk one successfully.

I planned to do some stalking where the traveling conditions were good, and to sit down and play the waiting game in brushy country where the animals, then in the tail end of the mating season, would likely be traveling.

The mating season is during the month of November. It is then that the big and wary bucks are traveling throughout the day to court as many of the pretty does as they can find. It also is the time when they are bull-necked and ugly and fight to the death if necessary with antlered rivals.

Those battles of the bucks are fierce encounters. The enraged animals fight for hours while a graceful doe stands by watching, and waiting for the winner. During these wilderness brawls the antlers of the bucks frequently become locked together and one or both of the animals eventually die.

I once came upon a giant buck in the northern Maine woods that had won a locked antler battle and was dragging his dead victim around with him. The poor thing had paid dearly for his victory. He was hiding in a fir thicket. Well-worn trails revealed that he was able to travel only a very short distance for food, and down to a nearby brook for water. Everywhere he went he had to drag his heavy victim with him. I called my hunting companion and we shot him. We judged by the signs and his condition that he had been dragging the other deer around with him for more than a week. We guessed his weight then at two hundred pounds, and in full flesh before the fight at about two hundred twenty-five pounds.

We were unable to pull or pound the antlers apart and had to shoot off one of the dead buck's. Although having lost considerable weight the flesh of the victorious buck was good and we dragged the big carcass to camp.

I recalled that day—that strange sight—and wished that I might again find tangled bucks. I wanted and needed the meat that much. Fresh signs were few in the area I prowled through and at noon I was still facing a winter menu of vegetables and the pithy flesh of what rabbits and pickerel I might catch.

I returned to the canoe and gnawed up a brace of carrots, hauled thoughtfully on the old corncob pipe, and paddled back a mile on the stream to hunt the bog and the woods that sprawled between the stream and George Pond on the other side.

A great smother of large, wet snowflakes that swirled down suddenly from a blanket of dirty blue clouds for about a half hour caused me to get turned around in that vast maze of chest high swale grass, clawing brush, and dwarfed trees. I sought shelter under an old pine that towered above a thicket of bushes and small white maples and wondered as I crouched there half wet and half frozen how such a splendid tree happened to grow there.

The squall finally ended as suddenly as it had begun. Only scattered flakes drifted down. I was soon able to get my bearings again and pushed on toward the woods that were still quite a distance across the desolate bog. The soggy snow that weighted down the tall swale grass also trimmed the naked branches of the hardwoods and powdered the green boughs of the firs, pines, and spruces in the distance. There was very little snow on the ground, however, save for the unprotected shore muck. It was covered with the ermine of the freak storm and made the stream appear like a huge black serpent coiling slowly through the great bogs.

I found several small poplars and maples that had been rubbed clean of bark in spots by the antlers of the bucks. Buck deer shed their antlers during the winter and sprout new sets in the spring. The new antlers are quite soft for a time and are covered with a soft, protective substance called velvet. As the antlers harden the bucks remove the velvet and polish them by rubbing them against small trees. They rub again during the mating season in November, perhaps to make them more attractive to the does and to sharpen their weapons for the fighting that takes place during that period.

The rubbing scars I saw were both old and new. The new ones encouraged me and I moved slowly onward through the tangled wasteland. But as the small fall day began to fade my hopes faded with it. My wide and straining eyes scanned the great and homely sprawl and my ears were cocked for any sound that might be made by a deer sneaking through the deep grass or one of the many islands of brush and discouraged trees.

It was deeply depressing as I stood there in the singing silence. And again I was heading toward the woods, dragging heavy and tired legs away from the clutching bushes. Then suddenly I thought I saw a deer come out of the woods and move down toward the far side of the bog. Nerves absorbed all moisture from my mouth. It was fiercely dry and felt very small, like a hole a broomstick would make in a pumpkin. My heart pounded so hard I could hear it in my ears, which became plugged for a time and hissed and sang like steam radiators. My chilled hands clutched the rifle until they hurt.

Then I mused that perhaps like men dying of thirst on the desert see shaded pools that do not exist, I, too, was looking at nothing more than a creature created by intense desire, and concentration of thought. It was a mirage, that's what it was, I concluded.

But somehow I couldn't turn away. I moved toward it slowly and with short and careful steps. Then as suddenly as it had appeared it was gone. Having hunted deer successfully since I was fourteen years old I knew that one would be very likely to see a deer at such a spot at that particular time of day. They would be coming out of their daytime hide-outs in the thickets to cross the bog for a drink at the stream. I had shot quite a few of them at drinking places in the early morning and late afternoon.

I pictured myself as a lean and hungry predatory animal. On hands and knees with the wind in my face, I crawled slowly and silently toward that bare spot on the bank where the forest came down to meet the swale. Cold water and black bog slop oozed over my left hand and my knees as I eased forward. I hated it but I was very near the spot and had to keep out of sight if I hoped to get a shot at what I thought was a deer. When within about a hundred yards of it I sat down in a fairly dry spot to regain my wind, check the rifle, and try to steady my shaking hands.

Then peering over the top of the grass I saw it. It was a deer. A real living thing and not something molded by my imagination. It was a doe. She had been feeding out of sight in the tall grass and bushes at the foot of the bank. She walked slowly back toward the woods and turned to survey the bog. Then suddenly from the dark woods stepped another. It was a buck. Bucks, being extremely wary, often push the does into the open to look for enemies before coming out of hiding. It seemed that was what she was doing.

I wished Pop were along with his old .38-55 rifle that we might blaze away together and perhaps both bag the meat we would need for the winter. Although deer of both sex, even fawns, are legal in Maine, like all hunters I wanted a buck. With the sun flashing its flaming farewell through a break in the dirty blue snow clouds there was no time to waste for darkness settles quickly in November. I realized that would probably be my one and only opportunity to bag a deer that season and I decided not to take the risk of trying to crawl any closer but to blaze away from where I crouched in the soggy swale hay and brush.

Although never in the Daniel Boone class as a marksman I could always shoot well. My confidence in the old .30-30 helped a lot in bolstering my own and I squirmed into position for the one chance, the one shot that would mean so much to me.

The rear sight was carefully set for one hundred yards although the two deer seemed farther away. The buck was standing broadside behind the slightly turned doe. They seemed to be still undecided about going into the bog. Then suddenly they moved slowly down the little slope. Apparently they were finally satisfied that the coast was clear. The doe disappeared and the buck hesitated at the edge of the bog and looked back. That was my chance—the only chance, for once in the tall hay and bushes they would be out of sight most of the time. The little rifle came slowly to my shoulder. I took careful aim on the buck's right fore shoulder, held my breath, and squeezed the trigger. The roar of the gun smashed the ringing silence and rolled like thunder on and on over the bog and into the woods.

A deafening silence followed and the buck was gone. I waited about fifteen minutes to give him a chance to lie down, bleed, and stiffen up in case I had hit him. It wasn't easy and the minutes seemed like hours. But that's the usual procedure and I wasn't taking any chances. Finally I moved slowly toward the spot where the buck had stood when I fired. There was blood and hair on the wet ferns and grass. Quite a lot of it in fact. The blood trail continued through the bog but became lighter and harder to follow as I moved slowly forward. I had just begun to feel the crushing pressure of failure, the same pressure I had known so long, when the badly wounded deer staggered to his feet in a little stand of alders about twenty yards away. A slug in the butt of the neck piled him up for good and the quest for meat in my quest to live was over. He was an eight pointer and weighed about one hundred sixty-five pounds. I slumped down on the huge, warm carcass and watched the stars come out.

# 15

I HAVE ALWAYS regarded sleep as a sample of death. And because of the complete escape from pain, problems, and toil it provides I never have dreaded, even for a moment, that day when I will have reached the end of this earthly journey.

This thought along with simple but true old sayings such as "We only live once," "We are all traveling on a one way ticket," "All a horse can do is his best," and the like have always brought encouragement and peace of mind.

I used to sit at night by the blazing fire and on the loom of deep thought produce bits of such homespun philosophy when the awful ache of frustration had me down. The thought that provided the most soothing balm was: Security beyond prison or the grave breeds contentment and, knowing what contentment had done to the cow, I was sure I wanted no part of its cushions and warmth.

Memories are strange little things. Some are like fine, hot wires bound tightly about the heart while others are like cool dew on hot and tired feet, or like a refreshing shower on a dusty lane. One that has remained bright these many years is of that desperate struggle against time, the weather, and scarcity to hunt down and kill a deer.

It was nearly midnight when dead tired, torn and wet, I finally reached camp with the fine buck. I had dressed it in the dark, dragged it what seemed like miles through the hateful, brush-choked bog to the waiting canoe, and fought my way with the paddle and the weight of my cargo through stubborn ice fields, up the stream, across the head of Hammond Pond, into the other section of the stream, and on up the lower lake to the cabin.

I didn't have strength enough left to hang the carcass on one of the big limbs of the huge old pine that towered brooding over my squatty little log home. I dragged it onto the veranda and actually staggered into the cabin and devoured wolflike a hasty supper that featured deer liver and onions. I kept the large heart also, to be boiled, chopped, and mixed into the dogs' food. The dogs and the hens, too, got a hasty meal that night and the dishes and pans were left heaped in the sink. My ripped and soggy clothes lay in a heap on the floor where they fell. Sleep came instantly, and completely exhausted I snored it out until nearly noon the next day. For nearly an hour I lay there in the blankets reliving again and again the hunt, the shooting of the deer, and the hard and hideous journey back to camp.

My clothes would need drying and mending, and I would need a bath. The deer would have to be hung up, and there were many other things to be done to put the cabin in shape for the winter. Those thoughts snapped me from toying with that fresh and pleasant memory, and sore muscles lifted me slowly from my bed.

The sewing and the bath were postponed until night for there were more important chores to be done and the afternoons were short. By using a couple of four-inch trees as rollers and a smaller one as a lever or pry, I managed to get the long and heavy boat slip out of the water and well up on the shore where it was fastened securely with rope and wire.

Hanging the deer was much more difficult and called for greater effort—tremendous effort. It had to be done. If it were left on the ground it would soon be chewed up by the dogs, Waldo the skunk, and those flesh eaters that would smell it and come out of the woods at night.

It was a big job. I simply had to have help and I called on a couple of tall slim white birches. By shinning to the top and using my weight I was able to bring them one at a time to the ground where I attached the deer to the tops with stout ropes. One tree when released lifted all but the head off the ground, and the two of them hoisted the carcass high enough to enable me to attach the hind legs to the limb on the big pine. It required a lot of figuring and pull hauling before the heavy carcass, which then weighed about one hundred fifty pounds but which seemed to weigh a ton, was finally suspended with head well above the ground, hindquarters spread with a length of maple sapling, and the belly cut held open with sticks that the air might circulate through the cavity. The birches, released from their toil, snapped back with a mighty rush to their full proud height as though enraged for having been put to work.

After a week or so of aging I would skin the carcass, split it in halves, and cut it up to be hung in chunks for the winter. I planned to use the feet for gun hooks on the wall and the antlers for decoration over the door.

During the next few days the weather turned bitterly cold and the lake and all of the other waters, save those parts of the stream that moved, were sealed solidly by winter. Now and then small, hard snow flakes slanted down to bring further warning of what was coming. As I worked furiously banking the cabin with spruce boughs, and tightening the calking between the logs, I thought of winter as a great white monster that would soon attack me and against which I would have to fight continuously day after day, week after week, month after month, until the arrival of a merciful spring.

As I rushed squirrel-like about the place, I could see during the days the smoke rising from the chimney of old Pop's cabin far across the closed and freezing lake. At night I watched the light that blinked like sparks from his two front windows. I wondered if he had bagged a deer before the season closed, and doubted it knowing how scarce they were and of Pop's rheumatism, which made it difficult for him to travel far in rough country.

There were a few new splits in the old roofing that needed patching lest I be pestered and probably soaked by the rains and melting snows, and with what odd pieces of the same material and tar I could find around the place they were finally sealed.

It seemed that I was pretty well fortified against the great white enemy except for the big wood for the fireplace that my farmer friend would bring with the coming of stout ice, and some kind of a good heating stove. The three feet of boughs banked around the base of the cabin made it much warmer but as the cold became more severe I realized more and more that the little cookstove in the kitchen and the old fireplace couldn't possibly pump out enough heat to keep me warm when winter cut loose with both barrels.

I was worried sick. I knew if I didn't get a two-fisted heater of some kind and very soon that I would either have to call it off and go home to admit defeat and probably be miserable in some store or factory job, or be equally miserable living in a cold cabin. I could have moved in with old Pop if it became too bad, but I didn't relish the idea, and probably Pop wouldn't either. I was again up against it and my new problem became greater as the days rolled on and winter tightened its grip.

I shot a handsome male fox ahead of the hounds early in December and the following day caught a smaller but equally handsome fellow in a blind set (using no bait), at a little spring not far from camp. It was the first of the red rascals I was able to outwit. Those pelts with others I hoped to get with the dogs and traps would add more dollars to my little nest egg.

I had a few sections of old stovepipe, which were in the cabin when I moved in, and I had picked up several more at abandoned shacks back in the woods. Brisk massaging with kerosene and sand removed the rust, and a couple of coats of stove blacking put them in almost first-class shape. I had that much of my final weapon to be used against the winter, but the stove was the principal thing, and finally in desperation I decided to hike around the freezing lake and see if my good friend the station agent could help me.

He said he was pretty sure a friend of his who lived on a small farm farther up the stream had an old ram-down he didn't need. If I would come back in a few days he would have it for me, he said.

"There ought to be enough ice close to shore to walk on by that time, and if you've got some kind of a sled you can haul the stove down to your place slick as a whistle," he said with that same warm and friendly smile.

I waited four days during which I built with cedar saplings, nails, and haywire, a crude but surprisingly stout sled on which to haul the stove. I would have waited longer before going after it but fine flakes that came tumbling down at noon of the fifth day looked very much like forerunners of a two-fisted storm, and I struck out with my funny looking sled, a kerosene can, and the two hounds.

I traveled slowly and very close to shore. There seemed to be plenty of ice even well out on the lake, but I wasn't taking any chances. The dogs, however, ran all over it sniffing furiously at trails of scent probably left by foxes that had crossed the lake in the night or early morning.

The ice cracked and buckled a bit as I circled close to the open water at the mouth of the brook that curled in from Ben Annis Pond. The head of the lake was wide open for a long distance down the middle where the stream came in, and I steered clear of both danger spots.

The stove was waiting for me at the station. It was an old ram-down built to take two-foot wood. It was red with rust and had only two legs and no pipe. Otherwise it was in good shape and I gave the station agent the three dollars the farmer asked for it. Kerosene, groceries, pipe tobacco, a bottle of stove paint, and matches bought at the store were shoved inside and piled on top of the rusty relic, and I hustled back through a snowstorm to camp.

It took a lot of kerosene, sand, and elbow action to change the complexion of the old stove. The paint and a good polishing finally made it look almost new. For safety I built a frame with old two-by-four joists the size of the stove bottom, nailed it to the floor, removed the two legs from the stove and substituted old red bricks, two under each corner and resting on the frame, which was then filled with sand from the shore.

It was quite a job hacking a hole through the old fireplace chimney, but I finally found a rock of about the right size that came out easily, and after a long and tiring struggle the pipe was finally fitted and strongly wired to the roof rafters.

The test fire was a very small one of birch bark and a few pieces of cedar kindling. I opened the dampers and stood back to watch. It drew well and sent off waves of heat along with a cloud of smoke from the kerosene and stove paint. It was burned off and blazing full blast that night and pumping sweet smelling heat all over the place. And at the left of the fireplace, in the middle of the living room, it didn't look bad at all nor was it in the way. It wouldn't have made any difference if it did look bad or if it was in the way; it would have stayed where it was for without it I wouldn't have lasted long there.

You couldn't do much cooking on it because most of the heat came out of the sides, front, and back. It wasn't made for cooking. It was a heater, and a good one. And it would take large wood including old stumps, knotted chunks too tough to split, and other such fuel almost as well as the yawning fireplace. If I didn't go to bed until late and got up early it would hold a carefully banked fire all night and keep the place fairly comfortable.

But whether it would do it when the mercury plunged far below zero and blizzards howled was doubtful.

But during the last of December when it never got colder than fifteen above there were many nights when cooking supper on the kitchen stove and when the heater and the fireplace also were blazing, that I had to open the front door to cool the place a bit.

The dogs liked the old heater. I let them sleep in the cabin on very cold nights and they sprawled on the floor close to it and snoozed. They liked it better than the fireplace because it never spit hot sparks on their pelts.

I again hiked through the woods and up the little road to see my farmer friend to inquire when he was going to deliver the big wood for the fireplace. He told me not to worry, that he had plenty of it and that he would haul it down just as soon as the shore ice was stout enough to hold his horses and the loaded sled.

I was surprised when three days later I heard the clanking of the bells on his horses coming down the shore of the lake. Three very generous cords of the three-foot stuff were dumped onto the ice in front of the camp. He charged me less than five dollars a cord and said that if I didn't have the money it would be all right. He was a wonderful person.

In a few days I had the large, sweet-smelling dry sticks of beech, rock maple, and birch piled neatly behind the cabin and covered with a thick layer of boughs. That wood had beauty all of its own. I was rather proud of it for it was all mine and was bought and paid for with money I had earned with my hands out there in the woods.

The old canoe was turned upside down on log rests in a nearby fir thicket and it, too, was covered with protective boughs. By the time this work was done the ice on the lake was four inches thick and the same amount of snow blanketed the woods. It seemed that finally I was ready to meet the winter—the winter my father said would murder me.

# 16

THERE'S SOMETHING strangely fascinating about the beginning of a snowstorm in the woods. I was standing at the edge of a frozen spruce swamp listening to the yodeling of Jack the hound as he trailed a big and very crafty buck rabbit, when in the dim light of the December afternoon I saw the first flake of what was to be a stout northeaster.

That little flake falling in bold contrast against the dark green of the forest giants was followed by others. They were small and innocent looking, like bits of white ash from a campfire. On and on they came, drifting down aimlessly to settle quietly and become lost in the white blanket already on the ground. Then suddenly, as though they were scouts and had found things suitable for an attack, they signaled others that came by the millions in a great white smother. I could hear them whispering as they sifted through the crisp dead leaves that still clung trembling to nearby beeches.

All wildlife, save that rabbit who was bounding ahead of the baying hound, was in hiding. The bell-tone baying of old Jack sounded deeper, softer, and farther away as the fall of the flakes increased and finally formed a slanting white wall obliterating all but nearby objects.

I pushed quietly into the swamp, missed a shot at the speeding bunny, grabbed the dog when he came up, snapped on the leash, and headed back to the cabin. Jack seemed peeved at me for having missed, and was reluctant to leave the trail. Good hounds are like that—they love their work and put all they have into it. Man would do well to follow the example. I would have followed it gladly had I known the kind of work I wanted to do.

It was the first big storm of the winter and when the last few flakes floated down the next afternoon more than a foot had been added to the old four-inch blanket. That was quite a bit of snow to wade through. My little world wore a gorgeous ermine robe, and even the poorest twig on the scrawniest tree in the woods was beautified. The frozen lake stretched away like a great basin of heavy cream and the firs, spruces, and pines stood ghostly and slope-shouldered.

The roof of the cabin wore a creamy crown and every tree stump sported a fluffy beret. It was weirdly beautiful yet it was a grim reminder that the siege was underway— that I was about to face the test, the test my father said I couldn't take. It also reminded me that my snowshoes and parka were at home in Bangor, and, too, that Christmas was but a few days away.

There would be other storms, many of them and much more severe, and the snow would become steadily deeper, making it impossible to move about without snowshoes. I would have to have them. The parka, too, with its hood for covering my head and neck would be needed during blizzards and when the air was fiercely cold. They were equally as important as my ax and guns.

The problem of how to get them and what to do about Christmas gifts for my parents and young sister haunted me as I shoveled away, making paths to the back and front doors of the cabin, out to the headquarters of the hounds and hens, and to the little relief station where the winds rushed up through the holes.

I had received no word from home for a long time. I was sure that my father and my mother, too, had washed their hands of me. And it was Christmastime when everybody who could went home to share with their loved ones that joyous season and holiest of days. The peace of mind I had known only a few hours before was destroyed by two little reminders produced by a snowstorm. That night was one of the worst I had ever experienced. It was filled with little mental pictures, some pleasant, others horrifying, and with thoughts that gnawed at my poor head like the deer mice that gnawed at my food chest.

I thought of my mother, father, and sister shopping with hundreds of others in downtown Bangor, and of the lights and laughter and the shouts of "Merry Christmas." I thought, too, of the excuses my mother, father, and sister must have been making for me, and finally of the gaily decorated balsam in the living room, on and under whose boughs there would be gifts for them from everybody but me. I saw in my troubled mind little candles burning brightly—millions of them, then suddenly their tiny flames were one great flame that came straight at me while a chorus of voices rose steadily to tremendous volume. I tried to run. Then darkness settled. A heavy thud ended the wild singing and I was suddenly free from a nightmarish nap, sweating and frightened on the floor in front of my chair.

The winter wind that was bringing colder weather whined like witches at the windows, as I sipped hot tea and miserlike counted my money. I had decided to make a Christmas package of pretty white birch bark which would include fifty dollars for each of my parents and my sister, and a large fancy greeting card also of bark, with verse and illustration of my own creation.

I could afford the gift of one hundred fifty dollars. I would have enough left for my small needs out there in the woods and there would be a little more coming from the sale of the two fox pelts I had and others I hoped to shoot ahead of the dogs during the winter.

The package was ready by noon the next day. I selected the largest and freshest bills, attached them to slits in the corners of three birch bark cards marked "Pa," "Ma," and "Sis." The tiny tip of a fir bough in the shape of a cross was also attached to each card. The large greeting card was made and addressed to all three and everything was placed in a large envelope fashioned from the white bark with its ends sewed up with red yarn pulled from an old sweater. I did some sketching on it, addressed it, wrapped it in heavy paper and wallowed through the snow up the lake to the station where I gave it to the conductor of the evening train to deliver to my father. He was an old friend of the family and was glad to do it.

I thanked him, and as though it were an afterthought I said, as the train started to pull out, "Oh, Dave, if you happen to think of it would you ask my father to ship out my snowshoes and parka?"

He nodded, smiled, and waved. I watched the train curl around the bend, snow and steam swirling behind it, and wondered if perhaps I should be on it and going home, at least for Christmas. The snow was not nearly as deep on the lake as it was in the woods because of the sweeping winds. But it was deep enough and would soon be a lot deeper—too deep if the snowshoes didn't come.

The winter sun went down in the west with a grand show of color and the purpling white hills stood out sharp and silent against the brass and apple green of the afterglow. Cold shadows crept like purple ink out of the woods and across the snow, and the lake grunted and burped like a gluttonous monster. The evening star, like a bit of hot steel, burned a little hole in the cold blue sky. A wisp of moon floated high over the woods and somewhere back in the sleeping hills a fox barked.

The fragrance of neither blossom nor bottle was ever so sweet to my nostrils as that of wood smoke. It has a certain something that entrances all who love the woods. The sweetness of that smoke from my cabin fires crept through the trees to meet me as I trudged around the point and into the cove. It seemed suddenly like an old friend welcoming me home.

The temperature dropped rapidly during the next two days then climbed suddenly back to create a drooling thaw that decorated the eves of the cabin with long, pointed ice daggers. And it was snowing again Christmas Eve. Big soft flakes tumbled down to patch the wind-torn ermine robes on the evergreens and deepen the blanket that covered forest and lake.

I watched the flakes from the window and saw in the flames of the fireplace little pictures of what was going on at home in the city. I made no effort to celebrate the sacred night—to have a tinseled tree, or a feast with Pop as I had on Thanksgiving.

My thoughts and those flame pictures scratched my heart like the old needle was scratching the record on the phonograph. I shut it off, banked the fire in the ram-down, and escaped from the torture in the velvet folds of merciful sleep.

That Christmas storm brought nearly a foot of fresh snow. As I again shoveled out the paths and piled the snow high over the bough-banking against the cabin, I thought of home and wondered if and when my father would ship my parka and snowshoes. I could, if I had to, get along without the parka, but I would be licked without the snow-shoes. As a matter of fact I would have about all I could do to wallow up the lake to the station to get them. I felt pretty sure though that he would send them the more I thought about it, because my kind and understanding mother would insist on it. But I didn't know when and I didn't want to make more than one trip up the lake.

It would make good reading and add a lot to my prestige as a resourceful and capable woodsman if I could truthfully say that I ploughed into the woods, whacked down a couple of ash poles, shaved them, bent them into snowshoe frames, and filled them tight with narrow strips cut from the hide of the deer. An Indian could have done it. But I wasn't an Indian. As a matter of fact I never could do much of anything with tools.

With the snow heaped deep on the roof and shoveled high against the low sides, the little log cabin appeared squattier than ever. It made it a lot warmer, too. I liked the looks of the deep paths shoveled out around the place.

They showed that somebody lived there—that it was a real home, and that the somebody wasn't a lazy person. In fact I kept the place, inside and out, as neat as possible. Not only because I like neatness but because I had a strange feeling that my father might at any time step into the little clearing.

The big spring in the woods behind the cabin never froze completely, even during the coldest days. Shell ice would form around the sides but the middle was always open. It was wonderful water. I gulped down several quarts of it every day in summer and winter. Besides keeping the contents of my food box cool and fresh in summer it was an ideal place in winter to keep a supply of live bait for pickerel. The live bait were small silvery fish that are called "shiners." Those from two and a half to three and a half inches long are the best for pickerel fishing through the ice. They were quite numerous in a deep spring hole that didn't freeze over down on the stream between the lake and Hammond Pond.

Pop and I caught all we needed there with a net made of cloth screening attached to a four-foot-wide hoop made with several lengths of heavy and very stiff steel wire braided together. Four pieces of rope, each about four feet long were tied to the hoop, brought up to a peak, and attached to a stout iron ring. Another piece of rope, this one about ten feet long was tied to the ring for lowering the net down into the water and hauling it up again.

The spring hole was about six or seven feet deep and the net was lowered down near the sandy and weedy bottom. Bits of boiled potato were then thrown into the water to sink slowly down and attract the shiners. After waiting a few minutes for the little fish to get over the net we would haul it up, hand over hand as fast as we could. Shiners are as quick as a flash and of course many of them escaped each time, but we always managed to get all we wanted on every trip. We each carried two ten-quart pails in which we transported the swimming shiners back to our respective camps and dumped them into our springs.

We had all we needed for our own fishing and sold quite a few to fishermen who came out from the cities and towns. The bait dealers were getting three cents apiece for them in Bangor, but Pop and I offered a two-cent bargain with a few extras thrown in for good measure. Most of the bait was sold on Sundays and holidays.

It would have been impossible to get bait if I didn't have snowshoes. As a matter of fact it would have been impossible to get out of the camp yard. I would have been snowbound. Pop had an old pair of those tailless rigs called bearpaws. Mine were tail-shoes with the pointed snout turned up slightly to prevent tripping.

I was glad and greatly relieved when after trudging through nearly two feet of snow up the lake to the station I found the shoes and the parka waiting for me. The train conductor had delivered my message and my father had shipped them out to me. There was a letter there, too, and a big Christmas card signed by my mother, father, and sister. A wave of happiness swept over me as I finished reading them there in the warm little railroad station.

The letter was from my father. He said that my Christmas package came as a pleasant and rather startling surprise. I had made them all very happy, he continued. He went on to say that they were all very much surprised that I did so well trapping and were wondering if I had any money left for myself.

Both my mother and father were still strongly opposed to my living in the woods all alone, and he again begged me to give it up and come home. He warned that the winter was just getting underway and that when the real cold and blizzards came I would have a bad time of it. He suggested that I put in one more week fishing, and hunting with the dogs, and then "get out while the getting is good!"

I scribbled a reply there in the station, thanking him for sending the snowshoes and parka, and for the card and kind letter. I told him I was getting along fine and not to worry about me. I sent love to all, and closed with a sort of comforting line telling him that if the winter did get too rough on me I would hit the trail for home.

It did get rough on me, and on everybody else in the region I guess, for it was one of the worst in years. But the only trails I hit were those to the bait hole, the fishing grounds on the lake, and back into the rabbit swamps.

Despite what I had told my parents to soothe them, I was determined that the last trail I would hit, come hell or high water, was that wide and unobstructed one that would lead me home. And I was equally determined that I never would hit it until I had first found one, or blazed one, that would lead me to my goal—whatever and wherever it was. I still didn't know.

# 17

JANUARY LET GO with both barrels and by the time it had crawled over the halfway hump the snow was over three feet deep on the level in the woods, almost twice as deep where it had drifted, and nearly two feet deep on the lake where the broom of the winds swept hard.

Unlike people living in the city I didn't try to fight winter, but lived with it, by wearing the proper clothing, eating the proper foods, and getting plenty of fresh air and exercise. The proper clothing makes a great deal of difference if one is to meet winter face to face, in all of its moods as I had to.

Discarded business suits, sweaters, street shoes with rubbers, and other such combinations are worthless. Such garb may be good enough while shoveling a path at a city home, but it's as worthless in the Maine woods as an air rifle on a bear hunt. I've seen many a tenderfoot dressed in such rigs who was absolutely miserable on late fall hunting trips and while fishing through the ice.

The winter rig that I swear by after trying them all down through the years, and the rig that I wore during those two winters alone in the woods, includes a snug fitting silk and wool union suit with long legs and sleeves; a wool sweat shirt, and a heavy plaid or checked all-wool lumberman's shirt. Over these I haul a heavy wool parka with a roomy hood for protecting the head and neck, and with a skirt that reaches nearly to the knees. Large slash pockets on the breast are handy for warming chilled hands and for carrying small articles. On my head, whether the hood is up or down, I like a snug-fitting knitted cap like those worn by sailors in winter. I decorated mine a bit by sewing the fluffy, boned tail of a red squirrel to the top.

My mittens were of heavy wool yarn and carefully knitted by hand. They were worn inside unlined leather mittens called choppers. The choppers kept the wool mittens dry and protected them against wear and tear. South of the breastbone my garb consisted of a pair of red and black plaid breeches cut army style with snug fitting lower leg and slightly flared hips; a pair of cotton socks over the ends of the union suit legs; then two pairs of thick but short, all-wool socks hauled over the snug fitting leg of the breeches; and finally a pair of red rubbers with crepe soles and very soft elk hide tops about ten inches high. For additional warmth I wore thin felt innersoles in the rubbers. This type of rubber is not to be confused with the heavy and clumsy things worn by farmers and called "gum rubbers." They're a light, well-made sporting rubber and are sold under the trade name of "Hunting Shoes."

The elk-hide tops were kept soft and waterproof with frequent massages of skunk oil I bought from Pop. I hasten to add here that by skunk oil I do not mean the foul smelling musk that the skunk uses for protection. The oil that I used on my boots and that Pop rubbed on his old joints to ease the agony of rheumatism is obtained by heating in a pan the thick white fat cut and scraped from the skunk's carcass. It is a golden liquid when warm but hardens quickly to a white grease when cool. It has an odor not of powerful skunk musk but of just plain grease. When my supply of the oil ran low I melted deer fat with it. Deer fat isn't a very good lubricant for leather, but mixed with the skunk fat it worked out all right.

When the snow was deep and very dry and I was traveling on snowshoes I wore ten inch moccasins with a very light and pliable sole. High shoes and boots are okay on the magazine-cover sportsman and woodsman but they're a joke in the winter woods. They are stiff, tight, and cold, and hard leather heels will soon chew snowshoe filling to shreds.

Another thing that is very important in footgear is the height. Those long-legged things whether rubbers, boots, or moccasins that come all the way to the knee look good but that's all. Years of traveling about in the outdoors in all seasons has convinced me that the top that comes to a halt under the calf of the leg is the proper one. That big leg muscle expands at every step, and if it has to shove out a wall of tight-fitting leather every time it soon becomes tired and the traveler suffers.

I have used parkas made of several different kinds of material but the one I like best and wore during those two winters was made from a heavy all-wool Hudson Bay blanket. It was bright red with a wide black band around the bottom. It was soft and very warm even on the coldest days. I always thought it was rather pretty. Anything red—whether parka, shirt, blanket, or bandanna—is pretty in the woods. I have always admired beauty whether it was in a winter sunset, a fox pelt, or the face of a girl. I could always find beauty wherever I turned in the outdoors. And I have always been a stickler for neatness in clothes—even those worn in the woods. I never was, nor do I ever want to be, in the dude class, but neither do I want to look and feel like a slob.

The proper outdoor clothing and footgear according to season that fits neatly not only makes the wearer more comfortable but seems to give him self-confidence and a feeling of well-being. At least that's the way they affect me.

Although ice freezes very slowly when blanketed with deep snow, it did a pretty good job that first winter when the temperature hovered close to the zero mark much of the time and frequently plunged from five to twenty below. On several occasions it went down to thirty and a bit more and remained there for days at a time.

I chiseled through twenty-four inches of hard blue ice when I took my first fling at the pickerel off what is known as Green Point, about halfway up the east shore of the lake. Gnawing out five clean funnels each about ten inches in diameter was tough on the arms, back, and wind. But that was the last hard cutting I had to do at that spot for on the following visits the newly formed ice was only a few inches thick.

Old Pop preferred to do his fishing off Birch Point, another tongue of land and ledge but studded with gorgeous white birches instead of the oaks and pines, which towered on Green Point. It was only about quarter way up the lake on the same side and much nearer to his cabin. In summer both places were hot spots for large white perch, bass, and pickerel, and in winter they were equally good pay-off spots for the latter. Pop loved Birch Point as though it were something warm and alive and friendly. He once told me that when his earthly journey was over he hoped to be buried there.

For the sake of company I fished there with him occasionally. But like most old hermits Pop was a bit queer and there were times when he wanted to be alone. He didn't try to hide the fact either, and on such occasions I would find some excuse for leaving, slip quietly away, and remain away for several days and sometimes weeks. The next time our trails crossed in the woods or on the lake he would be sickeningly friendly.

I cut up my deer before the coming of real cold weather but the carcass was frozen plenty stiff and I had my hands full taking it apart. I had cut up deer before so knew how to go about it, but I had never worked on one that so closely resembled a rock.

After a long session of cutting, clawing, and yanking out there under the big pine, the skin was finally peeled off. I split the backbone all the way down with a hand saw, and with the help of an ax, belt knife, and the saw I managed to hack off the hindquarters, forequarters, tenderloins, rib roasts, chops, and the thin bony flanks. The pieces were hung from the veranda rafters away from the hounds and the forest prowlers.

The neck of a deer, particularly a buck that is killed late in the mating season, is rather tough and stringy and if used at all is ground up and put into mincemeat. But I had neither the knowledge nor the desire to make mincemeat. It was set aside with all the scraps to be boiled and mixed with the dogs' food. The feet and ankles were crudely cured, bent, dried in the hide, and shoved into holes bored in the living-room logs where they served as hooks and hangers and added a certain something to the old place.

The top of the skull with antlers attached was sawed off, cleaned, and spiked to a fat log over the living-room door. Like the feet, they too added what I thought was a bit of rustic beauty, and served as a hanging place for everything from old hats to abandoned bird and hornet nests.

Pop was having one of his friendly spells the day I crossed the lake with a bundle of meat for him. He was shoveling a fresh path to the woodshed. Only the shoulders of his old red Mackinaw and moth-gnawed muskrat cap showed above the heaped-up snow. He was talking to himself and didn't hear me coming on the snowshoes.

"I brought you some deer meat, Pop," I shouted as I eased up behind him. He leaped almost two feet in the air, turned like a flash, and stood glaring at me with his red and watery eyes.

"Wal, wal, son, it's you is it!" he gasped, and let a slither of tobacco juice fly from his toothless mouth. It formed a little bushlike design on the smooth white snow.

"Yer almost sceered me outa my drawers," he squeaked. "I ain't laid eye on yer fer quite a spell. But I allus knows yer alive and kickin' when I kin see the smoke risin' outa yer chimney, and the lights at night. Alls I been doin' is fishin' and shovelin' snow. I'm sick of the damn stuff—wish it would rain hot water ter beat hell fer about a week and take it ter hell away!" he squawked as he took a vicious kick at the snow. We went inside and I pulled the meat from my pack and placed it on the table. Pop was glad to get it. He told me he had been living on beans, potatoes, and pickerel. He said he had sold five dollars worth of pickerel to a man from Bangor a few days before and had a standing order for all he could catch.

He had quite a few, some very large ones, outside stuck in the snow. Frozen white they looked like a little picket fence. He explained that the man who was buying the pickerel was selling them in Bangor. He came as far as Hermon Center on the train, picked up a big frame sled he kept at the station and hiked in four miles to the camp. Sometimes the fish buyer stayed overnight, and sometimes he went right back with his load of pickerel to catch the night train, Pop said.

I had tried many times to convince the old fellow that it was wrong to slaughter the pickerel and sell them, and that if he and others who were taking too many continued, the lake would soon be cleaned out. But it did no good. He insisted that there were millions of them in the lake and more coming in all the time from the outlying ponds, and that they never could be cleaned out. I often wondered why the state didn't protect the pickerel with a law calling for a certain bag limit and prohibiting their sale. I swore that someday, somehow, I would fight for and get such protection for a truly great game fish that was sadly underrated.

Snow fell often that winter and it became much too deep to run the dogs on foxes. I did, however, enjoy plenty of sport and kept the larder well stocked with the big snowshoe rabbits down in the frozen swamps. The rabbits tramped down deep runways in which they traveled back and forth at night. They looked like little streets. It was in those runways that the galloping rabbits and the hounds traveled most of the time in the long and merry chases during the day.

The study of wildlife continued and I learned many interesting and sometimes amazing things about the wild things, also the trees, storms, clouds and other things that made up the strange and silent world in which I lived. I made more and more notes and sketches in the rough. They were heaped high in the cabin. One of the most interesting of all was how the native ruffed grouse, that grand king of all game birds, keeps himself warm and comfortable when the night is bitterly cold and the snow lies deep over forest and clearing.

Day after day when the sun was floating low in the west I watched them, the ruffed grouse, with feathers fluffed for insulation, enjoying the evening meal of buds high in the poplars and yellow birches. And when their crops were filled and they had gone to an open spring or naked brook shore to gather grit, they would again go into the trees where the snow was deep and untrampled and dive at terrific speed straight down into it and disappear. There, under the deep snow they would sleep until morning when out they would come in a great white explosion to greet the warm sun and seek their breakfast.

The always hungry red fox, who hunts by night as well as by day, knows of this trick of the grouse and I have seen them hunting in such places. But the grouse is an amazingly smart bird. He knows that the fox and the horned and snowy owl will be hunting him as he snoozes under the snow. And pouncing on the scar where the grouse entered the snow blanket seldom pays off, for the wise old bird usually ploughs a few feet away from the entrance before settling down for the night.

## Nature I Loved

I traveled on the snowshoes far and wide in storm and sunshine, and many times at night, hunting, exploring and prying into the affairs of the wild things. My snowshoe floats curled away from the camp in all directions.

The trips to the head of the lake were made only when I needed supplies and that was very seldom. On a few of those jaunts I found letters or cards from home along with copies of the Bangor newspapers. My good friend the station agent saved his copies of a Boston newspaper for me, too. I read every inch of them, advertisements and all, then stacked them up to be used for starting fires and to catch the drippings of my washing, which had to be hung inside.

When I wasn't reading during those long, cold winter nights I was listening to those raspy old records and tying flies. And when I tired of that I would often strap on my snowshoes and hike over my old trails on the lake and through the woods. I enjoyed those nocturnal jaunts especially when a full moon flooded the outdoors with its pale and ghostly light.

I enjoyed listening to the many strange night sounds and trying to find out what was making them and why. They included the roaring and cracking of the great ice field in the lake, the frost and cold splitting the trees, the crashing of a dead tree stub in the wind, and numerous calls and yelps from the throats of those wild things that prowl when it is dark. There was only one night sound I didn't like. As a matter of fact I hated it. It chilled my heart and seemed to rip straight through my very soul, as a motor-driven saw would rip through a knotted beech. It was the awful, high, piercing scream of a snowshoe rabbit suddenly seized by a great horned owl or a fox. I heard it quite often not only on my nocturnal jaunts but while sitting before the blazing logs in the cabin and while lying in bed. It's an ungodly sound, like something that might be uttered by a maniac at the height of a tantrum, an infant in great pain, or what one might expect to come from the caverns of hell.

Every time I heard it I experienced a strange mixed feeling of fear, hatred, and fierce anger. I wanted to run at full speed to the spot where it came from, breaking down all barriers as I went, and beat to a pulp with my fists the owl or the fox, and the damned cowardly rabbit that was making it. I did once, but used my revolver instead of my fists and killed only the owl. It was a white cold night lighted brightly by a bloated, full-faced moon. Traveling swiftly on the snowshoes through a spruce swamp with that hellish screaming in my ears I came suddenly upon the huge owl and his struggling and yelping victim. The scene was a rabbit runway in a small moonlit opening in the heart of the snow-choked swamp. The screaming was deafening at close range. The big bird's sharp talons were embedded in the back of the rabbit and it was trying to kill the squirming thing before taking off, by raining hard blows on its head with a powerful beak.

The gun roared three times in rapid succession, smashing to bits the silence of the great swamp and drowning out the screaming and wing beating at that particular spot in its heart. The third slug nailed the huge bird through the back and a deathly silence settled over that lonely yet lovely place of ghostly moonlight, weird shapes and shadows, and sparkling snow. The only sounds were my breathing and the rabbit kicking his last on the blood-drenched snow. The big wings of the owl were spread and spiked on the wall of my cabin and the rabbit went into a stew for the dogs.

I learned a lot about Nature and the wild things on those day and night jaunts. The book was wide open for me to read and I made the most of it, loving it more and more as time rolled on.

Most of the nights, however, were spent close to the fireside with my good friends the hounds. Streamer flies weren't very popular at that time. As a matter of fact they had been on the market but a short time. It was my father, a skilled and ardent angler, who introduced me to the huge feather and hair lure that is supposed to resemble a minnow or other small forage fish. With the white hair from the tail of the deer, also squirrel hair, feathers from the hens, and what materials I had in my kit, I was able to turn out a large number of streamers, also wet flies and tiny dry flies. My flies were far from first class. They would never have sold in the stores. But they weren't tied for fishermen, they were tied for fish and they caught them and stood up well under the punishment. Most flies I have seen in the shops were tied to attract the fishermen. And they buy them at prices I have always thought were much too high. The flies are gaudy and usually too heavily dressed to fool fish, particularly those wise old guys on waters that are fished hard.

The old fireplace in the cabin, although pretty and cheerful with its huge throat full of blazing logs, was a flop as a heater. It threw out about as much heat as an elephant's breath. Most of it went up the fat chimney with the smoke. But it threw out plenty of sparks and burning embers that after a time created a pattern of little brown and black burnt spots on the big braided rag rug that sprawled in front of it. I had to keep an eye on it at all times and never dared leave the camp long or go to bed while a fire blazed in it. A screen would have been the answer but you can't get fireplace screens in the woods.

I couldn't have stayed there without the old ram-down stove. It poured out sweet-smelling heat in great quantities, and when going full blast along with the little kitchen stove and the fireplace the cabin was very comfortable. But it was far from comfortable on those sub-zero mornings when the fires had burned out in the night. And they usually did unless I banked them carefully, went to bed late, and got up early. But it seems that all people who live close to the land, as the man in the woods and the farmer, retire early. It was like getting up in a huge icebox on those very cold mornings. I could see my breath in clouds over the blankets. The windows that had been warm and wet the night before would be heavily frosted in pretty and fantastic scenes and designs.

The spring water in the pail by the sink would be frozen, the butter would be harder than flint and the floor would be so fiercely cold you couldn't tell, if you were blindfolded, whether you had placed your bare foot on a hot stove or a cake of ice.

Sometimes I would jump out of bed with a blanket wrapped around me, kindle a fire in the heater, and dash back to bed until the place warmed up a bit. But usually I faced it bravely, and shaking like a corn popper, lighted all three fires, washed in cold water, and kidded myself until the place finally was filled with heat.

There were times on such mornings when I wondered if I could hang on—if it were worth it, and if, perhaps, after all, my father and mother were right. I don't know whether it was pride or just plain mulish stubbornness that kept me from packing up, piling onto a train, and going home. But that hollow feeling of defeat and despair always melted a bit before the fresh heat, the warm red flood of the morning sun pouring in the front windows, and hot breakfasts of broiled deer steak, fried potatoes, or pancakes with honey and bacon, and of course big cups of powerful coffee. So I managed to hang on. When a man is warm and his belly is full it takes a lot to crush him.

Cutting that deermeat, which was frozen as hard as iron, was quite a chore whether I wanted chops, a roast, tenderloin, or steak off the rump. It required the services of the belt knife, ax, handsaw, and plenty of elbow action, and then of course a session of thawing. The steaks came off looking and feeling exactly like slabs sawed from a tree. Sometimes I thawed them a bit by soaking in a frying pan full of water on the stove. On those occasions when I was in no hurry to eat I would let them soak in a pan of cold water. They never were thawed completely for fear of draining them of the blood and ruining them. Most of the time, however, they were just slapped into the broiler just as they came off the leg and held over the fireplace coals. They did a lot of dripping and sputtering as the frost ran out, but were always tender, juicy, and delicious.

Many times, especially on those days when blizzards howled, I baked beans in the oven of the kitchen stove. The beans, which were bought at the store, were sometimes the large yellow eyes and sometimes the small California pea beans. I liked them both. Baked with plenty of salt pork, molasses, and a whole onion on the bottom of the kettle, and of course watered and watched, and watered some more, they always came out tender, golden brown, and swimming in juice.

Baked beans is the favorite food of most men who live in the woods, whether baked in the camp stove, in the ground nearby, or forked from a can. Beans are inexpensive and as old Pop used to say, they stick to your ribs.

Many of those stormy days were also devoted to experiments in cooking various dishes described in an old cookbook I found in the cabin. Some of the finished products were pretty bad at first but they really weren't wasted for the dogs and hens, who also had to eat, always gobbled them up. I had to go easy on those recipes that called for eggs, for the hens were then producing only two or three a day. I wanted to kill one of them to stuff and roast to be eaten hot and later sliced cold for sandwiches, but by the time I had finally found and marked the birds that weren't laying at all, it was spring, and all were producing again. I learned many things that winter—all of them the hard way.

# 18

I GUESS just about everybody has at one time or another, in moments of discouragement, expressed a desire to die and have it over with. But very few really mean it any more than I did during the frequent mental depressions into which I slumped in that blind and bewildering search for something I couldn't name. I never lived in fear of death but neither would I seek nor invite it. I hoped, however, that when it came it would be merciful.

That was all I asked. Perhaps all this was just a part of being young and frustrated.

I didn't have the slightest idea how I would react if death were suddenly reaching for me. I guess I never thought much about that. That is, I didn't until that cold February day it stalked me in the icy waters of Hammond Pond. Then I knew. And those awful years that were but minutes, when I fought frantically on the brink of the dark chasm of the great beyond, will blaze always in my memory.

I had become tired of fishing in Hermon Pond. I had all the pickerel I wanted to eat. But I had heard much about the old whoppers in Hammond Pond to the south, and I wanted to try for them. The little basin of weedy water was seldom fished and that of course was the reason for the fast and furious fishing I heard about.

The little thermometer outside the cabin door said it was twelve below zero the morning I struck off on my expedition. It wasn't good fishing weather but I had made up my mind and was ready to go. It's when a thaw is underway, the wind weak, and the snow water running in the holes, that this particular brand of angling is at its best.

But I could try anyhow, and besides, I could do a bit of exploring and check up on the doings of the wild things. The cold weather wouldn't bother me. One gets used to it living in the woods.

The knapsack that rode high and heavy on my shoulders bulged with lunch, cooking tins, three-piece pipe, ice chisel, fishing lines, a blanket, and a small ax. The .38 revolver was strapped to my hip and I carried a small bucket of shiners in one hand and a slush scoop in the other.

The snowshoes were strapped on and I scooted swiftly away through the woods. I enjoy walking on snowshoes. It isn't, as many think, difficult and tiring. I have seen beginners make an awful mess of it. They seem to think that one must walk with legs bent and sprawled like ice tongs to keep the shoes apart, and then just pick them up and lay them down. That clumsy procedure of course is very tiring and causes many a spill. It's easy and good sport when you swing freely from the hips with the inside halves of the shoes passing over each other, and the body slightly forward. One can travel that way all day and not be too weary when night falls.

Flaky frost sparkled on the ermine of the last storm that still cloaked the trees and bushes of the woods. It was beautiful outdoors and I was glad to be alive as I swung quietly along through the fantastic fairyland. Frost stung my cheeks like needle points, and burned my nostrils. Only the whispering of the webs on the snow and the squeaking of the tight and straining leather pack straps broke the ringing silence.

The fiercely cold air warmed by the blood-orange flood of the rising sun was like spice. I never felt better in my life. I traveled swiftly through the swamp, over a poplar ridge, and across a sprawling bog generously spiked with scrawny white maples and alder islands. Then, up, up again over a knoll of proud old oaks that overlooked the foot of the sleeping lake, and down with increased speed to continue the journey through a great stand of towering pines, spruces, firs, and cedars.

Rabbit trails curled away in all directions, and here and there the snow was dotted with the single file tracks of hunting foxes, and the meandering trails of wandering grouse. The climbing sun finally poured crimson banners down through the snow-mantled evergreens. They were pretty and warm, and here and there broke like brittle Christmas candy to scatter ragged pieces along my trail.

It seems the sun's warming flood brought life to the woods. Curious little chickadees, nuthatches, cedar waxwings, noisy blue jays, and other little feathered things were suddenly flitting from tree to tree in search of food for breakfast. Both gray and red squirrels, too, were scampering about, the latter bawling me out as I trudged along.

After a long haul through the dense stretch of woods I emerged flushed and puffing into an old field. It rolled away like a sea of milk, unmarked save for the buttonlike tracks of foxes that had passed in the night.

A small and tired looking old bridge spliced a narrow road across the stream that flowed into Hammond Pond. I walked up to it and rested. The little artery of travel through that sprawling region was marked only by the tracks of a heavy horse and a sled that passed the day before.

I crossed the road into another field—another expanse that looked like a sea of sparkling milk. It rose quickly like a great wave to meet a towering knoll crowned with a dense mixed growth. The stream twisted slowly along at my left. Like everything else it was white and appeared to be frozen tight. At the far end of the knoll I brushed a snow beret off a stump and sat down to puff on my pipe and with a twig, punched out the ice that had formed in the little air holes in the cover of the bait bucket. Shiners, like everything else, must have oxygen to live, and only living shiners darting about on the end of a line will attract pickerel.

Before my squinting eyes stretched a meadow and the pond. The glare of the sun on the snow was fierce. Without the large, dark glasses, which rested on my red and dripping nose, I would have been snow-blind in a short time. I had been before, and fearing it ever since, I always carried a good pair of the eye protectors.

The wind, which gets a free sweep at the pond, had packed the snow quite hard and I was able to travel about without the snowshoes. I decided to set my lines a little to the right and out about thirty yards from the wide mouth of the incoming stream. The gear was piled on the snow, and with the ax in hand I started for the woods to gather poles and spruce boughs for building a lean-to to break the cold wind that was coming out of the northwest with steadily increasing velocity.

The work warmed me and I removed my heavy parka. Firewood would be needed too for a blaze in front of the lean-to, and I headed, ax in hand, toward the meadow on the other side of the stream mouth where a number of old dry maples and cedars bristled. It was the same meadow and almost the exact spot where I had set the canoe in after the carry around the ice on the deer hunting jaunt that fall.

I didn't know that although looking exactly like the rest of the big pond with its snow covering, that that area is where the stream curls slowly along to the east shore where it leaves the pond on its journey to the Penobscot River. It is, I was later informed, the "channel," which never freezes more than an inch. I was pretty well out on the pond and crossing at that point where the current turns toward the outlet. I did notice that the snow was damp and not nearly as deep, but thought it was just a prank of the winds. I heard the ice cracking under my rubbers as I walked along but paid no attention to it. Then suddenly, the thin ice let go with a crash that sounded like a piano being thrown through a plate-glass window. Making the sound even more horrifying was the awful gurgling and sucking of the cold greenish water.

My arms flew upward and the ax went into the air. I was very fortunate that it didn't come down and split my head like a squash. It flew back and landed on the snow beyond the current. I guess it wouldn't have hit me anyway for I plunged quickly out of sight into the twenty feet of water that was so cold it felt like fire. It gave me quite a shock and my mind was almost a complete blank as I sank, half tipped over, deeper and deeper into the gloomy depths.

By instinct I kicked my heavy feet and pushed my mittened hands downward. I bulleted to the surface and my drenched and bewildered head popped out. I looked quickly about me. The hole where I went through was broken twenty times larger by the waves and crashing slabs of ice. I tried to swim but because of my soaked clothing and numbed body it was like crawling through soft tar. I couldn't make it and went down again. I reviewed my entire life in those few minutes. I thought of my parents and my sister, and of Big Jim. I thought, too, of a funeral, of the little cabin, the hounds, and old Pop. There was music, sweet and far away. I saw big greenish bubbles gurgle from my mouth and nostrils and my lungs felt as though they were about to burst. I was looking straight into the awful face of death. I saw it as a great gray thing that smelled faintly of decayed flowers. That was death. It was taking me and it seemed I was going quietly along with it without so much as a struggle. I was quitting I guess. Then suddenly I was fighting—fighting with every ounce of my ebbing strength—fighting as I never had fought before. I was on the surface again, this time nearer the edge of the ice. I splashed and struggled toward it but it broke off in large sheets under the weight of my grasping hands. Then finally I felt solid ice. My arms worked farther out on it. The soggy mittens and shirt sleeves froze to the slushy snow and I was able to rest a little and regain my wind. Finally I was able to haul myself out and I lay there half drowned, chilled, and exhausted. I coughed violently and heaved up my breakfast and what seemed like gallons of water.

I tried to pray while in the water. I did the best I could, which under the circumstances wasn't very good. But I made up for it when I found myself on solid ice. After regaining my wind I staggered to my feet and gazed about me wondering what to do. By the time I had found dry wood and built a fire big enough to undress by and sit wrapped in the blanket while my clothes dried I would have frozen to death. When a good woodsman goes overboard in cold weather he immediately looks for a huge, dry cedar, whacks it down quickly with a sharp ax, cuts it in chunks, splits those chunks, and builds a huge and fast fire. His clothes are hung to dry on nearby branches while he crouches on boughs wrapped in his blanket or sleeping bag.

Although I don't rate myself with those very tough and very capable veterans of the big woods, I had done just that on several occasions following crashes through ice that dunked me in water anywhere from my knees to my waist. But this was different. I had gone in all over, I was exhausted, dry wood was scarce, and the wind was tearing at me across a frozen pond, and the temperature was well below zero.

No doubt the first-class woodsman traveling in heavily wooded country with the proper equipment would have made out all right. He would have to or freeze to death. I realized that I would have to do something, and do it quickly, for my clothes were frozen stiff and I would soon freeze in them. I could feel my body inside of them. They were like a suit of armor.

I squinted into the stabbing glare of the sun on the snow across the meadow, and for the first time I realized that I had lost my sun glasses in the plunge. There, far across the meadow and a field that came down to meet it, stood a long and squatty white farmhouse. Plumes of white smoke hurried away from its two fat chimneys on the wind. That farmhouse was my only hope. But it was far away, looming more like a child's toy than a home in which people lived.

As far away as it was I had to get to it and as quickly as possible. But I would have to get there without the snowshoes which were on the other side of the stream current. I couldn't get to them. My legs, hands, and face were becoming numb. It seemed they were no longer a part of me. Frightened and desperate I struck off at a trot across the snow-packed pond and wallowed into the meadow. The snow was up to my knees in places and up to my waist in others. The winds had played tricks with it.

I tried to find the thin places and wallowed on and on toward my goal—that little farmhouse that seemed to move farther and farther away from me. It was like chasing a will-o'-the-wisp in a black and tangled swamp. I was breathing through both nose and mouth and the bitterly cold air burned my lungs and caused me to stop and cough violently. I was badly winded and half numb. The mad race continued and I ran, fell, floundered, and crawled on and on into the slashing wind and the terrible glare. I made it somehow and fell half dead onto a steaming dung heap that towered behind the barn. I wanted to remain there and rest forever.

What caused me to get up and stagger on through the yard and up the steps to the farmhouse door I shall never know. Perhaps it was the strength and fire of robust youth and the desire to live that really goes with it—the desire I had thought before wasn't too strong.

Through squinting eyes that were squirting hot water down chilled cheeks I saw the pleasant face of a man above some potted plants that lined the window sill. He was looking at me with eyes widened by surprise. He raced to the door and opened it. I floundered inside—into a blast of heat and piled up in a huge rocking chair. I could feel two men walking me into another room, removing my clothes, and rubbing parts of me with snow.

It was late afternoon when I awoke in an old-fashioned but very clean and comfortable bed. I looked up to see the smiling faces of the man who looked at me from the window, and a very husky fellow a few years older than myself. They had hot soup and crackers for me. They had dried my clothes over a large radiator in the hall that carried heat from hard wood chunks that blazed in a big one-pipe furnace. The man was Orin Bowley and the boy was his son Arno. Later I met Mrs. Bowley, a dear little woman who, too, had assisted in saving my life. That was the beginning of a strong and wonderful friendship that I have cherished down through the years. Perhaps the kindness shown me by those fine folks is responsible in a large measure for my love of all farm people.

I was very nearly gone when I staggered into the Bowley home and, as Mr. Bowley later told me, I wouldn't have made it if I had another quarter of a mile to go. But fortunately except for a frost-nipped left ear, a couple of toes, and one finger I wasn't much the worse for the horrible experience. The cold they said I was sure to catch didn't come either. I didn't even get the sniffles.

They insisted that I remain at the farm overnight but I finally convinced them that I was feeling much better and that my cabin was warm and well stocked with food. And too I had my dogs and hens to look after. The day was old when I said good-by to those fine folks. I walked slowly on legs still a bit shaky down the little road, crossed the bridge over the stream, picked up the snowshoe float I had made that morning, and headed back to the pond to gather up my gear. I got along fairly well by walking lightly on my packed trail and soon was strapped into the knapsack and snowshoes and on my way back at a fairly fast clip.

I relived that awful experience a hundred times as I traveled through the woods back to camp. The faithful dogs heard me coming and sent up a boisterous welcome. It was good to be home. I stood in silence at the edge of the dark swamp to look up and thank God and watch His stars come out.

# 19

IT WASN'T until the day after my extremely unpleasant experience at Hammond Pond that I really felt the full effects of it. I discovered much to my amazement that the toes, fingers, and left ear, which the Bowleys thought were only frost bitten and which they rubbed with snow, must have been in the last stages of freezing. The ear was nearly twice its normal size and was quite black. It stuck out from the side of my head like a playing card inserted in a squash. And like the toes and fingers, which also were slightly in mourning, it was very tender. I discovered too that the bridge of my nose had been gnawed by the fangs of the frost, and I was lame in the shoulders and arms. The ear, also nose, fingers, and toes, were kept greased to prevent cracking and excessive peeling, and recovery was quite rapid.

When the soreness had left my toes I made a trip up the lake to the little store with the old sled, knapsack, and a large burlap bag to get supplies for Pop and myself. On the return trip I saw two men setting fishing traps near the mouth of the stream that flows slowly in from Ben Annis Pond. The movement of the incoming water prevents the ice from freezing there for quite some distance out on the lake. It dances blue, cold, and forbidding all winter except during extremely cold weather when it skims over. And the ice for some distance around that opening is always very thin. It's a tricky danger spot and many an angler has taken a cold plunge there.

I saw one of the men walking briskly toward the open water with a fishing trap in one hand and an ice chisel in the other. He was going to set the line near it—too near it! I was quite a distance from him, but I cupped my mittened hands and shouted at the top of my lungs for him to go back. Both of the men heard me but apparently didn't understand. I guess they thought I was another fisherman shouting a greeting. I motioned with my arm for the man to go back. He still didn't understand what I was trying to tell him. He waved at me, took another step, and the lake opened up under him. Down into the cold water he went but managed to turn halfway around and slam his arms down on ice stout enough to hold him. He shouted, and I shouted to his partner near shore. We arrived at the spot at about the same time and hauled him out. And again, for an instant, I relived my experience on Hammond Pond.

"Are you all right, Tom?" the other man shouted excitedly, as we helped him toward their shore fire. It was a pitiful, smoky little heap of soggy, half-rotten pine limbs and sections of green alders.

"My Gawd!" gasped the drenched man's friend, "this will never do. There's no good fire wood around here any place. What in Heaven's name will we do?" he roared at me.

They were both badly frightened and excited, but the poor fellow who took the plunge was too busy shivering to talk. Suddenly I was something better than just a young hermit for whom a mother and father had given up all hope. A man's life depended on me. I was the only one who could save it. I was a sort of hero and really enjoyed the role in the little drama out there on the frozen lake.

I told them of the cabin, which was a little more than a cold, white mile down the lake, and that they were very welcome.

"Thank Gawd, thank Gawd!" gasped the freezing man's funny little friend. He was a small, frail-looking man of about fifty. His friend whose age I guessed at near sixty was quite robust and about my size, but a bit taller.

We had to act quickly. There was no time to lose. I was well aware of that fact following my experience. And the poor fellow was complaining of his feet feeling numb.

"Strap on his snowshoes quickly!" I ordered his nervous and very excited little friend.

He plunged for the shoes and finally got them strapped on.

"Now what? Oh, my Gawd, now what?" he screamed womanlike.

"Have you got any whisky?" I inquired.

"Yes—er yes, we have. Why, do you want a drink?" he gasped breathlessly, with a look of terror in his small, cold face.

He fished a pint bottle out of their pack basket and handed it to me. I broke the seal and passed it to his shaking pal who gulped down about a quarter of it. My bulging knapsack was quickly roped to their full and very heavy basket and with some grunting and struggling I managed to swing the load onto my shoulders. The little fellow finally got around to strapping on his own snowshoes and with my loaded sled and their bait bucket, followed us down the lake. Their chisel, a brand new one, was somewhere on the bottom of the lake.

If it had taken us half as long to get started as it does to tell about it the poor man would have frozen stiffer than a fish in an Eskimo's front room. Actually we were underway in a few minutes. I set a fast pace but dropped back now and then to help the soaked and freezing man along when he seemed to be tiring badly and about to fall. He talked very little. Just a few words now and then. The whisky and the fast pace on the snowshoes were making him sweat. It dripped from his forehead and around his eyes. But he said his feet felt like "blocks of wood."

Finally at the cabin I shoved open the door and rushed him in, hauled off his frozen parka and helped him strip down to the suit he was born in. He was completely exhausted. Although numb and a bit on the blue side, his feet and hands were all right after a thorough rubbing with snow. After a vigorous rubdown with a rough towel and another drink of his whisky, this time in hot water, he was very comfortable wrapped in a heavy blanket before the blazing logs of the fireplace.

"I can't imagine what has delayed my friend George," he said with a small smile. "Would you mind taking a look up the lake, son? He's an old friend, and my secretary, and although highly nervous and excitable, he's really a fine person," he explained, and returned his gaze to the fire.

George was no doubt a good man in a steam-heated office but he certainly was a misfit in the woods. He was just coming around the point into the cove. He was dragging the loaded sled and carrying one of his snowshoes under his arm. The other was still strapped to his foot, and with that foot riding high and the other plunging through the deep snow at every step his gait was like that of a bent hoop rolling down a hill.

"This confounded sled just wouldn't stay off the tails of these things and after several bad falls I finally broke the strap on this one!" he explained breathlessly. He was as mad as a tormented hornet.

I took the sled and the little man limped behind. Tom, the other man, turning in his chair at the fire, laughed heartily when his friend came floundering through the door. That was a golden opportunity to unleash the laughter I had been fighting back, and I roared.

It was a little past noon when we sat down to the last of my venison steak. With it we had fried onions, boiled potatoes, warmed-up biscuits of my own making, store doughnuts, tea, and canned peaches. We ate like wolves and George helped me with the dishes.

That afternoon I set two of their lines in the water hole in front of the camp, and several others in freshly cut holes farther out. Feeling much better after a dinner about which they both exclaimed, the two men began fishing. I didn't think they would get much action down so far on the lake but they did, and took a fine catch of large green and bronze pickerel. They were pleased and so was I.

The night was fiercely cold and I suggested that instead of wallowing up the lake in the dark to take the night train to Bangor they remain at the cabin and take the morning train. After a good supper which consisted mostly of the huge lunch in their pack basket, the little man who reminded me of a chipmunk went to bed. The other man, Tom, whom I liked very much, and I sat late before the blazing birch and beech logs and talked of many things.

He explained that he lived in Chicago where he had a business and that he was in Bangor on a sort of combination business and pleasure trip. He said he had hunted and fished in Maine quite a bit and shortly after putting up at the Bangor House had inquired about ice fishing. He was told, he said, that Hermon was a red-hot pickerel water so he decided to buy some equipment and hit the trail with his friend and secretary George, who didn't care for outdoor life.

He thought, as did other fishermen with whom I had talked that winter, that my living alone out there in the woods was escapism—that I was running away from something or everything in general. "A great many people do that," he said.

I didn't bother to explain to any of the others. I figured that it was none of their business and that they couldn't help me one way or the other. But he was different. He didn't try to pry my story from me with the bar of curiosity. As a matter of fact his approach, which reflected a sincere interest, caused me to pour it out without much questioning. I really seemed to enjoy telling it to him. It was like rolling a huge stone off my chest.

When I had finished the story a heavy silence fell over the little cabin. He was staring thoughtfully into the fire. Then turning slowly, he said, "I think I understand clearly, son, what you're up against and what you are trying to do. You're not running away, but running after something. I'm sure your parents will, in time, understand too. Many others have experienced this very same problem and have come through all right. You're young, stick to it for a while longer at least, and I'm sure you'll finally make it and be happier and better for it. It's your problem, your fight, and only you alone can solve it," he concluded.

We sat in deep silence listening to the ticking of the clock, and gazing wide eyed at the fire. Then suddenly he spoke again, "Money, fame, and power aren't everything in this world. Many men of only very moderate success who live in comparative obscurity, but who enjoy what they are doing, are very often the happiest." And then he told me a little story—a story that proved his point, and made my uncertain journey a little easier.

He said that if all who because of money, political connections, and social standing regard themselves as men of tremendous power, influence, and importance could become lost alone in the woods for just one day and one night they would be better men for the experience.

He was, he said, a member of a deer-hunting party several years before in one of the wildest regions of Maine. On the morning of the third day at camp he wandered off alone with the intentions of hunting an old road and being gone but a short time. But he wandered away from the road in the direction of a low beech ridge, which he could see plainly, and on which he planned to sit for a while and "keep an eye peeled" for a traveling deer. But, as so often happens to the man untrained in wilderness travel, he soon lost sight of the ridge. It had vanished completely, he explained. So he tried to get back to the road. But, lo and behold, that, too, was no longer there. But he knew that wherever it had curled it was much nearer than the ridge. So he tried again to find it but wandered into a deep and very dark cedar swamp. And to make matters worse the sun that had come up so brightly behind the camp that morning had been blotted out by thickening snow clouds. Finally it was noon, and then suddenly afternoon, and the perpetual twilight of the forest swamp was growing deeper.

He hadn't planned to leave the road so he left his compass at the camp in his heavy jacket. He tried to hurry this way and that, but finally winded and weary he realized that he was hopelessly lost. He shouted through cupped hands and with straining ears listened for a reply. None came.

None but the mocking singing of the cold wind in the trees. His signal shots brought no reply either.

He had been walking for hours and was very tired. There was nothing he could do but prepare as best he could to spend the night and wait for the other members of the party to find him if they could. He found a dry knoll in the swamp and began to gather all the dry wood he could find. He collected quite a pile of blowdowns, bark, limbs, and old stumps. Cedar and spruce boughs were heaped up for a bed near the place he had cleared for his fire, and suddenly he couldn't see his hand two feet in front of him. Night had moved in—a cold, starless November night. The creatures of the day had retired to their resting places and their nocturnal relatives began to prowl. The sound of their movements in the brush and fallen leaves were magnified by the night, and caused chills to race over him. He soon developed the creeps and was tired and very hungry.

Fortunately he had taken along a good supply of matches, a few cigarettes and his belt knife. His unskilled hands finally got the fire started and he fell back exhausted on the boughs. The flames burned a small hole in the black velvet of the night and tiny explosions sent sparks floating skyward. Something dug into his hip as he lay there on his back and he reached into a pocket to remove it. It was his wallet, he explained, which held, among other things, his hunting license and nearly four hundred dollars in bills.

He had only a few cartridges left after his afternoon signal shooting and decided to keep them for protection, killing something he could eat and for answering the signal shooting of his party, which he felt certain would come in the early morning.

Once he thought he heard a voice far off behind him. He sprang to his feet to answer, but it was only the cry of a night creature. It was from then on through the long, cold night, humped over the sputtering and smoky little fire, that he realized, he said, how small, helpless, and puny even the greatest of men, as their greatness is so foolishly measured on this earth, really are.

He thought how quickly a little root could snap his ankle, and how any one of the dead trees that towered like hideous black skeletons about him could, if suddenly felled by the wind, crush the life from his body; how the little flames if he slept, and rolled too near could burn him to a crisp. And how any of the larger flesh eaters of the forest could, if they so desired, suddenly jump him and kill him.

And he also thought of how absolutely useless were the money that bulged in his wallet and the fortune he had back in the city now that he was alone and hopelessly lost in a growth of trees. That money in his pocket couldn't bring up the sun to light his way, nor could it hire anybody to lead him out of the woods. And the whole kaboodle couldn't buy him an ounce of food.

"Those bills," he went on, "were of no use to me except perhaps to stimulate my fire should it burn low and fail to warm me. And they wouldn't serve the purpose nearly as well as bits of worthless birch bark!"

The wind came up during the night and toppled a huge cedar stub nearby. It fell with a resounding thud. Startled from his dozing he leaped to his feet. His heart was pounding furiously, he said. He placed his hand over it and felt the throbbing, and for the first time in his life he realized that there was another thing that his money couldn't buy— that man couldn't make, and that when it stopped he would be dead, and his brief little journey on earth would be at an end.

"I wondered," he continued, "as the night wore slowly on and my supply of wood dwindled, if I ever would be found!" And he went on to tell me unashamed that he became frightened, and like all men in trouble thought of God, and began to pray. He prayed as well as he could remember how, as a little boy, his good mother had taught him.

"I was thinking of how little this whole thing called life amounts to," he drawled, "when I slumped into deep sleep. I was completely exhausted."

Then leaning forward to knock the ashes from his pipe into the fireplace my sportsman friend told of being awakened by the warm flood of the rising sun and the shouting and shooting of his three companions and the guide.

"Those friends, too, are very successful as men are measured," he snapped. "They had plenty of money, too, but they couldn't have helped me a bit. They couldn't have found me in that trackless wilderness. But that poor little guide, who only the night before was telling me how he had to count his pennies to support his fine little family, could and did! Yes sir, he saved my life, that little guy who, on the yardstick by which the greatness of men is so foolishly figured, would be close to the bottom.

"He put a buck deer onto me the next day that I might shoot it, and when we left the little cabin back there in the big woods I hauled out my check book and gave him some of my so called greatness!"

I loved that story. It has stuck with me and helped me through the years. It was particularly helpful at that time when life and the world looked desperately dark.

We had fried pickerel for breakfast the next morning. Both men tried to pay me for what I had done for them, but I refused. I really enjoyed them. But when they insisted quite forcibly, I did accept the bright new ash pack basket, which I admired and needed badly. The contents went with it too. In it I found a big bundle of winter fishing traps, yards and yards of fishing line, a metal slush scoop, a new short-handled ax, cooking tins, lead sinkers, lead depth sounders, hooks, a big belt knife, a quart thermos bottle, and other odds and ends.

I snowshoed with them up the lake to the station in plenty of time for them to catch the train, and returned at a slow gait reviewing the story the man Tom had told me, and taking from it much encouragement that stood by me during the remainder of those lonely winter days. And I wasn't very much surprised when that night I found a ten-dollar bill stuck in a lamp chimney.

# 20

THE REMAINING WEEKS of winter dragged like the tails of the otters I had seen on the stream. Time was heavy on my hands. The one thing that eased the monotony was the study of wildlife and the outdoors in general. More and more birds flocked into my little feeding station in the camp yard as the winter waned. At first, in the early part of the winter I just tossed out bread crusts on the snow for a few hungry little chickadees. But as the days rolled on and natural food became scarcer they came in great numbers along with other little feathered things, which included woodpeckers, nuthatches, blue jays, cedar waxwings, pine grosbeaks, sparrows, purple finches, and red polls. I built feed trays and boxes in the firs and spruces near the cabin, and kept them well filled with table scraps, boiled rice, rolled oats, and some grain.

The birds became very tame and after a time I was able to walk very close to them. Some of the chickadees would perch on my head and shoulders while I was filling the trays and boxes. Then the red and a few gray squirrels muscled in and fought with the birds over the food. I made many sketches of my forest friends and enjoyed their screamingly funny all-day vaudeville show. I learned to love the little things—even the fresh little squirrels—and they seemed to love me.

My store of vegetables was getting low and sank even lower when in making a check I found many that had either wizened almost to nothing or were rotten. Some were boiled for the hens and the others were carried back to the camp dump and thrown away. The woodpiles, too, were shrinking but there seemed to be enough to hold out well into the spring.

But to make sure, and also because I had nothing else to do, I cut down and sawed up in lengths for the ram-down, cookstove, and fireplace all the old dead stuff I could find near camp. Some young white birches, white maples, and oaks also were harvested. I devoted a few hours each day to the harvesting.

My visits to Pop's cabin across the lake were few and far between then. I didn't enjoy him as much as I had at first, for his rheumatism was killing him and he was grouchy and irritable much of the time. I did, however, call at his place every time I went to the store to see if he needed anything. I knew the long hike was too much for him.

I fished when I needed fish and hunted rabbits with the hounds when I needed meat to supplement my very low supply of venison, which by that time consisted of a couple of small roasts, a few chops, and a stack of stewmeat.

Foxes and a few ravens visited the fishing holes on the lake in the very early morning to pick up the dead bait fish I had thrown away. The little fish would be frozen into the slush and ice but the hungry brushtails and the big birds always managed to dig them out. I saw them many times, and one morning, in the late winter when a thick fog crawled across the lake, I sneaked up to within a few yards of a huge and very handsome old dog fox who had his back to me gnawing one of the little fish that was stuck fast in the ice. I didn't dare stretch my luck any farther so drew the revolver and blazed away. The slug missed by inches and threw snow all over him. I wanted the big and very beautiful pelt to have made into a rug for my mother. And although my aim was bad I thought I was going to get it anyway when the badly frightened fox came very nearly jumping right out of it. Taken completely by surprise he leaped high in the air at the roar of the gun and started to run before his feet were back on the snow. I was laughing too hard to try a running shot. And after the big fox had streaked away across the lake and into the woods I was glad I missed. After all, he was one of the wild things that lived with me out there in my silent world of trees and waters. Like all of the many other creatures he was a sort of neighbor. More and more as time rolled along I came to regard all of them as my friends. I lived as close to them as I could—the bugs, birds, fish, and four-footed things. And many of them accepted me as such. I was pleased and quite proud. From then on I killed sparingly, scientifically, and mercifully, and only when I needed them that I might live. By scientifically I do not mean that I killed them with gasses or strange weapons. I still had only the guns and the steel traps. But I tried to kill in season of course, in places where long periods of observation and study told me they were too numerous—where the populations of the various species seemed to be out of balance with the natural food supply. Nature in her wisdom usually takes care of this, but there are times when she falls down on the job. But whether I was right or wrong in my wildlife management, the taking of those things was easier for me. I had no feeling of guilt.

I had become pretty well toughened to the winter as it reached the long downhill haul toward spring. One day was pretty much like another with either high blue skies and floods of golden sunshine, or squatty gray ones filled with tumbling flakes. The nights, too, were pretty much the same with ghostly moonlight, smothering darkness, or storms. They were deadly quiet and sometimes I was very lonely. There were long lamp-lighted hours before the blazing fireplace when in meditation I struggled with my thoughts. Some of them lifted me like bits of thistledown onto the soothing winds of encouragement, certainty, and ambition, while others spiked me to the big pine outside the door.

Before me on the table were letters from home—from my father and mother who had finally abandoned all hope for me and made it known in no uncertain terms. And there were clippings from the Bangor newspapers telling of the progress some of my friends were making in the world. One had been promoted to the job of shipping clerk for a local company. Another was a cashier at a bank. Another had become a "full-fledged" cigar maker, and still another had accepted a bookkeeper's job in Boston. If my good parents thought for a moment that such bits of news would act as barbs to prod me into the pursuit of similar city jobs they were mistaken.

Any faint desire that I might have had for such work had been devoured by that summer and winter of complete and wonderful freedom in the open. That life convinced me of one thing at least: that I could never be happy locked in the shackles of whistles and clocks, and struggling with others to win and hold the favor of a boss who would probably be struggling equally hard to win and hold the favor of one in a higher position.

Such an existence, it seemed, was much like that of the wild things that lived near me by that oldest of all laws, survival of the fittest. Then there would be the rut, which except for being longer, is a grave. Such an existence wasn't for me, of that I was certain.

During those many hours of deep and serious meditation before the old fireplace, the trailside fires, and on long walks in the woods, I wondered again and again if perhaps that life in the open was the one I wanted—the one I would eventually follow. It seemed to be tightening about me more and more, like a vine to a tree, as time went on. But the thought of the uncertain, hand-to-mouth existence and perhaps finally winding up like old Pop in a purgatory of poverty and pain cut such dreams adrift along with those of eventually getting a farm for myself.

The winter crawled on and then, suddenly, like all things that are old, it collapsed and passed on. The end came before I realized it. The snowdrifts slumped and drooled under a mounting sun. Patches of brown needles showed under the pines. Skunk cabbages bulged green and smelly in the bogs, and the raspy call of returning crows rode the warm winds.

Early spring in the woods, particularly following a winter of great snows and severe cold, is not entirely pleasant.

It's extremely messy with slush and water everywhere over land and lake. And because of its sloppiness and the fact that there is little to do, it seems to drag snail-like.

One thing that must be done when a lake stretches between a camp and a store is to put in a supply of food that will hold out during that period when the ice is too weak to walk on and the time it is wide open and ready for a canoe or a boat. I called on Pop to get the list of things he wanted but this time he went along with me. Walking on snowshoes over my old trail was easy then; the day was mild, blue, and golden, and Pop thought the jaunt would be good for him. I shouldered my new pack basket and took a burlap bag, the big kerosene can, and the old sled. Pop took his knapsack, a bag, and his sled.

I've heard it said that a man living alone eats but very little. Pop was proof of that, but I certainly was an exception. There were days during the winter when upset by my problem or stinging letters from home I ate mouselike, but in between those spasms my appetite was like that of a bear coming out of hibernation.

In addition to the food for myself I had to get a supply for the dogs and hens. I found neither newspapers nor letters from home. Pop knew how my parents felt about me living in the woods alone. We had discussed it several times. He noticed that I was disappointed upon finding no mail, and dropping a heavy gnarled hand on my shoulder as we rested on the lake shore, he blurted, "I wouldn't let it bother me a mite, son. Chances is yer father did what he wanted ter do about goin' ter work and they's no reason under the sun why you can't. With all respeck to yer dad and yer mother I wouldn't let 'em lead me by the beak inter somethin' I didn't want ter work at. Allus remember thet a good woodsman finds his own way out. You kin do it, too. You got plenty of time. What in hell's the hurry?"

We trudged along with our supplies in silence for a while then Pop started again. "First thing yer know they'll be pickin' out a wife fer yer. Then she'll start bossin' and slatin' and tellin' yer what ter do and when yer'll do it. And then, son, yer'll be a damned fool for fair. I'd sooner tie a rock to my neck and jump offen old Birch Point!" he roared.

At Pop's suggestion we set up a little sugar camp in a stand of maples back in the woods on his side of the lake. We erected with poles and boughs a fairly large shelter and, with an old wash boiler and all the pails, jars, and bottles we could find, pitched into the work of gathering the sweet sap from the fat trunks of the trees. March with its warm sunny days and freezing nights is ideal for that sort of thing. It takes a tremendous amount of sap to make syrup and even more to make sugar. We soon gave up the idea of making the latter and decided to halt operations at the syrup stage.

It was hard work wallowing back and forth through the melting snow to gather the liquid and the wood for the fire that blazed steadily throughout the days under the old boiler. It was interesting though, and I enjoyed it. We hadn't been in business long when Pop's rheumatism became aggravated by the wet snow and dampness and he was forced to quit. We each got about a gallon and a half of syrup. It was delicious on hot flapjacks and every time I sat down to such a feast I wished I had stuck to it alone and made a lot more of it.

The streams coming into the lake were the first to shake off the bonds of winter. They cut farther and farther into the ice field. Soon the ice over the springy spots opened. They were like sparkling blue eyes peeking out at spring. Then gradually the field became black, and suddenly it was gone. The waves borrowed beauty from the blue sky and the sun, and danced wildly with the wind.

Nature's method of clearing the ice from the lakes and ponds is very interesting. It has caused many heated arguments some of which I have heard and enjoyed. I have heard some people claim that the ice field breaks up in great sheets, then smaller pieces, and rides away down the outlet streams. Some said it sank to the bottom. Others insisted that the chunks were carried onto the shores by the wind and the waves where they gradually melted. And I've heard a few other explanations equally far off the track by persons who really didn't know.

Rain, fog, sunshine, and wind are the forces that free the waters of winter's bonds. Little by little, day after day, they gnaw away at the ice until it becomes soft and finally honeycombed. It is then very black and is nothing but a great mass of long tinkling needles. Then the wind steps in for the final blow. The millions of needles are separated and suddenly, like magic, the ice vanishes before your eyes.

I repaired the old canoe as best I could and varnished the badly worn paddles. It was too early for fishing on the lakes and ponds of that region for the bass and perch were protected until after the spawning period, and the pickerel, too, although not on the protected list, were reproducing their kind.

I wished more than once that I were living on the shore of a trout and salmon lake. And then I began to wonder and have wondered ever since, why Nature arranged it to have the salmon and trout spawn in the fall and the bass, pickerel, perch, and some other species spawn in the spring.

But there would be good trout fishing as soon as the water in the brooks and in old Souadabscook Stream dropped and cleared. Plans to trap a few muskrats to replenish my dwindling supply of cash were knocked spinning by a half-dozen Indians who suddenly appeared on the scene and strung their steel all over the region. They were Penobscots from the Reservation on the Penobscot River at Old Town, twelve miles north of Bangor. I learned from the station agent that members of the tribe came every spring to trap rats. Their canoes, heavily loaded with camping equipment, traps, and food were put into Black Stream at Kenduskeag and down they came, trapping as they moved along and finally reached Souadabscook Stream and the lake, where they camped for two or three weeks and harvested the rats.

The Indians didn't trap the rats in the fall. They sought them only in the spring when the pelts are at their best and bring the top prices. They pitched three soiled canvas tents and one wigwam in a stand of huge pines less than a mile from my cabin. One of them, a young fellow, whom I met on the narrow stream flowing out of Ben Annis Pond tried to get rid of me as a competitor by telling me there were not many rats in the section and that I would be wasting my time. I knew better but thanked him and paddled on.

When I walked into their camp one day about sunset I was given a very cool reception. All of my efforts to make conversation were met mostly with grunts and grins. I noticed that they were enjoying considerable success in their trapping. Whole rats and stretched pelts were hanging near the tents and a number of skinned carcasses dangled from a tree limb. Others stewed in a huge iron kettle over a crackling fire. They didn't want to make friends. That was certain. The Indian name for muskrat is *musquash* and I understand the flesh is quite delicious. The Indians ate a lot of them out there and they also ate a lot of pickerel.

Curious to know how many rats they were taking I crawled to the top of a knoll a couple of times just before sunset and watched them coming into camp with their catches. I watched them skinning the rats, building fires, cooking, eating, and everything else they did. I can't remember ever seeing any one of them wash his hands and face, comb his hair, or brush his teeth. But perhaps they took care of such things when darkness came and I had gone back to my cabin.

Although my days of playing cowboys and Indians were far behind me, I experienced quite a thrill during those sessions of snooping around the camp of real and very unfriendly Indians. It was easy picturing them in beaded buckskins, moccasins, and swaying eagle feathers. I don't know what would have happened if they had caught me spying on them. Perhaps it's just as well I didn't have a chance to find out.

I noticed among other things that one man, an old fellow, always remained at camp; perhaps to guard the furs. One day in the late afternoon, before the others returned, I watched him as he squatted cross legged before a small fire and with a stick beat softly on a little tomtom drum.

It was weird music yet it fascinated me strangely. Finally he sang softly in the Indian tongue. He pulled himself to his feet and walked into the wigwam when the trappers began to arrive. I crawled quietly away and dreamed all night of fighting Indians.

One afternoon I saw two other Indians paddling swiftly down the lake. I found them the next day camped halfway down the stream leading to Hammond Pond. They, too, were trapping, but were a bit late arriving in that region. Everywhere I went I found the traps of the Indians. There were very few places where I might squeeze in a set. So rather than get tangled up with them I took only half of my traps and set them back on the small brooks and bogs. They didn't bother me in there, but my catch was pitifully small. I was glad when the trapping season was over and the Indians broke camp and went away.

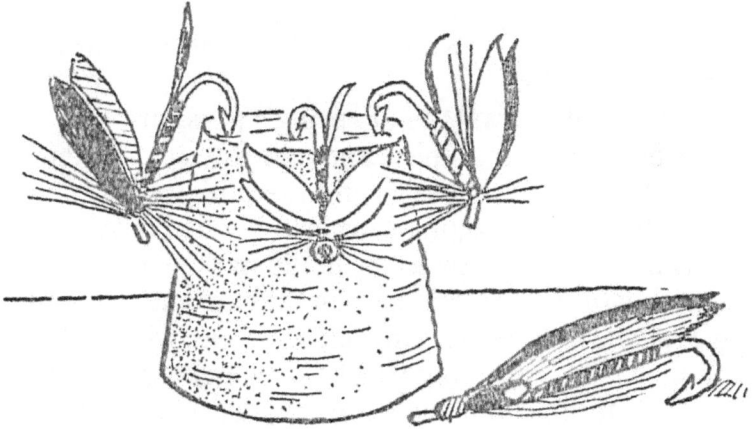

# 21

SPRING BECAME more ambitious after the rat-trapping season and seemed to be rushing to put her house in order. The buds of the poplar trees burst their tight corsets to produce bits of pearly plush; the poor alders along the shores shook out powdery curls; the wild ducks, the loons, and the herons swooped in; and the choir of the songbirds became sweeter with each passing day. And down in the bogs young ferns were in the fiddlehead stage. And it wasn't long before the cheery symphony of the peeper frogs was rising in great volume from flooded fields and meadowland. The land was coming to life. All wild things were mating and love rode the fragrant winds. And suddenly young dandelions, like little green octopuses were spreading their scalloped tentacles in the high, grassy places, and Waldo, whom I hadn't seen all winter, was underfoot again.

I took full advantage of spring's gifts, drinking sweet sap from the sugar maples, and upholstering myself to the bursting point with greens and the pink flesh of sluggish trout that took wriggling worms in flooded brooks.

A man takes a new lease on life in the spring. It is the season of the resurrection, when the bare and sleeping land lives again. I talked with my farmer friend who said he was going to plant corn in the big field again before resting the soil, and that I could again have my garden.

All of the hens in my small flock were producing eggs every day. I ate them fried, boiled, and scrambled until I feared I would soon sprout feathers and begin to cackle.

The old canoe was launched, and finding it tight I paddled up the swollen lake to the store where I got a free seed book and borrowed a fat catalogue issued by a Chicago mail-order house in which were advertised ram-down stoves nearly twice as large as the one in the cabin. I would need a much larger one if I lived in the little place another winter. The bigger the better. Firewood of any kind and size was cheap. And there was plenty of old dry stuff standing around in the woods that I could have for the taking. All I needed was a stove big enough to shove it into and that would hold a fire through a long winter night. I decided on an old whopper and planned to send for it as soon as I was able to pay for it without leaving me flat broke.

I would soon be guiding fishermen including the wealthy old fellow I had worked for the summer before. And, too, I would be selling eggs, flies, and bait to him and a few others. And there might be other ways of scraping in a few dollars. My friend the station agent and the folks at the store would be in contact with all fishermen and campers and they promised to send them to me. I was as happy as a pickerel in a pool of stranded minnows despite the fact my parents were bitterly opposed to my way of life and were just about all through with me.

A man who was at the store that day told me that the annual spawning migration of the smelts from the ocean up the brooks and rivers was underway and that good catches were being made with large dip nets along the Hampden shore of the Penobscot River. I don't give a rap for the tiny fresh-water smelts of the salmon and trout lakes that some people rave about. They are too small to clean and have a flat taste. But the big fellows that swarm up from the salt water are my favorite fish. I would rather have a feed of freshly caught sea smelts rolled in corn meal and fried in pork or bacon fat than brook trout or salmon, or anything else wearing fins.

With time a bit heavy on my hands I decided to have a go at the smelts. I didn't have a long-handled dip net, but I did have an old and unusually large landing net with a fairly long handle. The mesh was much too coarse for holding smelts but with pieces of string and old fishing line I filled it in; and with a burlap sack, pack basket, lunch, and a lantern, I was away in the canoe in the late afternoon on the journey to the river.

I paddled as far down the broad shouldered stream as the wild spring rapids would permit, beached the canoe, and struck off with my load. I passed through bogs, woods, and farm fields and, finally just before dusk, arrived at the bridge and the dam on the main road in Hampden.

Smelt dipping is done at night when the smart and very swift fish can't see the fisherman or his net. It was but a short walk to the mouth of the big stream at the river. Three other fishermen were there ahead of me. They were sitting by a small driftwood fire. They informed me that the run had slowed down but that I could probably dip a "mess" if I stuck to it long enough. But on seeing that I had no wading boots and only an oversized landing net, they were extremely doubtful if I would catch any at all.

I laughed, thanked them, and walked down the shore where I sat alone watching the black river racing past, and hauled on my pipe. Night—a thick, black-velvet night—came quickly. I had dipped smelts many times before so knew what it was all about. I waddled slowly down to the river's edge, climbed onto a greasy low-water ledge, and plunged the net into the swift current. After several dips I brought up one smelt. It was about eight inches long. The tide had about another hour to run out before it would be dead low. By that time my total catch amounted to only eleven fairly large smelts. That was very poor fishing.

Other fishermen began to arrive. Their fires burned ragged yellow holes in the blanket of night. I talked with several of them. They, too, were finding the pickings rather slim. I moved up the rocky shore to the mouth of the stream but could find no ledges or large rocks on which to stand.

In desperation I waded into the cold black water. I went all the way to my knees then a bit higher. The swift current of the river and that of the stream coming into it created a mighty pull against which I had all I could do to hold my feet on the slippery bottom. The fiercely cold water numbed my legs and ran down the net handle to drench sleeves and arms as I swept it up from the depths. The smelts were coming in close to avoid the fast water and business was picking up. I dipped from one to a half dozen at a time. By ten o'clock, according to the watch of a passing fisherman, I had, heaped on the rugged shore, nearly a bushel of squirming silver. I didn't know I had so many of the little fish. They pile up fast.

Men who go fishing are usually friendly fellows, and I was invited to join a party of four for a smelt fry. I contributed my share of smelts and we all ate ravenously of the crisp little fish fried to a golden brown in a huge iron pan, and potatoes baked in the coals of the fire. I enjoyed the feast and also dried out my trousers, socks, and leather-top rubbers.

During that session around the blazing night fire I was informed that Atlantic salmon, some of them of considerable size, were running into the stream all the way to the dam at the highway bridge and that a Hampden fisherman had landed one of eight pounds a few days before. That interested me and I was still thinking about it when at daylight I arrived, dog tired and damp, at the cabin on the lake.

Every spring the Atlantic salmon swarm up the Penobscot River more than two hundred miles to spawn in the fall. On the way up they stop for a time in the wild waters of the Bangor Salmon Pool below the Bangor Waterworks dam. This great sprawl of turbulent water has long been world famous as a fishing grounds for these finned aristocrats. The members of the Penobscot Salmon Club ride the rips in canvas boats and, with expensive rods, reels, and flies, take salmon up to twenty pounds. In the early days of the Pool, salmon up to thirty pounds were not uncommon.

The next day, following that night on the river, was devoted to cleaning all the smelts I could use and placing them in cold storage in the tin-lined box down by the spring. The others were cleaned and delivered to old Pop, the station agent, and my farmer friend who owned the cornfield. How I forgot the Bowleys who cared for me after my plunge into Hammond Pond, I don't know. It really bothered me for a time.

The urge to try for an Atlantic salmon was too much for me and a few days later I was away again in the old canoe for the mouth of Souadabscook Stream. This time instead of a net, my gear consisted of the five-ounce rod, a level "D" line, a seven-foot, six-pound test leader, and a few camp-tied flies which included crude copies of the Jock Scott, Durham Ranger, Silver Wilkinson, and Dusty Miller. I fashioned a gaff from a length of broom handle and a piece of very stout wire which was barbed and sharpened just in case I did tangle with a salmon. My chances were slim, I knew, but it was worth a try.

It was still dark when the canoe glided away from the landing. The sun rose in a blaze of glory just as I walked onto the shore of the stream's frothy head but it was quickly devoured by dirty shower clouds that cluttered the sky throughout the day.

Carefully scanning the curling water of the stream between the highway dam and the river I thought I saw a fish roll at the head of a pool near the other side. Forty feet of line were stripped off and a Dusty Miller floated through the early morning to alight daintily above the spot. It rode the current into the pool and over the exact spot where I thought I had seen a salmon roll. I got set for the rise, but nothing happened.

The little fly made the same trip more than a dozen times with no better results. Perhaps I should explain here that when traveling up the fresh-water streams to spawn the Atlantic salmon does not feed. A feeding fish would have grabbed the fly on the first cast. But old Salmo salar, the fighter from the Atlantic, both male and female, strikes at a fly only because it is bothering them and they want to kill it. I've heard some salmon fishermen say that the salmon takes a fly because he or she is in a playful mood. I don't agree. But I guess nobody really knows or ever will know because salmon can't talk. But anyhow, I do know that if you cast long enough over a salmon it will eventually rise and take the fly.

Thinking that perhaps what I saw in that little pool was not a salmon after all I moved upstream to cast in the crazy water nearer the dam. I had no action there either. I fished all the way to the river, whipping every pool thoroughly and to the best of my ability. And I used my four favorite flies and a couple of others. It seemed hopeless—a waste of time and energy.

The incoming tide was rapidly filling the pools and I knew that if I didn't snag onto one within the next half hour or so I would have to wait until late afternoon when the pools would be showing again. Returning to the place where in the early morning I thought I saw a fish rolling, I put the Dusty Miller into action again. I must have made about thirty casts and was just about ready to call it quits, when I saw the line suddenly tighten and heard the reel squawk. Something had taken the fly. I was sure of that but I wasn't sure whether the taker was a fat old chub or a fine salmon.

I had tangled with Atlantic salmon before and knew that the rod never should be lifted to set the hook as in other types of fishing until the salmon is at the peak of that first sprint. I waited with pounding heart and impatient hands. The line was pulled out slowly then like a flash the fish was away, out of the pool and into the fast water. The little single-action reel screamed as the line was whisked off its arbor. I feared for a moment that backing and all would be ripped off and that the fish, which by that time I knew was a salmon, would go dashing away with it into the river. Wading into the stream I lifted hard on the rod. I gave the little stick all it would stand. That halted the sprint and a handsome sagging bellied salmon, whose weight I guessed at ten or twelve pounds, smashed the water wide open and leaped high into the air.

The battle was on, a long and hard battle that with the light rod took me up and down the stream and into its cold and rushing water up to my chest. My heart pounded so furiously I thought it would stave out my ribs. My mouth was small and dry and I was drenched with a mixture of sweat and water. I never wanted anything so much in my life as I wanted that handsome finned warrior. I used every trick in my personal piscatorial satchel and he used all of his. He sprinted, leaped into the air, sulked, rolled, yanked, and several times bulleted straight at me while I stripped line furiously to take up the slack. The little reel wasn't equal to the task. And suddenly it was all over and a tired and crestfallen fisherman reeled in his fly. The salmon had finally succeeded in throwing it after what I guessed was a twenty-minute struggle. I couldn't have felt worse if I had lost a hundred-dollar bill.

I tried for salmon there three more times that spring and on the second attempt raised, hooked, fought, and lost a much smaller fish. It was a difficult place to fish for those huskies, especially with trout tackle, but I sure did enjoy those two skirmishes.

At the risk of drawing the fire of those brother anglers whose quarry is the salmon species of the Pacific, I rate the Atlantic salmon the king of all fishes. He's a handsome and courageous aristocrat who makes not one, but at least two trips to the spawning beds, and who knows no master but death.

I never have killed one after a long, hard fight and watched the blood streaming from the gaff wound in the silvered side without feeling sorry, and regretting a bit my act that took the life of a thing of such beauty and magnificent courage.

I found it difficult settling down to trout fishing after those two action-packed sessions with the salmon. But a few successful trips with both worms and flies took care of that. There are very few things that good trout fishing won't cure.

# 22

THE SUMMER, which we in Maine wait and yearn for through the long and cold winter, comes all of a sudden and is gone just as suddenly, leaving us wondering where it went and wishing we had made more of it and had accomplished more during its brief stay. Maine summers are really beautiful. The long blue and golden days are warm and filled with the songs of a million birds and the fragrance of twice as many flowers. The short and deep-blue nights are star-studded and cool—sometimes cool enough to cause the northern lights to reach with great green claws for those stars. And there's nothing more thrilling and refreshing than one of those booming and drenching thundershowers.

June found me fighting black flies and mosquitoes while I planted my garden, which had been enriched with manure from the roost boards of my hen house. I continued with the study of Nature, and added to my mounting knowledge that the black flies are humped-backed, and that only the female mosquito stings. She stings to get blood that she must have to lay her eggs, and in the process injects into her victim, whether it's a two-legged or four-legged animal, an irritant that causes the blood to flow freely. It's that irritant that also causes the sharp little pain and makes one scratch the wound.

The fields and clearings were generously dotted with the little white blossoms of the wild strawberry. I never saw them more numerous. There would be a bumper crop of the delicious little red fruits and I would enjoy them for dessert until the coming of the raspberries, the blueberries, and finally the blackberries.

The wild apple and cherry trees in their scented garments of white and pink blossoms were like lovely ghosts in the old clearings, here and there, back in the woods. It seemed that Nature's horn of plenty would be filled to overflowing that summer. I hoped that my vegetable garden would be equally productive. I would need all I could raise for the winter that was moving toward me with every tick of the clock—my second one out there alone in the woods.

I helped Pop with his garden for the poor old fellow was pretty badly crippled with rheumatism. It was almost impossible for him to enjoy his favorite sport—skipping cut bait with the long bamboo pole for pickerel. One day one of the men who came from Bangor to buy pickerel from him poured a lot of nonsense into his good ear to the effect that a sure cure for rheumatism is the sting of the honeybee. He explained, and unfortunately convinced the old man, that something the bee injects into the blood stream drives out the agonizing pain of the disease.

Pop believed him. He gobbled it up hook, line, and sinker, and nothing I could say to the contrary could change his mind. I told him that there was no known cure but that he could get relief from bakings in the sun and massages with oils and liniments. I offered to catch a couple of skunks, melt the very penetrating oil from the fat and give him daily massages with the stuff. He delivered a long speech of appreciation but said he was sure the bees would take care of it just as the fish buyer said they would.

He tried to pick a fight with the few bees that visited the wild flowers near his cabin. One of them did sting him on the thumb and another drilled him on the leg but that was all. And that wasn't enough, according to the fishmonger. Those stings were only samples, he said. What Pop needed was a full-sized dose, he explained, and Pop was determined to get it. He did, eventually, and good! I gave up and went back to my cabin and my garden while Pop, the poor old fool, desperate with pain, devoted the days to hunting bees. Finally he found a tree in which a large swarm had set up housekeeping and was storing honey. It was about a mile and a half from his cabin near the shore of Tracy Pond. The tree was a huge old beech and the entrance, which was a wide crack, was about four feet from the ground. He could see the bees coming and going and could hear their buzzing symphony inside. That was it. That was what he had been looking for. There were the mean-minded little doctors that could cure him, he thought. Old Pop returned to the tree the next morning, hauled off all of his clothes there in the silent woods and stark naked walked boldly up to the tree, and with a stick stirred up the busy bees. When he had them boiling mad he closed his eyes and stood in front of the opening. The snarling honey makers came out in clouds and went to work on him from his head to his heels.

I don't know how he managed to get dressed and crawl back to his cabin. But the thing that puzzles me most is how the poor old fellow lived. Every part of him was twice its natural size, and he suffered terribly for nearly a week.

The fool who told him to do it found him the next day sprawled flat on his back in his bed. Frightened stiff he and his partner took Pop's boat and rowed across the lake to my place. They said they thought Pop was dying and pleaded with me to go to his cabin as quickly as possible. I leaped into the canoe and standing in a crouch paddled as I never had paddled before. The old fellow was in bad shape. Both eyes were closed tight and his face and other parts of his body were badly swollen. His breathing was heavy and fast and he groaned with every breath. He appeared to be more dead than alive. After telling the boss fish peddler what I thought of him I told the pair of them to get to the nearest phone and get a doctor out there as soon as possible.

I made packs with all the soda I could find in the place and paddled back to my cabin to get what I had. Later in the day I paddled to the store for more of the soda. The doctor and the fish peddlers whom he had picked up on the way in arrived in a dust covered automobile shortly after dark. The doctor left medicine and told me to continue with the soda packs. He said he thought he would be all right but instructed me to phone him if the old man took a turn for the worse. I saw to it that fish peddler number one paid the doctor.

Pop hated that fellow after that and when he and his partner again called to buy pickerel the old man drove them away, and in no uncertain terms told them never to come back. I enjoyed that. I didn't like the looks of them in the first place and that dislike was inflated by the fact that they were enticing Pop to slaughter fish.

Pop was a tough old fellow and he recovered rapidly. And by midsummer daily bakings in the sun along with liniment rubdowns had taken quite a bit of fire out of his joints. He was feeling much better and was able to go after the pickerel with his long bamboo pole. He didn't kill so many because he had banished his best customers, but he always managed to find a few luckless fishermen who would buy those of unusual size. His awful experience with the bees remained fresh in his memory and he had a terrible fear of them the remainder of his days.

I developed a very strong love of Nature and lived close to it day and night. The woods, waters, and the creatures in them seemed to become closer to me and to fascinate me more and more. The sun that blazed its welcome in the east in the morning and bled to death in the west at night; the rainbow that bent colored bars across the sky; the clouds; the winds; the moon and the stars—all put their mark on me as the lumberman's ax would mark a pine. That was his. They were mine. Or perhaps I was theirs. But regardless of ownership I would have to live with them the remainder of my life. That was one of the very few things I was sure of.

Many times during the long summer Pop took care of my dogs and hens while I wandered back in the woods alone and, with scanty equipment and very little food and sometimes with none of either, lived close to all of those things for days at a time. Nature provided me with soft boughs to sleep on and shelter me when a shelter was needed. There were berries and apples in the clearings; trout, chubs, and fat frogs in the brooks; and cold, sweet water in fern shaded springs.

Cups and buckets were made from the bark of the white birch and spoons and forks from the branches of the maple. There was firewood to warm me, old pine knots for candles, cool brook pools to bath in, wild things to entertain me, and honeylike air was my sleeping potion. And I hasten to add here that if you've never sat naked on the sandy bottom of a cold, neck-deep pool on a woods brook when the summer day is blazing hot, you've really missed one of life's most pleasant sensations. It's a grand and glorious feeling.

Most of the stinging insects are gone by midsummer and it was very comfortable most of the time in the cool, green woods. After several such jaunts I thought seriously of going into them stark naked and, with nothing but my two hands and my knowledge of woodcraft, try to live off Nature for a week or maybe more. I didn't try it but I still believe I could have done it.

After the mating season in the spring, Waldo my skunk showed up at the cabin, but although just as friendly as ever he didn't stay around much. I'm sure he had a family and the responsibilities that go with one. I didn't envy him. I don't envy anyone who has responsibilities. They are like hard little hammers that crack you on the head every time you try to relax. But we all have a few of the hellish things.

Fly-fishing for bass and white perch was usually good that summer. I enjoyed many action-packed sessions on the lake and at Hammond and Tracy ponds. Ben Annis Pond was strictly a pickerel water, and the other two, George and Patten ponds, were too far away and too hard to get at for the few small pickerel and perch they had to offer. Ben Annis was alive with large pickerel, also giant yellow perch and sunfish. Sometimes I caught them among the white water lilies with a little Scarlet Ibez wet fly. They were delicious fried and in chowder.

Both Ben Annis and Tracy ponds, which were reached by poling a canoe up crooked little bog streams, were also the stamping grounds of many black ducks, bluebills, and both blue and greenwing teal, and large flocks of golden-eyes, or whistlers, as they are called in Maine, poured into them to rest and feed in the fall. Pop and I decided to build shooting blinds on the soggy shores of both of them but we never got around to it.

I saw a lot of wildlife on my jaunts during the spring and summer. Deer appeared to be more numerous and the fur bearers were everywhere. I saw a number of otters on the stream that curled into the lake. One day Pop and I saw a whole family of the handsome, seal-like creatures. The fur of the otter was very valuable and Pop suggested that we go after them that fall, and we planned to but, like building the duck blinds, we never got around to it.

Frost doesn't bother peas, and as my garden spot was high and dry early that spring, I planted my seeds about the middle of May. Spurred on by the hen-manure fertilizer they came fast and the lush and fiercely green plants were wearing white blossoms by early June. Pop had peas, too, but they were much later than mine. We had several good feeds of fresh green peas and brook trout. Green peas and salmon is the traditional late spring and early summer feast in Maine. It is particularly popular on the Fourth of July. But if we were to have salmon we would have to cast our flies on the wild waters of the Bangor Salmon Pool for a denizen from the sea or drag our lures on some far away lake for the landlocked variety. And then we couldn't be sure. So we substituted trout, which I caught on the lower Souadabscook and the woodland brooks. The plump, pink-fleshed beauties were a very good substitute, too. As a matter of fact I think I would rather have them. I would rather have sea smelts than either salmon or trout. They have a certain something found in no other species of fish. Also high on my list of food fish is the young smallmouthed black bass, skinned and fried immediately after catching.

Rolled in corn meal and fried very slowly with a strip of bacon in an uncovered pan, they are extremely delicious.

The ugly horn pout, or bullhead, as it is called in some parts of the country, is also a surprisingly excellent food fish. Those I caught at night in the depths of Tracy Pond were plump, pink fleshed, and very tasty. All fish, even the lowly sucker, if bled and dressed and cooked soon after catching, are good. I like all species of fish and believe that we would all be much better off from a health standpoint if we ate more of it.

Old Pop, who too was a fish eater, agreed with me and said that too much meat, especially red meat, is bad.

"If yer wants to keep yer blood pressure where it belongs and keep from gittin' a shock or kidney trouble, cut down on the meat and eat fish and vegetables!" he used to tell everybody.

I've always believed that if and when we are completely civilized we won't kill to eat, not even fishes, and, too, that there will be no wars.

I would like to see wars done away with, but I sure would miss the fish and meat. It would be pretty difficult if not absolutely impossible to beat broiled trout, a platter of crisply fried sea smelts, or a slab of broiled venison steak plastered with butter and smothered with onions. But I'm not worrying about it for it probably never will happen. At least not in my time. And speaking of venison, I saw twice as many deer as I did the first summer at the cabin. I hoped that when the hunting season came I would be able to bag the handsome buck I had seen several times in the dense woods along the upper Souadabscook.

I wasn't at all surprised when I received neither letters nor newspapers from home that summer. I was hurt, to be sure, but I could appreciate how my parents felt about the whole thing. I wished they could have appreciated how I felt. I don't think they even tried. This seeming unfairness of my father and mother fanned up fierce little flames of anger that burned to a cold ash the sorrow that gnawed at my heart during the frequent sessions of meditation—of thinking it over.

They were, I knew, still interested in my welfare. I knew, too, that the broken link in the family chain could be welded only at the hot forge of success—my success. At least enough of it to prove that I had found myself—that I had a definite and worthy goal, and was driving steadily toward it.

# 23

I MADE FRIENDS with several gray and red squirrels and a very handsome little chipmunk that summer. They came to the cabin for food every day. I would sit motionless and talk softly to them and after a time they would come scampering inside. The chipmunk would finally eat out of my hand.

When my frequent jaunts on the waters and through the woods took me to the head of the lake I always climbed to the top of the big wooded ridge where I could sit in wonderful silence and gaze out over the gorgeous panorama of woods, waters, mountains, meadows, and faraway farmlands. It fascinated me strangely. The huge, age-cracked boulders plastered with lichen, and the old weather-toughened stubs and stumps of the pines and spruces that cluttered the ridge also cast a spell over me. They possessed a weird kind of beauty all their own. I seemed to gain strength just by looking at them.

Above me, fat and fleecy cumulus clouds, looking like huge puffs of freshly washed wool, floated slowly across the bright blue meadows of the sky. I watched them dreamily day after day, through half-closed lids and wished, as the wind piled them into huge and creamy castles, that I could fly up to them and drift in their soft folds for the remainder of my life, or better still until the end of time that I might watch how other bewildered wanderers like myself made out in the brief but mixed-up journey to the grave and beyond.

One day I remained there and watched huge thunderheads building up for a storm. They bulged upward in great white billows for several miles and grew steadily darker. Finally towering majestically and forbidding into the heavens they released from their shadowed bowels deep growls of thunder. That warning of the thunder, the bully of the skies, was followed by a strong dry wind that swept dust, sand, and dead leaves before it. It attacked the trees and caused them to bow before it. And it swept down the flank of the ridge to maul the woods of the lowlands, the bogs, and the meadows and to make crazy water on the lake and the ponds. Lightning flashed and snapped like a great red whiplash and all hell broke loose. Cold rain smashed down in a blinding gray wall. I watched it from the rocky mouth of a small cave into which I had dashed for shelter. It was wild and crazy. Nature and the outdoors were at their worst yet I loved it—all of it; the roaring and crashing thunder that shook the ridge under me, the fierce red lightning that split the black sky, and the drenching rain that belched from its wide, hideous mouth.

And finally, almost as suddenly as it had begun, it was over. Nature's awe-inspiring demonstration of might had moved on to disturb and frighten those who lived away from her, and entertain those who like myself suckled at her great breast.

The outdoors had been washed. The sun dashed down through the clouds with her warm mops and I walked loose-legged down the ridge through the dripping trees feeling small and puny.

On the way back down the lake I ran into the fastest fly-fishing I had ever experienced. Thunderstorms usually frighten fish and send them to the depths where they remain for at least several hours. But apparently it didn't bother those perch. The small Grey Ghost streamer, which I was trolling on a short line, was suddenly snatched by an unusually large one as I entered a shaded cove on the west shore. That fish weighed three pounds and put up a rugged battle before he was boated. There was a large school of the big fellows in there feeding on shiners. They ranged in weight from a strong pound and a half to nearly three pounds. Never before had I caught such large perch in the lake. And while a rainbow bent its handsome body across the sky I fished with the smart rod and the little fly. I took the rugged scrappers until my arms ached. Every cast brought a boiling rise. And finally having my fill of the fun of catching and releasing the finned gamesters, I paddled slowly down the lake with three large ones for supper. The daily bag limit allowed me twenty-five of them. I never could understand what a man could do with that many fish. To me there is nothing more beautiful than an unusually large and well-proportioned specimen of game fish, nor is there anything more sickening, more disgusting than a boat load of the slimy things. And that includes trout and salmon. Yet there are many who call themselves sportsmen who strive for such slaughters.

Early that evening I walked with my dogs through my friend's yawning cornfield and up to the dusty little road. I kept them on their leashes for I didn't want them chasing the wild things out of season. I did unhitch them though when I saw a fat old woodchuck dash out of my garden. It was a furious race but the old chuck succeeded in reaching his nearby den in the nick of time.

The woodchucks gave me quite a bit of trouble in the garden during the days and the rabbits moved in for the night shift. They kept me and my dogs pretty busy. It was all a part of my fight to live. The destructive crows that I bagged in the cornfield were suspended on sticks here and there along the rows as a warning to others of the tribe coming down for a snack. The plan worked pretty well, but crows are bold thieves, and I had to shoot many others until the corn waved its green arms well above the ground.

I received a letter finally from the old fellow I had guided the summer before. It came in July. I had expected it much earlier in the summer and began to wonder if he had decided not to come to the lake or had passed away. I was a little worried, too, because I would need the money he paid me to buy my new stove and other things for my fight against the long cold winter.

I met him at the station a few days later. As usual he had too much equipment. It was heaped high on the platform at the station, and after carefully loading the old eighteen-foot canoe and wedging him in with a few extra boxes and bundles I had to paddle down the stream and across the lake to his camp with a heavily loaded pack basket strapped to my shoulders. That's the trouble of most fishermen and campers, they carry too much equipment. I had earned every penny he paid me the previous summer and my guess that I would have to work even harder that summer turned out to be correct.

I took him fishing from two to five times a week for the same pay I had received the year before. And I earned a few more dollars by working around his camp. I washed floors and walls, blacked and polished his stoves, sawed and split wood, patched screens, put out his boat slip, patched the roofing, repaired the chimney, and did a lot of other things I didn't know much about. But it's surprising what a man can do when he has to—when it means bread and butter and a few other things.

There was one job that I refused to do and the old guy got as mad as the proverbial hornet. That job was cleaning out the old outhouse. He finally hired Pop to do it. There is one job that makes me squirm all over. I just can't stomach it. I could clean out my own with less discomfort because I had placed a strong wooden box under the holes and attached a long and stout rope to it. When it was time to remove it I would go to the far end of the rope and haul the box far back into the woods and bury it. Then a new box, which was easily made of scrap boards, was put in its place. I used wood ashes after each visit to the place. But the job at the old fellow's place was too much for me. It was a shovel and wheelbarrow job. But Pop didn't seem to mind it. I guess he liked it better than he did his employer who in turn had no love for him either.

I sold quite a lot of live bait to fishermen who came out from Bangor and other towns, and picked up a few more dollars selling streamer flies that I had tied during the winter. And on those days the crabby old sport across the lake didn't want to go I was sometimes hired by other parties who sought fish on the lake and ponds.

My hens produced fairly well throughout the summer, and the eggs, most of which were sold strictly fresh to my regular employer, added more to my personal gold. He ate them boiled, fried, and scrambled, and he also used them in cooking. I figured that a good haul of fur in the fall would give me quite a little bank roll—all I would need. A person living as I was—where things such as fish, meat, fruit, vegetables, and some other foods, and most of the fuel needed were free—didn't need much money. As the grouchy old guy once said to me, "You're a king. A young and extremely fortunate and wealthy king, but you don't know it!" I guess maybe he was right.

One night when rain and wind lashed at the windows I read several old copies of sportsmen's magazines. I had browsed through them many times before but this time I read the feature stories and some of the departments very thoroughly.

After I had finished and lay resting on the couch I began to wonder if perhaps I could write something for one of those magazines that might be accepted and bring in a few more dollars. I continued to think about it long after I went to bed. I didn't know then nor will I ever know why I had that sudden urge to try my hand at writing. It came suddenly, like a summer shower, and clung to me like lichen to a stone. Before I realized it my feet were on the floor. It seemed that unseen hands had wiped the cobwebs of sleep from my eyes and lifted me gently from the bed.

I had no story to tell. At least I didn't think I had. Nor did I have photographs to illustrate one. I decided finally that I would write of the many interesting things I had learned about the wild things and others of Nature's creation. They interested me so why wouldn't they interest other people, I reasoned. Squaring off some sheets of cheap white paper I went to work with a pencil. The blaze in the fireplace flickered out and I was a bit chilly; and my fingers ached but I continued to write furiously—as though I had much to say and very little time to say it.

A drenched gray dawn tumbled in the windows to challenge the yellow flood of my lamp as I completed my literary brain storm. Twenty pages were loaded with little paragraphs. In bold strokes I lettered at the top of the first page, "Nature Snaps by Bill Geagan." I decided that the then flourishing *National Sportsman*, published in Boston, would get the big break.

Perhaps I decided on that one because it was nearer than the others. Or perhaps the same unseen hands that seemed to lift me from the bed, and that pressed me into action, had something to do with it. I felt like a puppet moving at the bidding of manipulated strings. A brief note told the editor how I dug up the interesting facts and how and where I was living. I mailed the stack of pages in a huge, homemade envelope that afternoon and paddled back to Green Point to sleep in the sun.

One afternoon two well-known Bangor sportsmen called at the cabin and informed me that my father had told them I would help with an experiment they were working on. They explained that they were sure the Ring-necked pheasant could be successfully introduced in Maine as a game bird and that they wanted to try it on a small scale in that area where somebody could keep an eye on the stock birds and make reports that would be mailed to them in Bangor. They said they would ship me any food the birds might need during the winter and would pay me three dollars a week for my trouble.

The experiment interested me and so did the three dollars a week. I accepted the job and walked down to the landing to look at the birds. The men had a flatbottom boat with an outboard motor attached and at the end of a stout rope behind was another boat on which rested two large flat crates of pheasants. There were two dozen in all, fifteen hens and nine roosters. They had hatched and raised the birds themselves, they explained, but those were only a part of the large number they had produced. They had released a greater number in a cover nearer Bangor, they said.

They were handsome young birds, especially the very gaudy males with their long tail feathers. We toted them about a half mile from the cabin and released them in what they agreed was excellent cover. They also agreed that foxes would probably get a few of them during the winter but they were confident that the survivors would reproduce the following spring and that in a few seasons that section would be quite heavily populated with strong wild birds capable of taking care of themselves.

I was instructed not to mention to anyone the fact that the pheasants had been liberated there for, as they explained, although they were primarily interested in establishing the pheasant as a game bird in the state, and believed they could in time obtain the co-operation of the Department of Inland Fisheries and Game, they also wanted to establish some immediate shooting grounds for themselves and their dogs. They figured that by fall the released birds would have become wary and would provide good sport. They planned to kill only three apiece in that cover and said that I could kill two for myself after they had bagged theirs. That was all right with me. It was something new and I was quite enthused.

I checked on the birds several times during the summer but they were quite widely scattered. And it seemed that foxes had snatched a few of them. Later I was convinced when I found small bones and two leg bands at the entrance of a den. I got my three dollars every week and I sent them reports according to our arrangement. When the bird season opened that fall I received a letter telling me to line up the pheasants for they were coming to hunt them in a couple of days.

I knew where the birds were and led the two sportsmen and their handsome English setters over frosted fields and through blazing October woods to the cover that bordered on a great swale. It was early morning when the classy canines began to cast and point and the twin-tube scatter-guns began to roar, and by midafternoon each hunter had his quota of three. That was all for them, they explained. I could bag my two any time I cared to. When I questioned them regarding a legal bag limit they said there wasn't any bag limit nor closed season either because the birds belonged to them. They were pleased and very enthusiastic and instructed me to keep a close watch over the birds during the winter and to bring as many through as possible. The money and the grain would be sent to me every week, they promised.

It seemed that the bombardment had scattered the surviving birds and driven them farther back in the woods and swales. It was almost impossible to get within shooting range of the very wild things without a dog. But I continued to try. And one day with the help of a light tracking snow I scored. It was a big, handsome, and very crafty old rooster. I flushed him several times and finally after hours of figuring, tracking, and matching wits with the old boy I put him up in a stand of little snow-mantled firs. He roared up with a squawk less than fifty feet ahead of me, but he lost no time in stretching that distance. The twenty-gauge double gun covered him in mid-air and wobbled him with a charge of number 6 pellets. The second shot brought him down. I felt kind of sorry for the poor thing when I saw him sprawled in the snow.

I shared it stuffed and roasted with Pop and saved the feathers for tying more fishing flies. The big bird made a delicious meal and I decided to go after my second one very soon, but I never did. I did feed the starving few I could locate and it wasn't long before they, too, vanished and with them went the experiment and the three dollars a week.

But getting back to the summer and the nature notes I had submitted to the Boston magazine, I received a reply from the good editor two weeks later, and lo and behold a check for ten dollars. I also received about half of the copy I had sent to him along with a note explaining that although the material was "very interesting" he was using only the best of it because of a lack of space. He also explained that what he wanted most were stories about fishing and hunting experiences and with pictures if possible. "Surely, a fellow like you living out there in the woods alone must have a good story in him somewhere," he concluded.

Perhaps there was a good story in me but I wasn't writer enough to know it. But I did want to write one. I wanted to write one more than anything else in the world. Interest in everything else seemed to have vanished like dew before the sun. It seemed those same ghostly hands were again shoving me forward.

One cool morning before the sun had come up I sat silently in the canoe at the foot of a large quiet pool far up the stream. The water was like black glass and the trees, crowding down to it as if to watch me, cast their leafy beauty in its depths.

Lovely white water lilies were yawning and beginning to open after the long night of sleeping, and a fat frog burped in the pickerel weed. That deep and silent bulge in the stream held a huge, wary, and very powerful old bass who knew all the tricks. He was one of the smartest things wearing fins I had ever encountered. He had to be to live so long. I had battled with him on two occasions but each time came out on the short end with damaged equipment. And perhaps others had too. A third attempt to capture him a few days before was a complete failure. I couldn't even raise him. But I was ready to try again and with all the tricks I possessed. I wore dark clothes and took my stand in the canoe against a dark background of firs and spruces. The equipment consisted of the five-ounce fly rod, a tapered HDH amber-colored line well greased, and eight feet of tapered leader. My lure for the first attempt of the morning was a small cork stopper into which was secured a strong and sharp hook. The rig was decorated with chicken feather wings, and a tail of white deer hair. I had used streamer flies on the old warrior on previous visits to the pool but the last time none of the many patterns in the book could raise him.

I thought that perhaps the little plug being something new might do the trick. Carefully scanning the pool and the woods behind me that I might not hang up a back cast, I was ready. One sloppy cast would ruin my chances. I had to make it good and with all the skill at my command I put the smart little rod into action and the funny looking homemade plug floated out fifty feet over the slick water of the yawning pool. A couple of feet of line were stripped in and the lure alighted softly in the cool, black shadow of a huge water-killed maple stub that rose four feet above the surface.

That's where I had always found him. It was a perfect cast. Slight twitches of the rod tip now and then caused the plug to struggle a bit—like a winged insect that had fallen onto the water and was trying to rise. Nothing happened but I knew he must be watching it closely from his lair down in the roots of that old tree stub. Again the plug wiggled and again it failed. I took it in and hauled on my pipe. Ten minutes later another careful cast placed the plug at the desired spot. I twitched it in fast little spurts toward the middle of the pool. Then suddenly it rested and just as suddenly it started to wiggle and sprint again, this time down the pool toward the canoe. It seemed hopeless and I was about to strip in the line when the middle of that pool exploded as though a case of dynamite had been touched off. His highness, the old warrior of the stream, was mad clear through. The lure vanished, the hook was quickly set and the battle was on.

I handled him carefully and with a light hand. Keeping him away from the stub roots, sharp rocks, and out of the lilies and pads was a real test. The big gamester was in the air almost as much as he was in the water. His numerous leaps were high and spectacular. I was thrilled to the marrow. Each time he went up he would shake his big head violently as he tried to throw the plug and its stinging hook.

He even surged straight away upstream on the surface kicking up a frothy wake and looking like a speedboat with bow high. And quickly reversing his field he came dashing back toward the canoe in an effort to gain slack line and shake out the plug with a sudden leap.

He bored into the depths, too, to sound, yank, and sulk. He tried desperately to get into the cluttered shallows to snag the line. It wasn't easy holding him out with the light gear. But finally after a strong half hour the great strength of a great fish could no longer support his magnificent courage and a tired and trembling hand slipped the landing net under the exhausted bronze body. He was a whopper and a beauty as smallmouths go. The pocket scales gave his weight at a little better than six pounds. That's a lot of smallmouthed black bass.

I sat sweating and trembling and admired my gasping victim. He never left the net until after a few minutes when it was slipped back into the water and he was permitted to fan out and go home. It was his life and my fun that we had fought for. He gave me what I wanted and I gave him what he wanted. We were all even and I paddled slowly away.

# 24

THERE'S SOMETHING about scoring a victory that stimulates and inspires me. Even a victory over a wise old fish like that big bass of the stream. It's like dry cedar to a dying fire, or salt to food that is flat. I fought that battle over and over for days; from the cast that raised him to the netting and his release. It gave me much pleasure and great satisfaction. I had planned that last attempt very carefully and I had followed those plans closely. I didn't make a single mistake. Just one, the slightest one, would have meant another failure. It wasn't a great or important victory to be sure, but it was a victory nevertheless. A man needs to win once in a while, if only over a fish, a spike that won't drive straight, or a chunk of knotted wood that refuses to split. Such little conquests are good for his mind and his soul.

Another bass of about two pounds was the principal item on my breakfast menu that same morning. He didn't of course weigh two pounds when dressed and laid in the pan, but the thick white meat was plenty along with the bacon, fried potatoes, dark bread toasted on a flat stone, a doughnut, and stout red tea. This morning meal was prepared and devoured on Green Point in the fragrant wind and golden sunlight. And as I ate I watched the birds, squirrels, muskrats, and fish as they ate too. They were all about me. I felt more strongly than ever that I was a member of their strange and wonderful world and that they were all my friends—friends that I hoped I never would lose.

Clean sand and water heated in the tea pail scoured and washed the cooking and eating tins. They were placed on a huge stone to dry and sweeten in the sun while I slept heavily under the oaks. I awoke about an hour later to find a curious little chipmunk looking me over from a nearby spruce bough, and another inspecting the tins on the rock. Juicy raspberries were numerous on nearby bushes and with no effort at all I filled a pint dipper and ate them. Off to the west, over the towering old ridge I loved, a thunderstorm was brewing, and piling into the canoe I was away on a fast paddle down the lake to the cabin.

It was a thrilling race with that storm. I really enjoyed it. It broke in all its fury just as I beached the canoe. That was my second victory of the day. I dashed for the cabin, slammed the door, and shut out the rain. It was quite chilly and like night outside. A lamp was lit and a brisk blaze started in the fireplace. Lounging before it I read again and again the letter from the magazine editor. That last sentence, "Surely a fellow like you living out there in the woods alone must have a good story in him somewhere," crawled about in my mind the remainder of the day. That night as I washed the supper dishes I decided that I did have a good story in me—the story about the big bass.

More paper was squared off and more pencils were sharpened, and I went at it. I told of the occasions when I had tangled with the old warrior and of how his tricks and great strength enabled him to escape, and of how I finally conquered, captured, and released him. It was a fast story packed with action and description.

I knew nothing about writing. I wrote it as I would have written a letter to a friend, or to my parents in those days when they cared about hearing from me. It contained about two thousand words. The following day was devoted to making three pen and ink drawings to illustrate the yarn. I was pleased with the whole thing but I doubted that the editor would be. A brief note was inserted and away went the package on the night train.

Ten days later I was just about the happiest person on earth when I ripped open a long envelope to find a letter from the editor telling me that he liked the story and the illustrations and that he was paying me twenty dollars. And there was the long yellow check attached to the back of the letter. I think I kissed that check. He said the only part of the entire story he was changing was the title. I didn't care. As a matter of fact I didn't remember what it was. The story, he said, would appear in the magazine the next issue. And he invited me to try again sometime.

Never before or since have I experienced such a feeling, such a wonderful sensation, such overwhelming joy. It was as though I had been bathed in cool dew and was floating naked on a high cloud that was fleecy and fat. I wanted to scramble to the top of the ridge, stand on the highest boulder, and scream my happiness to the sky and the winds. I didn't though. Suddenly I didn't have the strength.

Instead I slumped down in the tall cool grass and thanked God.

I turned to God many times during those two bewildering years out there alone. And I got the help I asked for in accomplishment and that greatest thing a man can know, peace of mind. He never failed me, and I never forgot to thank Him.

I felt always that He was close by me as I roamed the woods, and fought the wind and waves. I was never afraid. I pity the man who doesn't believe in God. To such a fool everything ends at the grave—there is no hereafter—no better life. If that were so then there would be no reason for trying to be decent and kind on this very short earthly journey. We might as well stone the churches and the good men who are supposed to represent Him on earth and go on to reap the pleasures and profits of a scoundrel.

But like a storm cloud suddenly blotting out the sun came a bit of bad news on the heels of the good. It was a letter from the tax collector in the town of Hampden informing me that taxes at the rate of five dollars a year on the cabin hadn't been paid for five years. A bill was inclosed. I owed for one year and the man I bought the place from owed for four years. He didn't mention that to me. Perhaps it slipped his mind. Anyhow the little place was still a bargain. So into a large envelope went twenty-five dollars to cover the back taxes and five more dollars for the next year. That put me in good standing, and a bit ahead of the game with the town of Hampden but pretty well behind financially. Fortunately I didn't need much money to live. There was no rent to pay, and most everything else I needed was mine for the taking.

The old actor and sportsman was both surprised and pleased when I told him of selling the pieces to the *National Sportsman*. He wasn't half as surprised and pleased as I was and I crouched on the proverbial pins and needles until I saw them in print with my name on them. Finally a copy came in the mail. Both were in the same issue. The nature bits were carried in a long bold face box with my name in heavy type over the top. The story on the big bass occupied a top spot up front. I read those pieces over and over and studied every detail of my pen and ink illustrations. I was extremely happy and, as might be expected, a little proud.

The old fellow told me what little he knew about writing and writers and urged me to stick to it. He said that perhaps if I teamed up the writing and the drawing with my knowledge of the outdoors I might plant the seed for a pleasant and profitable career.

"Everything has to start, son, even an ugly cabbage or a majestic pine," he explained.

My third literary attempt, which also was illustrated with pen and ink sketches, was a story on skittering for pickerel with cut bait and the long pole. It was about a trip I took with Pop who was a master at wiggling the big stick. That, too, was shipped to the Boston magazine and like the others was accepted and I received another check for twenty dollars. I was wild with joy. I had found a little gold mine it seemed. But that balloon of happiness was soon deflated when the next story, a good one I thought, on brook trout fishing, was returned to me.

"Not suitable to our present needs," was the editor's only comment. That story was later sold to another sportsmen's magazine. And I continued to play at the fascinating but sometimes discouraging game of shooting at a target in the dark. I scored a few times but the misses were many. But those I did sell were bringing more money—quite a bit more.

*Nature I Loved*

I tried out a few short nature stories with drawings on the *Daily Commercial*, Bangor's evening newspaper, and all were bought but at a very low rate. It wasn't long before I found myself with quite a few clippings in a homemade scrapbook, a neat little bundle of money and a wild desire to continue at that sort of work.

And finally my sudden although small success as a writer and artist melted my parents' cocoon of ice, and I received a long letter from my father. It was the first in many months. He said that he and my mother were pleased to see that I was at least trying to do something and that the stories and sketches they had seen in the magazines and the local paper were very good. But, he went on to dash cold water on my happiness and enthusiasm by saying that they hoped I wouldn't "play around with such nonsense too long," and that I would soon "stop my foolishness and come back to the city and get a nice steady job."

That letter maddened me to the core and made me more determined than ever to continue with my way of life until I could decide on a better one. I hadn't made much progress but I was confident that I would in time work out something by which I could earn a pleasant and substantial living.

I have always felt that a man can't be much of a success working at something he dislikes. Although it was of the hit or miss, hand to mouth variety, and although I was terribly lonesome at times, my life out there in the woods wasn't too bad. Anyhow my mind was set on sticking to it a while longer and I told my father so in a long letter. I wanted more than anything else in the world to prove to my parents that I was right, which would in turn prove that they were wrong.

I continued writing stories on hunting and fishing, also bits on the family doings of the animals, birds, and fish

253

that I shipped to the magazines and a few newspapers, including a few of the latter in Boston and New York. I sold a few but most of them landed back in my lap with little or no comment. A couple of magazine editors told me my copy must be typed and one of them said that he liked a particular story I had submitted and that if I typed it and made a few changes here and there and sent two photographs along with the pen and ink sketches he would pay me twenty-five dollars for it. Other editors—even the editor of the *National Sportsman* magazine—finally told me that I must type my copy and have good clear photographs along with my drawings to tie in with the stories.

I had neither a typewriter nor a camera but I was determined to get both and with the help of my good friend the station agent I soon acquired the former. It was an old-timer that had been used by a bookkeeper. I bought it for ten dollars and that was all it was worth. The carriage on the thing was the longest I have ever seen. It was forever banging into the wall or the window and once crashed into the lamp chimney and smashed it. It was a rather dangerous old thing. If I had been using it near an open window on a city street where people were walking past I would have been compelled to tie a red rag on the long carriage during the day and a lighted lantern on it at night so I wouldn't knock somebody's brains out.

I used the search system in my typing. I would search all over the keyboard, which seemed almost as big as one side of the cabin roof, and after a time locate the letter I wanted. It took me quite a while sometimes. But when I finally did find it, believe me it was really found! Then with my tongue sticking out of the side of my mouth and one eye squinted as though sighting a rifle, I would take a deadly aim and with the second finger on the right hand I'd come down on it with everything I had. And the finished product was much more than just a letter in ink. Oh, yes indeed, it was an engraving.

After a time I was able to operate the relic a little better and could use two fingers. My struggles with it sounded like an ostrich with eye trouble pecking at corn scattered on a tin platter. I called the thing the iron monster.

The camera, a cheap box affair, came next. I bought it from a mail-order house in New York. I didn't know much more about taking pictures than I did about operating a typewriter. But by following the instructions very carefully I was able to get some fairly good shots. I took pictures of birds and animals, the fishing spots, and the fish. Pop and the old fellow I was guiding took shots of me, and I wrote another story about fishing with Pop and took a few snaps of him in action with his long bamboo pickerel pole.

The negatives on the roll were about four inches deep and about two and a half inches wide. I used to send the whole roll along with the story and the editors would select and print the pictures they wanted. Most of them were pretty bad but the retouchers sharpened them up and they looked fairly good when printed. Most of the few magazine stories I was able to sell carried the following credit line under the title: "Photos and drawings by the author." The author—me—Mrs. Geagan's male child, an author. I couldn't believe it. God and the editors were good. I wasn't and I knew it.

I never got more than twenty-five dollars for a story in those days. Usually I got a lot less. But at the time it seemed like a lot of money. I had never made a dollar any easier but I still was pretty crude as a writer and had no dreams of following it as a career. But every once in a while the words of the old man would creep into my mind, "Everything has to start, son, even a lowly cabbage or a majestic pine."

My garden was quite beautiful with its lush green plants marching in straight lines along the rich brown soil. I had won another stiff battle against the weeds, the bugs, and the little forest creatures. It is difficult to understand how one tiny withered seed can produce a lovely green plant that in turn produces food for him who plants it. You can trust a seed, as small and insignificant as it might be. A seed is honest. What a pity we can't say the same for all men. But unfortunately the world and life are like that. And I have noticed as I travel along life's rocky trail that the things that are really great, like the seed, the sun, the tides, and the rain, perform their miracles in silence. Each has a big job to do and does it quietly and well, while the thunder, which shakes the earth and the drowned valleys of the sea, and kindles the fires of fear in the hearts of most living things, is but a boisterous good-for-nothing. Some people are like that, too. And, too, we learn, if we will but pause to look as we plod along, that after all it's the little things, like the seed, that make the big things we know so well.

I devoted much time to thinking along those lines— sometimes until it confused me, but it never failed to bring a strange sort of comfort and the encouragement I needed to continue my search for a way out of the forest of confusion in which I floundered.

Much of that sort of thinking, of being a realist, and of delving deeply into the farce called life, was done while quietly casting flies from my canoe in the languid lily coves. I was enjoying very good bass fishing one blushing morning in late August when the wonderful singing silence of the outdoors was suddenly broken by the chatter and laughter of girls. Turning I saw two boatloads of them coming down the lake. The two at the oars were older than the others and they knew little about rowing. I noticed that instead of feathering the oars along the water they lifted them high each time and brought them down with a heavy chop. There were twelve in the party, which I guessed came from some nearby town for a picnic. I learned later that my guess was wrong. I learned a lot of other things, too—things that changed my plans and my entire life.

I watched them as they splashed their way toward Green Point. They landed and unloaded what seemed like a tremendous amount of equipment for a picnic party. I watched them drag it back into the fierce green of the woods, and with a fat bass for dinner I paddled slowly back to camp and forgot them.

That night was beautiful. A full moon of unblemished brass pushed its bloated face over the pointed firs to the east. I love moonlit nights, so with my two faithful hounds for company I paddled up the lake to the store for groceries. Curiosity caused me to go out of my way, across the lake and past the point where the girls had a roaring fire. I heard them singing, and resting on the paddle well out beyond the light of their crackling shore fire, which was much too big, I watched them as they roasted frankfurters and marshmallows on long, pointed sticks.

They sang well as a group, such old songs as, "My Old Kentucky Home," "Sweet Adeline," and a few others. I listened for a while; then, hearing my dog Jack whimpering and fearing he would join in with his deep yodeling as he had many times before when people were singing, I dipped deep and moved on into the warm blue plush of the late summer night.

I learned at the store that the singing females on the point were girls from Orono, a little town about eight miles up the Penobscot River from Bangor. They were Campfire Girls, the man told me, and the two women were counselors.

While paddling past the point with the old actor early the next morning I saw, back in the woods, a couple of large sagging tents under the oaks. One of the counselors and several of the girls were dashing about a very smoky breakfast fire. The other counselor and several more of the girls were fishing with hand lines and worms from the two boats that were anchored a very short distance off the point. It appeared they weren't enjoying much success.

When I mentioned it to him and expressed a desire to give them a little advice, he broke into a lukewarm rage. "I'm paying you to help me not them. What's a bunch of women doing in the woods anyhow? It's no place for them, absolutely no place for them. Let them go back home to their brooms and sewing baskets!" he growled.

He made me pretty mad but I held my tongue for fear of angering him to the point of firing me, for I did need the money he was paying me for guiding him about in the woods and on the waters. And he had planned to stay through the month of September, he said.

As we passed the boats, the woman in charge cupped her hands at her mouth and asked us if there were any fish in the lake. She explained that they were trying to catch some for breakfast but up to then they hadn't had so much as a nibble. They all laughed. I laughed too but the old grouch didn't crack a smile. I told the woman there were plenty of fish in the lake and advised her to move farther out and anchor in deeper water. My hateful employer motioned for me to bear down on the paddle, which I did, and we glided in silence up the lake to the stream to cast little plugs for bass.

We enjoyed fast fishing and released all but two, which he ordered me to kill and dress. He later had a lively session casting a large red and white streamer for pickerel near a great weed bed at the head of the lake. He ate very little of the lunch I prepared on the shore and explained that his stomach had been bothering him for a couple of days. He ordered me to take him back to his camp where he planned to take some medicine and lie down.

Nothing could have pleased me more and after unloading him and promising to look in on him the next morning I paddled back to the point where the girls were camped. The boats had been beached and the place was very quiet. Then suddenly the counselor with whom I had talked that morning came down to the shore and dipped a pail of water. I hauled in the paddle and asked if they caught any fish. I was informed that they had not and that they were very disappointed and, too, that she didn't believe there was a fish in the whole lake. She seemed quite peeved.

"Can you fix a fireplace, young man?" she asked in a voice that snapped like a whiplash.

"What kind of a fireplace?" I inquired politely as I paddled very slowly nearer the rocky shore.

"Come on up. Follow me," she snapped.

I was as shy as a country bumpkin in the presence of all those females and they knew it. The camp consisted of the two large tents that hung loose and sloppy on their poles, a canvas fly over the long eating table made of poles that sloped badly, and a sad looking fireplace.

Turnip-sized rocks rimmed the spot, and two spindly alder limbs with crotched tops that were supposed to support a cross pole and the cooking pots had collapsed dumping the pots, food, and water into the fire and putting it out. That was the third time, the woman told me.

"I'll try to fix it," I mumbled softly, and hurried into the woods where with the dull and badly nicked camp ax I worried down two young maples about four inches in diameter at the butt and whacked them off where stout limbs formed crotches. They were four feet tall when ready to go into the ground. Another length of maple about three inches through was cut for a crossbar on which to hang the pots. A fourth length was cut and sharpened on one end for drilling holes into which to set the uprights, the bases of which were banked with rocks. As I worked there on my knees arranging the stones around the fire spot so there would be a good draught, I could hear the girls talking and giggling. All around me I saw their feet. Some wore sneakers while others wore low cut moccasins. I noticed one pair in particular. They were made of moosehide in the natural color. The girl that wore them was standing very near and directly in front of me. Slowly and slyly my eyes climbed up her legs, stumbled a bit on dimpled knees and stopped at a pair of khaki trunks. I couldn't look any higher without lifting my head, and I didn't want her or any of the others to know I was stealing a peek.

They were the most beautiful legs I had ever seen anywhere—at the beaches or in shows that feature that part of the female anatomy. Nothing I saw at art school could touch them either. They were well shaped, strong looking, and as brown as the summer rabbit. Completing my job I arose slowly and looked straight at the girl who owned them. As I had thought and, I guess, hoped a little too, she was equally pretty.

She wore a white, short-sleeved jersey, striped with blue. She was strong and wholesome looking. I liked particularly her round brown face with darker-brown eyes, generous red lips, and heavy dark-brown hair that shone in the sunlight. It was parted in the middle and neatly worked into a long and thick pug at the back of her neck. It seemed I had seen her many times before yet I knew I hadn't. Perhaps I had seen such a girl in my dreams or had carried her down deep in my subconscious mind.

My glance became a stare and she smiled showing handsome white teeth, as the counselor remarked, "I guess our shy young friend likes the looks of you, Alice."

The other girls laughed but Alice didn't. I guess she pitied me, or was too polite to laugh. They laughed again when after quickly whittling out a few pot hooks for the fireplace I tried to make a hurried and graceful exit but tripped over a tree root and went into a floundering fall. But I don't think she laughed. I was equally clumsy piling into the canoe and with a face still hot and blazing red I paddled slowly back to the cabin with her, Alice, burned deeply in my mind.

# 25

I USED every excuse I could think of to visit the girls' camp. And after a few visits I was accepted as a friend by the two counselors. By that time I wasn't known as the young hermit down the lake, but the young writer and artist at the little cabin in the cove. I heard it quite often and I liked it. My efforts at the typewriter and the drawing board were bringing me a reputation if not a lot of money. A man's success is magnified by the eyes of others. It will always be so.

My time was then devoted to peddling stories and pictures to the magazine and newspapers, guiding, and hanging around the girls' camp. I didn't like the two women in charge nor did I care a whoop for any of the girls but Alice. There were some other pretty girls that might have appealed to other young men, but most of them were terribly plain. A man sees a woman at her worst under those conditions. But Alice somehow was different. She didn't need to primp and powder—to fuss with her hair and face. She was the attraction at the camp. I would have gone out of my way to avoid the place if it hadn't been for her. She attracted me like the cold water of a brook spring attracts a trout in midsummer.

I did considerable work around the camp, which included tightening the sagging tents, rebuilding bough beds, fixing the crooked table, and building a long log slip out into the lake so that it wouldn't be necessary to haul the two heavy boats ashore over the rocks. I supplied the camp with plenty of fish, too, and showed the two counselors a much larger and better spring of drinking water right under their noses. I guided the whole gang to clearings across the lake where wild blueberries grew in abundance, paddled to the store for supplies, split wood, sat in on nature talks, and did many other little things to help. By that time I was getting used to the strange sweet odor of cold cream and talcum powder.

I accepted the criticism of Pop and my so-called sport with a grin. I didn't tell them why I was helping out at the camp of the females. I figured it was none of their business. After all, they were too old to understand although no doubt they, too, had known and liked girls in their youth. I never asked them about such things. I wasn't interested in their past.

After a few days around the camp I was taking a couple of girls at a time in my canoe for instructions in paddling, and finally I managed to get Alice out alone. I guess the women in charge trusted me. Or perhaps after looking me over carefully they figured that I was just a simple fellow who could do no harm. When I mentioned it to Alice she told me that the counselors did trust me and liked me, but she added that it wouldn't have made any difference anyway because although the rules were quite strict, she was old enough to select her own company and was leaving the organization after the group returned home. She had a job in Bangor, she said.

I never tried so hard in my life to make an impression. I didn't go in for rock throwing, tree climbing, or weight lifting, but I did just about everything else I could think of.

Although I saw her only occasionally during the two weeks the girls were camped on the point I shaved every day just in case I happened to meet her. In addition to keeping shaved and bathed I also wore the best clothes I had. They weren't much but they were clean and fit me well. I had a pair of gray wool sportsmen's trousers. Sometimes I wore a white, short-sleeved jersey, and so she wouldn't think that's all I had I shifted occasionally to khaki pants and plaid and checked sportsmen's shirts. Low moccasins and short, white wool socks, and a little gray hat decorated with fishing flies completed my raiment.

It required a lot of water, a bit of vaseline, and a thorough combing to keep my heavy thatch from looking like a haystack in the wind. When I told Alice I was going to try to find somebody who could give me a decent haircut she protested strongly. I was surprised. She said she liked it that way.

"It gives you a sort of mysterious and dignified look. With your very tan skin it makes you look like a young Indian guide," she exclaimed.

That mysterious and dignified stuff got me. And I always admired Indians. She couldn't have pleased me more if she had planned her flattery. Perhaps she did. But anyhow I liked it. When she could get away from camp after the nature studies and other duties were done I would be waiting for her in the lee of the point in the old canoe. She enjoyed canoeing and I enjoyed showing her how good I was, or how good I thought I was, on the paddle.

We went to the best fishing spots and I showed her how to take the big ones on the fly. She liked that. As a matter of fact she liked everything including searching for Indian relics along the shores of the lake and the stream. We spent a lot of time studying wildlife, trees, plants, clouds, etc. She said I showed her more about Nature in a day than she had learned in all the time she was a Campfire Girl. She was probably exaggerating to please me. But I liked it, anyhow.

One day we feasted on freshly caught bass, broiled on the shore. We selected a spot where lush ferns crowded around a deep, cold spring and where the sun spilled its warm gold down through the white birches. Alice said it was "a feast for the Gods."

While we were stuffing ourselves with the sweet flesh of the bass, my biscuits, potatoes roasted in the coals, juicy wild blackberries, fragrant red tea, and doughnuts, Alice looked up to see a deer watching us. It was the large buck I had seen several times before and that I hoped to bag with the coming of the fall. I hated to think of fall. The loveliest girl I had ever known would be gone with the leaves, the birds, and the long golden days of summer. Only memories and a gnawing loneliness would remain. It would have been better, perhaps, if I hadn't met her—if the little group hadn't come to camp on Green Point.

We made the most of those golden hours. It was all so wonderful—a girl and a boy enjoying God's great outdoors and living close to Nature and each other, yet clean and good. Then suddenly, as all things must, it ended. I couldn't realize it. It was as though the sun had been taken from the day—the moon and stars from the night. Summer was gasping its last, and already samples of autumn's artistry were visible on the sugar maples. Some of the birds had departed. The other winged migrants would soon follow. Then the trees would undress and stand naked and shivering while waiting for winter to spread its great white blanket. It was a sickening realization. The awful loneliness I knew would come arrived on schedule. It was armed with unusually long and pointed barbs. The days were empty, like a hazelnut in which bugs have feasted, and the upper part of my body felt the same. The nights, thank God, brought relief in sound sleep.

Although I knew my loneliness would become more intense I made occasional visits to Green Point where the girls had camped. Nothing remained save the smoke-blackened stones and crotched uprights of the fireplace, the old table and the faded squares of dead vegetation, and withering fir bough beds where the tents had stood. Sweet little memories, all carrying little spears, wandered over the place. I was living in a bit of hell that was hidden in the heart of heaven.

Finally the old fellow whom I guided packed up and went away. And the white water lilies rotted and died. The eager fingers of the wind teamed up with the frost to start the harvest of the lovely leaves, and the golden blond heads of the goldenrod were showing streaks of dirty gray.

The cricket symphony was loud in the clearings and a few of the little black musicians came to my hearth. The candles of the sumac were crimson on the altar of the outdoors and the mornings wore robes of fragrant frost. There were other signs of the approach of another winter all about me. I was soon to be alone again with only old Pop and my dogs and my wild year-round neighbors of the woods.

And finally came the letter that Alice had promised the day she left. The day of grouse hunting that we had planned together still interested her, she said. She would arrive on the early morning train the following Saturday. My misery melted like a brick of butter in the sun of a July noon. The days were eagerly counted and checked off on the kitchen calendar. I prowled the woods and located several flocks of grouse. I would be ready when she came. I wanted her to have good shooting. While waiting I also sold my old hens and bought a flock of ten young ones which I was told would be laying by November and would produce steadily throughout the winter. And I ordered the large ram-down stove I would need for the cabin during the winter. Instead of buying it from the mail-order house I took the advice of the station agent and bought it from a foundry in Bangor. I also dashed out a story on autumn bass fishing and mailed it with photographs and a few drawings to the *National Sportsman*. All this kept me busy—kept my mind off Alice—and finally the days passed and she came as she said she would.

She looked wonderful in the neat hunting outfit I had advised her to buy. The dawn was deep blue and cold as she stepped off the lighted train that morning. And the ride down the steaming lake in the old canoe wasn't pleasant, even for me in constant motion on the paddle, but neither of us complained. We talked and laughed and shouted "Good morning" to the muskrats swimming along the shore shallows, and the fat black ducks we flushed at every bend.

The sun came up to blush with us as Alice prepared the breakfast of bacon and eggs. I watched her every move. She was quick, neat, and capable, and once again that lovely odor of a dainty woman crept into my nostrils. We talked over our hunting plans and were off down the trail to find patches of light frost nestling in the laps of purple shadows. The woods were ablaze with color that dripped from the trees when the morning wind hurried through them.

Alice carried my single barrel 20-gauge and I toted the little 20-double. Although I am right handed I shoot from the left shoulder for some reason or other. With Alice shooting from the right shoulder we teamed up well as a shoulder-to-shoulder road-hunting pair. The birds were quite numerous along the old roads at those places where I had located flocks. They were breakfasting on green clover and defrosting their frames in the warm sunshine. Alice was to have the first crack at the birds while they were on the ground and I was to try to bag those she missed after they were in the air.

She went almost wild with joy and excitement when she finally toppled her first feeding bird. She missed many more shots but managed to bag another fat one before lunchtime. We rested by a spring on the bank of a brook. The water was fiercely blue and on the smooth places of the little woodland ribbon we watched curled leaves floating along like little ships under full sail. The smoke of our little cooking fire brought curious chickadees and blathering red squirrels that entertained us while we ate.

So high was her enthusiasm over the pursuit of the birds she could hardly take time out for lunch. The grouse were back in the woods in the afternoon and she got very few shots and no birds. I prowled through the dense covers and managed to bag two on the wing. And soon the pretty little afternoon was old and shadows wearing cold purple robes crawled out of the woods onto the roads. And with them came the grouse for the evening meal. Alice got in three shots and bagged one bird. It was good enough for a girl on her first jaunt. The chilly autumn dusk was settling when we reached the cabin, Alice with three birds and me with two.

She left with the five grouse on the night train after making me promise that we would hunt again the following

Saturday. That was easy. We did and again enjoyed good sport. My autumn bass story rang the bell with the Boston magazine and I received a check for twenty-five dollars and a request for a piece on duck hunting. Alice hunted with me once more that fall. Black ducks were our quarry and we sought them along the upper reaches of the winding stream that curled into the lake. She killed only one just as it left the water. I managed to bag another as it bulleted away straight up, above my head.

She came once more, this time to hunt foxes ahead of the hounds but because of her work was unable to visit me during the winter for the pickerel fishing we had planned.

And I was alone and lonely again and sought relief in harvesting wood for my fires and writing stories. I had several in the mail to magazines and newspapers most of the time. Those that some editors turned down would be accepted by others. It was hard work and my postage bill was high but it was fascinating and quite profitable. I did my best writing and drawing at night—especially on those nights when a storm snarled and howled around the little cabin. It was much more comfortable in the little place with the larger stove. One night I turned out a short piece on Waldo my skunk whom I seldom saw any more and sold it with sketches to a Nature magazine. I was paid very well for it and the editor said he would like to see more pieces along the same line.

I didn't trap that fall and winter, and hunted and fished only for food. And the big buck I had seen up the stream during the summer was finally bagged but it took a week of steady hunting, all the tricks I knew, and a great big dose of luck to get him. And I hunted with the benefit of a light tracking snow the last three days too. I didn't have a chance on bare ground. Like the wise old bass I finally took on the stream, the big buck was extremely crafty. I saw him several times but never where I could get a good shot at him. It seemed he knew I was out to get him and he was always on the alert and outguessing me at every turn.

Twice he waited until I was almost on top of him before bolting away from his hiding place in a thicket. And I saw him watching me from a knoll one morning but too far away for a shot with the rising sun blazing in my eyes. The first day I picked up his trail on the light snow he must have heard me stalking along and quickened his pace to increase his lead. I could tell by his tracks that he was hurrying. When he got far enough ahead the wise old fellow circled back and watched me pass by. I almost leaped out of my skin when after looking me over he snorted and went crashing away through the brush.

Like all wild animals he was curious and wanted to know whether the creature that was pursuing him was a bobcat, a bear, or a man. It became increasingly difficult to get within shooting range of the big fellow and I decided to give up the chase and try for one of the smaller deer I had seen.

It was old Pop who changed my mind.

"Don't give up now, son!" he spouted. "You've got plenty of time en yer young en stronger en hell. Stick with him a while longer. He'll make a mistake one of these days as smart as he is. They allus do!"

Two days later he made that mistake. I hadn't been pressing him so hard and becoming careless he came out of the dense woods, in which he always traveled, into the open. I was resting on a knoll overlooking a brushy clearing where several wild apple trees stood. I held my breath and listened to my heart pound as I watched him walking slowly out of the woods. He was the handsomest deer I had ever seen, along with being one of the largest and smartest.

He walked majestically up to the nearest apple tree and began feeding on the half-frozen fruit on the ground. I couldn't believe it. There he stood broadside less than a hundred yards away. Sweat beads bulged on my forehead and my hands shook. I feared I was going to have an attack of "buck fever"—go all to pieces like many novices when in the act of shooting at their first deer.

I steadied myself and took careful aim at the fat forward shoulder. The rifle's roar smashed the quiet morning and the slug smashed him. Down onto his knees he went but he was up quickly and, in high gear, bounded straight toward me. That was his second mistake. On and on he came. The second shot, a hurried one, turned him at about fifty yards and the third went wild. I fired a fourth as he bounced into the woods. I knew he was hurt but I didn't know how badly. And there was no telling how far he would travel before he would lie down to rest or die. I gave him twenty minutes that seemed like an hour and started walking slowly across the clearing. I found blood and hair on the few patches of snow that remained and guessed that he was hit hard. He was. I found him piled up only a few yards inside the woods. He was a magnificent specimen with a perfect set of ten-point antlers. I guessed his weight at a strong two hundred pounds. I experienced the great happiness that all big game hunters know when the quarry is finally bagged after a long chase, but at the same time I felt a bit sorry for the old monarch of the thickets.

It was hard and very slow work dragging the huge carcass. I thought I would never get him out of the woods to the canoe. It took the remainder of the day and all of the next morning. I laid awake most of that night worrying about my prize that I had hidden back in the brush. I feared that a bobcat, a bear, or foxes might find the carcass and tear it to pieces. I was glad when morning came.

Except for a porcupine that had come to gnaw at the antlers a bit where my perspiring hands had left traces of salt, nothing had touched the carcass.

Pop and I worked most of the afternoon hanging it from the pine near the cabin. I gave Pop the heart and liver and took a hot bath in front of the fireplace. A letter to Alice telling her of my success on the trail of the big buck was written with great enthusiasm and, too weary to be lonely, I plunged into bed.

At the station the next day to mail the letter, I found waiting for me three of my stories and the pink rejection slips. They didn't bother me much. I had received them before. And I still receive them, but they are now very few, thank Heaven.

The lot of the free-lance writer, especially one who is still wallowing in the swales of obscurity, is anything but a bed of roses. Writing is hard and tiring, and sometimes very discouraging work. It's hard on the seat of the pants, the eyes, and the nerves. It's as uncertain as fishing. Nothing could be more uncertain than that.

And the steady job on a newspaper where you're sure of a check every week is nothing more than a grind and not nearly as profitable as many less glamorous-looking jobs. You've got to turn out the daily column or feature no matter how you feel. You don't lounge about in a silk dressing robe looking bored and hauling on a cigarette jabbed into the end of foot-long holder, and sip drinks while waiting for the proper mood. That's movie stuff.

You just plank yourself down at your typewriter in a little corner of a noisy city room or perhaps a sports nook, roll up your shirt sleeves, and go to work just like the fellow on the factory machine, in the garage, or with the pick and shovel. You've got a job to do and a deadline to meet, and if you hope to hold that job you had better not miss.

I read in a book on writing and writers, which was sent to me by Alice, that a person who hopes to become a successful writer of books or magazine articles must first have a certain amount of training on a daily newspaper. That writing under pressure is absolutely necessary, the book said. It's experience, background—a foundation to build on. It's like a cellar to a house.

Kenneth Roberts, Maine's great historical novelist, and in my humble opinion one of the greatest descriptive writers of our time, insists that at least five years of newspaper work are necessary. Roberts worked for many years as a reporter and feature writer on the *Boston Post* before venturing into the uncertain field of book writing.

My love of the outdoors—the woods, waters, mountains, and wildlife—became more intense as time rolled on. And my writing leaned more and more to conservation. And finally one gorgeous day the next spring, as I gazed from my favorite ridge at the great expanse of land and water below me, I knew I could never be away from it all for very long. Not only that particular region but the outdoors in general. Then suddenly I believed that God had sent me to protect those priceless gifts from all who through ignorance, carelessness, or greed would destroy them, by preaching with the written word the gospel of conservation, and if necessary fighting for them in the same manner.

That, it seemed, was to be my work. I felt it strongly. I felt that it was a calling—that I was nearer to Him like those called servants who represent Him in His churches across the world. The long and discouraging trail leading out of my bewilderment to the high land of happiness—the sort of happiness I wanted so badly but couldn't put my finger on—lay suddenly before me. I would climb to those heights as I had climbed to the crest of the ridge that very day and devote the remainder of my life to work that was worthy and profitable, and that I would enjoy. My father had said such perfect arrangements didn't exist. But they do and they can be found by men who will search and who are not in a hurry.

My happiness was shared by my father and mother to whom I returned in early June. A year of hard work on a Boston newspaper followed. It was the beginning of my training to write. Then back to Bangor for a couple of years on the evening *Commercial* as reporter, telegraph editor, sports writer, artist, and finally outdoors columnist. And even today after these many years, but now as a free-lancer, I still write and draw for this fine and proud old newspaper.

I was living and working with written words. I then moved across the city to Maine's largest newspaper, the morning *News*, one of the very finest for a city the size of Bangor in the country. That move was one of the wisest I have ever made. The publisher, Fred D. Jordan, now gone, God bless him; the managing editor, John M. O'Connell, Jr.; and the sports editor, Jack Moran, a long-time friend, shared my love of the outdoors.

After a year of grinding away at all sorts of writing and desk jobs, along with a daily column on fishing and hunting and the outdoors in general, which leaned ever stronger toward conservation, I was told to devote most of my time to the latter. All three understood the importance of such writing and they swung wide the gates of opportunity for me. They liked my style of writing too, they told me, and gave me both time and money to travel about whenever and wherever I wished that I might gather firsthand, along the trails, material for such work. Nor did they frown on outside jobs I took to write and draw for the magazines, large city newspapers, and finally the big news services.

Instead they encouraged me. I shall always be grateful to those men.

The daily grind on the newspapers had enabled me to write much better, easier, and faster. Editors of magazines and some large newspapers to whom I sent stories liked them to the extent of ordering more. And there were offers of good jobs in other states. But Maine with its great, unspoiled outdoors was the place I knew and loved best, and the *Bangor News* was my paper.

My mail from readers, particularly of the column and features in the *News*, became increasingly heavy. It was all very encouraging and I dug in hard in an effort to make my writings even more interesting. I was very happy.

"Oh, why don't you write a book!" I began to hear that question quite often. For that I had the following stock answer, "Maybe I will sometime." But I never really intended to for two good reasons. First of all I didn't think I was capable of such a tremendous task, and second I didn't want to take the time away from my woods wandering and my pleasant job on the *News*. And finally there were offers from the publishers of books. I still wasn't interested. But now finally I am writing one out here in the woods.

Time, like the water of the stream, passes swiftly, and suddenly it was another June—lovely month of birds, and buds, and brides. Alice was among the latter. And a few hours after she had accepted me for better or worse, we were back in that region of lakes and woods where I found that Nature's horn of plenty will provide for those who will seek it in God's outdoors, and that a man can find himself in such an environment as I had found myself, and Alice.

www.ingramcontent.com/pod-product-compliance
Lightning Source LLC
Chambersburg PA
CBHW031425270326
41930CB00007B/582